In Search Of...

In Search Of...

LOST CIVILIZATIONS
EXTRATERRESTRIALS
MAGIC and WITCHCRAFT
STRANGE PHENOMENA
MYTHS and MONSTERS

by Alan Landsburg

Everest House
Publishers   New York

To Linda.
Thank you for your support,
your kindness
and above all, your love.

Author's Note

THE CHRONICLE of discovery amassed in this volume is the work of many people. More than a hundred researchers, scientists, and skilled filmmakers participated in the various quests. For simplicity's sake we have combined our experiences into a single first-person narrative so that we may share with you the essence and excitement of the hunt without a clutter of personal introductions. As author and chief chronicler of the work we have done, I owe an enormous debt of gratitude to those who joined me in the field to explore the world of mystery. To all of those dedicated workers committed to "In Search Of . . ." I say thank you. This book is as much yours as mine.

Contents

PART FOUR
Strange Phenomena

PART FIVE
Myths and Monsters

Introduction

Six years after I first set foot into the world of paranormal phenomena, radical archaeology, extraterrestrial influences, and black arts, I still find people who have known me for years asking the question "Do you really believe all this?" For a long time I evaded a direct answer by saying, "I write about it, don't I?" My reason for hedging has little to do with the veracity of the information I present in both the book and the television programs called "In Search Of . . ." but is a great deal concerned with the specter of quackery raised in the minds of the questioners by the words "believe" and "all this."

I take great pride in the results of the work that has been accomplished by a wonderful staff of researchers, writers, and film producers on "In Search Of . . ." Together, we have participated in the development of a television series and many specials for both television and motion pictures.

Our rule has been to check and double-check every fact. We have had grand and glorious feuds, and loud, raging arguments over the theoretical basis from which "In Search Of . . ." has operated. And that base is very simple. We are convinced that no theory which concerns any of the following is sacrosanct: the origin of man on earth, the manner in which intelligence, technology, and craft evolved, the possibility that individual events have been shaped by a remote force. If you ask me what I believe, I believe that there is more, much more, to be learned about the way we have reached our present state of development.

The other part of "all this" is the expectation on the part of the reader or listener that I accept all mystic advice as gospel, that I support every report of flying saucers, that I believe in the power of astrology and the prediction of anyone who calls himself a seer. I view all claims of such power with skepticism. I do not intend to be a repository of phenomenal oddments; I would rather have the responsibility for opening doors of radical theory, letting in light, air, and focusing attention on what has long been thought of as "far-out nonsense."

I am pleased that in the years since we began "In Search Of . . ." I am no longer ridiculed when I describe the machines that have been used to train students in extrasensory perception. When I discussed these machines five years ago, I was virtually hooted off the stage. Today I can show films of their successful operation with no outcry. I do not suggest by any means that I am alone responsible for the gradual adjustment of public opinion. In fact, I am but one of hundreds of writers, journalists, and filmmakers who have examined the field and found intriguing evidence that the boundaries of scientific investigation must be vastly expanded to explain an ever-increasing number of events that for years were not thought to have been possible.

Alan Landsburg

In Search Of...

Part One

LOST
CIVILIZATIONS

1

Where Did Everyone Go?

ALL DEAD CITIES are inhabited by some kind of ghosts, I think. When I wander through lonely ruins in far places of the world, something nudges my brain. Images crowd in. I look at a crumbled stone stairway and I imagine the courtiers and priests who climbed it. I look at a weed-grown tile court worked with images of mythical beasts, and I think I feel what the artisans felt when they laid the tiles a few millennia ago.

The thought of civilizations wearing out was a theme that haunted the Romantics and came to haunt me: the grandeur and desolation of history, the hint of evil behind stone facades, the thunder of imperial names dying away into everlasting silence.

I came to share the fascination that Byron, Delacroix, Shelley, and other Romantics of that period felt for royal names from the invisible past—some names perhaps imaginary, some handed down through the Bible or from persistent myths. The names evoked drumbeats, fanfare of trumpets, and clanging cymbals: Nebuchadnezzar. Belshazzar. Ozymandias. Herod. Hammurabi. Harun al-Rashid. Angkor Wat. Wassukkanni. Quetzalcoatl. Sargon. Priam. Minos. Zeus. Camelot.

I felt an impact when I read those strange names and whispered them to myself. I had to know about them. I felt a compulsion to go in search of answers to some mysteries of antiquity:
- What made a civilization vanish?
- What made thousands of city dwellers flee from (or perhaps die in) a splendid city that looked to be at the height of its grandeur?

- Where did they go?
- Was there a common pattern woven into massive disasters scattered across thousands of years? Perhaps a flaw to be found in our own civilization as well?

So long after the fact, answers to these questions might not be possible. But I would search.

One of the first facts I found, in a general scanning of the field, was one I'd half known but never fully grasped. Maybe it will help you, as it did me, to see mankind's long confused story more clearly.

Do you realize that as recently as the time of Byron and his contemporaries—even as recently as our great-grandfathers' day, in most cases—human knowledge of ancient history was just a few scraps?

Our forefathers spoke with certitude of "the dawn of civilization" and "the dawn of history." They were sure just when both dawns had come. Very comfortable they must have been to stand, as they thought, at the high noon of human progress, and glance back to watch the epochs of the past click into sight like a reversed chronometer, until the dial went blank in the small hours. Seen that way, it was quite tidy and gave an admirable stability to existence in the best of all possible worlds.

Lately this neat little horizon has widened awesomely. We see a timetable that keeps regressing. By 1860 the dawn of Genesis, dated at 4044 B.C. by Archbishop Ussher, was known to be much too late. Behind it was the dawn of Assyria, and behind that the dawn of Babylon, and behind that Sumer, a world of cities that rimmed the Persian Gulf from the Tigris to the Euphrates. Sumer was especially shocking to biblical scholars because it contained clay tablets telling a flood story much like that of Noah and the Ark, which, according to the Book of Genesis, was supposed to have occurred a thousand years earlier.

Thus, the "dawn of civilization" is slipping farther and farther back, already displacing all the darkness back to midnight. No sooner do we accustom ourselves to an earlier dawn than another brightens behind it, and we wonder how long this bewildering rearward progression really may be.

Suppose that the whole existence of man has been compressed into twelve hours, and we are living at noon of the long human day. Be conservative and assume that man has walked upright and thought creatively for only 240,000 years. Each hour of our clock would then represent 20,000 years. Each minute equals 333 years.

For more than eleven and a half hours nothing was recorded. We know of no persons or events, but we infer that man was here, for we find stone tools, bits of pottery, and pictures of mammoths and bison.

Not until 11:40 did the first signs of Egyptian and Babylonian civilizations begin to appear. Classical Greece, which we customarily call ancient, arose about 11:53. At 11:59 Sir Francis Bacon wrote his monumental *Advancement of Learning.* A half minute ago, man invented steam engines and began the industrial revolution. A second ago, he flew to the moon.

But the hour between eleven and twelve o'clock doesn't look as empty to us as it did to our forefathers. In the world of archaeology, the last few decades have been an age of exploration as rich in adventure and discovery as was the age of Columbus and Magellan.

Reports have come in from windy uplands of Anatolia, where a strange people, the Hittites, once ruled with formidable authority; from flowery jungles of Cambodia, where some unsung genius raised temples of dazzling and exotic beauty for the Khmers; from Central American rain forests, where the remains of white temple cities could be the work of Israel's lost tribes; from the shores of the Aegean, where the fabulous myths of our own classical past suddenly proved true.

The pick-and-shovel brigades have invaded Gibeon, where once the sun stood still for Joshua; they are groping for the ruins of Gordium, capital of Phrygia, where King Midas saw concubines turn to gold at his touch. The great Tower of Babel, the labyrinth of the Minotaur, the magnificent hanging gardens of Babylon, and other wonders from an unlikely past are taking the shape of historical reality.

The city of Ephesus, sacred to the goddess Artemis, and Aphrodisias, sacred to Aphrodite, are yielding their ancient secrets. Remnants of Hatra, razed long ago by the Persians, are being pieced together. Samarra, that lovely capital of caliphs who ruled the Near East during Europe's Dark Ages, is emerging from the dust. With the Bible's help, searchers have found more than a thousand ancient sites in Transjordan and have set a firmer date for the Exodus; they have located the long-lost mines of King Solomon and spotted the site of his port on the Red Sea.

Everywhere archaeologists, armed with modern science, are lengthening and widening history's view. Aerial cameras find the faint outlines of long-gone walls and canals. Magnetometers ferret out forgotten fortifications. Carbon-14 dating is causing consternation in museums by establishing accurate ages of artifacts back beyond any written record. Ultraviolet light irradiates reused writing materials called palimpsests, and shows words that were erased thousands of years ago.

Most of these discoveries are reported first in the pages of scholarly journals, but my television documentary crew was fortunate enough to be part of one of them.

The green leafed dome of the Peruvian rain forest shut out fresh air and wetness pervaded our senses. The click, whirl and hum of insects made us feel we were inside a gigantic loudspeaker broadcasting static interference. The physical effort of hacking through jungle enervated us. At times it was hard to recollect why we were here at all. The drudgery of the march replaced the bubbling optimism of the expedition's start.

We were seeking an X on a map, an X that we had reason to believe was the last undiscovered citadel of the ancient Incan empire. The damp heat of the trek had sapped our enthusiasm. We were making slow headway, some four to six miles a day.

The clang of a machete hitting rock snapped us out of lethargy. In the wake of the sound came a shout of pure exaltation. We had literally walked into a wall, a wall of a city that had not been seen or touched for four hundred years. It was the first major new Incan find since 1911.

There are explorers who spend lifetimes in the search for such a discovery and never realize their goal. We were lucky. The *In Search Of . . .* crew had made a major find the first time out. We take no special credit. We were along for the ride. The laurels belong to Professor Edmundo Guillen, a Peruvian archaeologist.

His quest was the famed Vilcabamba. According to legend, the last Incan ruler, Tupac Amaru, withdrew to Vilcabamba in the face of the Spanish onslaught. There the Inca nation made its final stand. From the day of the Conquistadores, it was believed that an enormous trove of gold and silver was carried to Vilcabamba by the Incas. The city, however, could not be found. It was lost. For almost four centuries adventurers and explorers, armed with the slimmest of accounts, launched expeditions into the foreboding jungles of the territory in east central Peru generically called Vilcabamba.

The belief that a lost city existed gave rise to the legends of El Dorado. For four hundred years the jungles of Peru were scoured for the actual fortress of Tupac Amaru. If found, it was believed that the city would yield untold treasure.

A startling announcement was made in 1911. Harvard's Hiram Bingham electrified the world of Incan archaeology. He claimed that he had discovered Vilcabamba. What he found in fact was Machu Picchu, a wondrous fortress perched on a mountaintop. While Bingham asserted as late as 1951 that his discovery was Vilcabamba, other historians declared that the splendors of Machu Picchu did not fit historical accounts of Spanish expeditions to Vilcabamba in the mid-sixteenth century.

According to the ancient tale, Vilcabamba lay in rich pastureland in a valley four miles wide by two in length. Machu Picchu, placed on the pinpoint of a mountain, hardly matched the description.

The lure of Vilcabamba drew Dr. Edmundo Guillen to the quest. He is a professor of archaeology at the University of San Marco and a specialist in sixteenth-century Peruvian history.

Polish archaeologist Elzbieta Dzukowska joined Professor Guillen in the hunt for the real Vilcabamba. The method he used was to construct, from letters and personal descriptions of the city, a portrait of the entire region surrounding Vilcabamba as it was seen in the mid 1570s. For ten years Guillen participated in aerial surveys of the Vilcabamba region, piecing together significant landmarks from the early accounts with parallel landmarks that exist today.

In April 1973 he had narrowed the field to a valley in the Vilcabamba region that was some ten miles long. It took until midsummer of 1976 for Dr. Guillen to decide that he could, armed with maps created from four-hundred-year-old accounts, find a city that fell to the soldiers of Spain in 1572. *In Search Of* . . . cameraman Tony Halik joined the expedition that would take twelve gruelling days of hacking paths through the jungle, and on the twelfth day, July 22, 1976, the machete cleaved through a vine and rang loudly against the wall of Vilcabamba. Dr. Guillen had made the most important archaeological discovery in Peru in more than half a century, and we were there. There is no thrill to match the moment of discovery.

Well, I'm no archaeologist, but maybe there's a side of archaeology that is more a matter of discerning and imagining than of digging and measuring. Maybe there's an art of seeing a whole camp site in a broken shard of pottery on the dull gray desert. Maybe there's an ability to hold a relic in the hand and hear in the mind's ear an echo of a forgotten language almost understood.

I wanted to see if I had such a sixth sense—to visit the places where civilizations had gone down in darkness, and ascertain whether I could feel or see anything there.

Where was the logical place to go first? Where was the first known civilization?

2

Atlantis

ATLANTIS MAY HAVE been the first great empire, the fountainhead for other civilizations. That theory might account for some curious facts, like the blue-eyed, blond tribesmen in the North African mountains; like the Basque language, which is so different from all others; like rabbits in the Azores, where the theory of evolution says they can't be; like beetles common only to Africa, America, and the Mediterranean region.

Examined more closely, the theory implies that sometime there must have been big islands where none are now. Geologists and oceanographers agree. There are underwater mountains and mesas in every ocean. Call them lost continents—Mu, or Lemuria, or Atlantis, whatever you like. The only trouble is that they've been submerged for at least twenty thousand years, maybe much longer. Even ten thousand years ago there were absolutely no cities, just Stone Age nomad hunters, according to the archaeological evidence. So if Atlantis had those blonds and beetles and rabbits, so what? It didn't have a civilization.

Plato, the one and only written source for the Atlantis story, told of a mighty seafaring people who lived beyond the Strait of Gibraltar on a mountainous continent bigger than North Africa and Asia combined—800,000 square miles, by his figures.

He said that the capital city was far grander and richer than Athens, with aqueducts and baths, bridges and docks and naval stores, and temples in which sacred bulls ran loose. They were "the fairest and noblest race of men who ever lived . . . but when the divine part began to fade away, they then behaved unseemly and grew visibly debased, full of avarice and unrighteous power." Therefore, Zeus decided to punish them, and "in a single day and night the island of Atlantis disappeared under the sea."

How did Plato know all this?

By hearsay. According to him, the story came from the great Athenian law-giver, Solon, who had served as high magistrate for twenty-two years, then retired in 572 B.C. and spent ten years in Egypt—long before Plato was born.

Solon too got the tale by hearsay (through interpreters) from Egyptian priests who claimed they had been handing it down verbally for a dim nine thousand years. He supposedly made notes and began to write it as an epic poem, which he never finished. No such writings were found by his family.

In fact, nothing else in ancient literature says in plain language that an island civilization sank beneath the sea. Solon returned to Athens as an old man and told the Atlantis tale to his brother—from whom it was passed along through 150 years to the brother's great-grandson, Critias, whom Plato quotes as telling the story in old age. Many other Greek writers quoted Solon, but not about Atlantis, as far as we can tell from the surviving scrolls.

Not reassuring, was it? On the other hand, Plato himself probably visited Egypt and could have picked up the Atlantis legend there. Why didn't he tell it on his own authority? Because first-person stories just weren't his style. He never mentioned himself in any of his writings. He put them all into the form of conversations between students and Socrates or other mentors.

He may have chosen a long-dead source in order to protect himself from accusations that he made up the Atlantis story. We know for sure that Plato had a fertile imagination. His writings included descriptions of islands floating in the sky, of Tartarus below Hades inside the earth, of primeval men with four arms and four legs. This was why I'd always suspected that Plato personally invented Atlantis and its destruction by earthquake and flood. His skeptical pupil Aristotle had been quoted as saying "he who invented Atlantis also destroyed it."

By the time Plato wrote about Atlantis he was in his seventies and had gone through a lot—including enslavement and liberation, a reign of terror in Athens, competitive wrestling, a battle with the Delians, which brought him a decoration for bravery, an abortive attempt to apply his theories of government at the court of the tyrant

Dionysus, and forty years of schoolteaching. Significantly, Plato's pre-scription for an ideal government, expounded in the *Republic* long before he wrote about Atlantis, is almost identical, word for word, to the political system described as an actuality in his Atlantis dialogue.

His physical description of Atlantis conflicted with facts discov-ered later. According to his dimensions, the continent would have been too big to fit into either the Mediterranean or the Aegean, which were the seas around which civilization had centered in classi-cal times. In the Atlantic Ocean—named after his legendary land—undersea explorers had no more luck than did Magellan or Columbus in finding vestiges of the continent Plato described.

The likeliest location seemed Galicia Bank, a flat-topped bulge twenty miles long, lying a half mile deep off the northwest corner of Spain. In 1958, the British research vessel *Discovery II* dredged the bank and took hundreds of underwater photos, finding nothing. No bits of pottery or tools, no signs of a drowned civilization. More recently, Dr. Maurice Ewing of Columbia University announced that after thirteen years of probing the mid-Atlantic ridge he hadn't located any clues to sunken cities—even though he'd taken sound-ings, combed with dredges, and plunged cameras and searchlights as deep as three miles.

The "day and a night" during which Atlantis supposedly sank would have been somewhere around 9600 B.C., as Plato told it. But if the highly civilized survivors fled to other lands—there must have been some at sea in ships when the land sank—why didn't scholars find clues to their existence? Egypt itself, where the priests sup-posedly had been handing down the facts ever since the cataclysm, wasn't even crudely civilized until about 4000 B.C., as far as scientists knew. Archaeologists all over the world were sure that mankind ev-erywhere was just beginning to emerge from caves during the Stone Age nine or ten thousand years B.C., and that the transition from wandering hunters to settled farmers took many centuries. So Plato's date seemed wildly wrong.

But what if Atlantis fell later instead of earlier? We could suppose that Plato—or Solon—saw Egyptian writings about Atlantis, and that he misread the Egyptian symbol for "hundred" as "thousand," thereby multiplying all figures tenfold. If we eliminated that extra zero, Atlantis would become eighty thousand square miles in area, which would fit several areas not very deep under water. The date of the cataclysm would become nine *centuries* before Solon instead of nine thousand years. This would put it in the fifteenth century B.C., when Egypt did exist.

There are three sites of undersea exploration where sunken cities seem to be. One is in the Bahamas, one in the Aegean between present-day Turkey and Greece, and one in shallow waters off Spain, west of the Straits of Gibraltar.

In 1940, Edgar Cayce, the "sleeping prophet," had predicted in a trance that part of Atlantis would rise from the sea around the Bahamas. He had even set an approximate date—1968 or 1969. In those years, aircraft pilots did begin to report glimpses of what looked like rectangular enclosures, or the foundations of big buildings, under the water. Maybe the sea bottom was rising.

I knew that there were massive walls off the shore of Bimini—I'd seen them a few years earlier, while filming a TV documentary. But this time, maybe I could see more. So we went down to take another look.

The seven-hundred-odd Bahama Islands are scattered across ninety thousand square miles of sunlit solitude in the North Atlantic basin, starting near the coast of Florida and running southeast almost to Haiti. The whole Bahama Banks area is fairly shallow, and might have been above water five or ten thousand years ago.

I put on a diver's mask and slipped under the glistening surface layers of light, sank down to the bottom, and wandered among the huge white blocks that the pilots had seen and the divers had studied. They were as square-cut and as smoothly fitted as parts of a modern edifice. They extended far beyond my sight, fading into the opalescent haze. Were they paved causeways, or plazas, or the tops of buried walls? I couldn't see enough to guess. Even the divers weren't sure, because drifting sand kept burying some parts and exposing others.

A deserted city might lie there, extending for miles among the coral and swaying seaweed. If so, the city was not recorded in any history that has thus far come to light. I knew that divers had brought up pottery and figurines that no museum was willing to classify as typical of a known culture. I knew that Pino Tarolla, one of the world's leading undersea researchers, had found a marble column that could be part of a temple or villa. He believed it was twelve thousand years old. Maybe scientific tests would fix a date for it.

Suppose there had been a civilization on the Bahama Banks. What became of it? Rather than simply moving to the higher ground that still shoulders up from the sea as islands, all the people must have been drowned, or must have fled far away. When Columbus reached those islands he found no stonework, no civilization —only primitive Indians in huts. Plato said that the Atlanteans were warned of impending disaster, and he implied that some escaped.

An Atlantis theory could explain those well-engineered stone structures in thirty-five feet of water. It might also explain what had been found under a sunken ship.

The ship had gone down in 1830. But it had crushed something beneath it that was more interesting: the remains of a smaller, much older ship. Studying the fragments, experts decided that this ancient ship was a typical vessel of the Phoenicians, those sea wanderers who built a vast network of small seaport towns.

The Phoenicians seemed rather uncanny and mysterious to the Mediterranean peoples, who could not understand how this tiny race could be so widespread. The Phoenician empire depended not on vast territories but on a fleet, a system of forts, and the good will of its customers. The Phoenicians had no army and no strong war galleys, but they had footholds on the Spanish and North African coasts, on the Bosporus, and in Italy and Sicily. Their agents were seen with the priests and pharaohs of Egypt, with the kings of Persia and Babylon and Assyria. They were in every port, but said little. They arrived, transacted business with memorable honesty, and disappeared again. They offered wares purveyed by no other nation, and sometimes hinted that they had traveled to lands unknown in the Mediterranean.

What had a Phoenician ship been doing so near the then undiscovered American continents?

At some time in the dim past, we know from historic clues, a few bold sea adventurers did move west into the broad Atlantic in search of a fabled continent. These men, mostly Phoenicians, left no record of finding Atlantis. But they found the Madeiras and the Canary Islands. And wherever they wandered, gossip sprang up of other island kingdoms west over the ocean—the Hesperides, where grew the golden apples, the Fortunate Islands, the Isles of the Blest, and somewhere out there the Elysian Fields, which became the abode of the blessed in Greek mythology. Perhaps legends like these led the Vikings to America about 1000 A.D.

But I was peering much further back. If venturesome early Phoenicians were in the Bahamas three thousand years ago, were they visiting the western edge of a continent of Atlantis? Plato's description, taken literally, would mean that part of the Atlantic was once occupied by a land mass linking the Mediterranean area to the Caribbean area. If the Bahamas were the western or Caribbean tip of this trans-Atlantic land bridge, where was the Mediterranean tip?

Somewhere off Spain? The broken remains of a city had recently been reported on the sea bottom near Cadiz—an old, old city that was originally the Phoenician port of Gades. Cadiz is in Andalusia, on the coast near the mouth of the Guadalquivir River. In that same river valley, probably, was the lost metropolis of Tartessus—which also may have been the biblical Tarshish, Jonah's destination. Ezekiel mentioned mysterious "ships of Tarshish" which sailed from the Gulf of Aqaba to the equally mysterious Ophir, and brought back "gold, and silver, ivory, and apes and peacocks" for King Solomon. (I Kings 10:22)

Were Tartessus and Tarshish the same or different places? Where were they? We know for sure only that they were in southern Spain. Herodotus told of a king who ruled over Tartessus, and therefore many have thought it was a country rather than merely a city. The country was rich—Strabo wrote of a river "with springs rich in silver" and other writers mentioned its "silver mountains." Those mountains are now known to be Spain's Sierra Morena.

About 500 b.c., Tartessus disappeared from sight so mysteriously that Plato was inspired—some say—to base his Atlantis myth on it. I wondered if the place had been a Phoenician capital. Wherever they settled, Phoenicians lived near the sea rather than inland. It seemed almost as if they mistrusted the firmness of the land. Their empire was elusive, founded less on settlements than on trading routes, and its chief manifestation was its fleet of fragile ships. Phoenician towns were walled settlements with watchtowers, barracks, and storehouses. The only traces left to us were a few statues and a strange many-colored bust in sandstone, "The Lady of Elche," carved in a strong and flowing Celtic style.

A town called Gades (which became the big city of Cadiz in the Spanish empire) was founded sometime before 800 b.c.—perhaps by Phoenicians, perhaps by Carthaginians. It may well have been a sort of suburb or satellite of Tartessus or Tarshish. German archaeologist Adolf Schulten wrote a book arguing that Tartessus was the key city of Atlantis. Near the mouth of the Guadalquivir he dug up blocks of masonry that, he thought, showed that two older cities had been there—one originating from about 3000 b.c., the other dating from about 1500 b.c.

The Bible said that Tarshish had a great fleet. Plato said that

Atlantis had a great fleet. Some occultists like Cayce said that its civilization dabbled in black magic near the end—and a ring inscribed with what looked like a magical spell was found deep in the mud of the Guadalquivir estuary. The characters, never deciphered, consist of a single four-letter word repeated three times, in the manner of many mystical charms and runes.

Schulten couldn't dig far, because water kept seeping in. The rest of Tartessus-Tarshish (or Atlantis?) might lie deep in the ooze offshore of Cadiz and the river mouth.

The legend of the golden land of Tarshish lived on in a sort of afterglow for many centuries after the Romans left. An Arab commander described it to his troops on the eve of their first invasion of Spain in 712 A.D.:

> Maidens as handsome as houris, their necks glittering with innumerable pearls and jewels, their bodies clothed with tunics of costly silks and sprinkled with gold, are awaiting your arrival, reclining on soft couches in the sumptuous palaces of crowned lords and princes.

Yet I saw no traces of sumptuous palaces in Andalusia. When I first went there I found bare brown and violet mountains, with tiny whitewashed towns at their feet. The land contained no pre-Roman ruins. I drove along 140 miles of Mediterranean shore whose dun sand seemingly had never been used for anything more than beached fishing boats and drying nets. Later, a land boom transformed that ribbon of shore into the fashionable Costa del Sol.

Cadiz—as the Spaniards renamed Gades—contained little that hinted at its centuries as a Phoenician and Carthaginian colony. Its antique splendors must have been hidden by the rising sea. Dr. Maxine Asher thought so. In 1973 she organized an expedition to dive two and a half miles offshore.

Some of the diving was to be done by twenty-five students from Pepperdine University, which granted them summer-school credits. Dr. Asher is an energetic advocate of the theory that Atlantis is a discoverable reality.

Although she had made many trips to Cadiz, members of her 1973 expedition found little of interest because they kept getting both official and unofficial notices that they couldn't dive, couldn't go on the beach, couldn't go in the water. Told subsequently that they were being chased out because there were United States nuclear submarines and missile bases there, Dr. Asher and her crew decided to go ahead with one dive without permission.

Selecting the six best divers, they sneaked out in the middle of the night and dived down ninety-five feet, taking three rolls of film.

"The water was very murky," recalls Dr. Asher, "very sandy— you're now talking about the Atlantic, not the Caribbean. . . ."

The crew came back to the hotel and reported that they had found an entire ancient site and had photographed it. It was the same site identified by Spain's only archaeological scuba diver of note, Francisco Salazar Casero—known as Paco. He had pinpointed four diving locations about twenty miles north of Gibraltar and had found the remains of an ancient city at one of these sites.

Unfortunately, very little of the film came out and they were unable to make any other dives. Police were all over the beaches; they felt they could not go on.

Since the Spanish government's treatment of Dr. Asher indicated that we too would be stymied there, I headed instead for the Aegean Sea.

The windy Aegean Sea is like a great lake, almost surrounded by land. Greece's jagged shores, on the mainland of Europe, lie to its west and north. To the east is the Asian part of Turkey. Along the south, like a breakwater, the long, narrow, mountainous island of Crete sets the Aegean apart from the rest of the Mediterranean Sea. South of Crete is nothing but ocean until you reach the coast of Africa—not a long voyage by modern standards, but in days when ships rarely sailed out of sight of a coast, it was enough to make the Aegean fairly remote from Egypt, the nearest civilized power from 3000 to 1000 B.C.

Myth said that a king named Aegeus once ruled over preclassical Athens. His son Theseus went to Crete and slew the Minotaur. On his return voyage, Theseus forgot to hoist white sails as the prearranged signal of success. The agonized King Aegeus saw the ship's black sails—the signal that Theseus was dead—whereupon he threw himself into the sea and drowned. It has been called the Aegean ever since. No one knows what it was called in the dim centuries before Greeks and Phoenicians, the centuries into which I now was questing.

I was bound for an island in the Aegean some seventy-eight miles northeast of Crete. It was one of two hundred twenty isles strewn in a great loose circle, and therefore called the Cyclades. They are mountain peaks of a land mass, now mostly drowned in the sea, that once linked the mainland with Asia Minor.

For centuries, beginning with the dawn of the Bronze Age about 3000 B.C., dwellers in the Cyclades had dominated the Mediterranean and outstripped Crete itself in commerce. The islanders were mining obsidian and trading in wheat, pottery, copper, and gems long before their neighbors in Crete or on the mainland. "Their weapons were of bronze, their houses of bronze, and they worked with bronze," the Greek poet Hesiod wrote of the men who lived thereabouts long before his own age. They slowly built up an elegant culture that would vanish suddenly, haunting the classical world, not to be found again until our own time.

My goal was the island that had been the crowning gem of this culture. The island was known by various names. Most people now call it Santorini, after its patron saint, Santa Irene. Legends gave it other names: Stronghyli, or Round Island, and Kalliste, or Most Fair. It has now been officially designated Thera, a name given to it by the classical Greeks.

Long ago Thera was a round, flowery island surrounding a conical mountain that rose a mile high from the sea. Today, most of this mountain is gone. As I stood at the rail of a motor launch I saw from afar what was left of Thera: a crescent-shaped mass with jagged ridges lancing into the sky. As we drew closer they loomed black and stark as battlements. The old island seemed a citadel under attack by the sea, with sloping rock sides that here threw back the surf and there had been breached.

Nearer yet, I saw cliff faces streaked with strata of black, white, pink, and rust red—marks of a turbulent past. From these strata, geologists deduced a brief terrible episode that had snuffed out civilization all around the Aegean. Now I was to see what archaeologists made of that same episode.

We landed at Thera from the west, within the incurve of its broken crescent. The curve was big—eighteen miles around the rim, and half enclosing some thirty square miles, according to the chart. It could have been a good harbor—except that it was far too deep. No ship's anchor could reach the bottom, thirteen hundred feet down. We had to tie up at a quay clinging tenaciously to the steep shore.

From there a cobbled path zigzagged upward like a staircase. A patient donkey carried me among whitewashed houses and steepled churches, up and up on a precarious climb that any sensible wild goat would have shunned. Santorini's donkeys were said to be inhabited by souls in purgatory, paying for their sins by toiling up that steep path.

I pondered what this strange sharp-edged land had been fifteen centuries before Christ. On these steep slopes, along terraces like balconies, vineyards would have been lush with figs and olives and wine grapes. People would have been bathing in warm springs that bubbled from the sacred mountain in the center of the island, or steaming themselves in yellow-white vapor from its fissures.

Thera's people probably didn't realize that they lived on the slopes of a mighty, slumbering volcano—as large or larger than Vesuvius or Etna. It was also an active earthquake zone. One fateful day, the earth's jolts evidently opened subterranean cracks, through which cold sea water seeped into the lava furnace under the volcano. For a period of hours or days, steam and gas pressure rose steadily toward the bursting point.

Lava welled up and broke through. People on the slopes saw a river of red-hot rock creeping toward them. But there was a lull, giving everyone time to snatch up belongings and hasten downhill. Inside the mountain, the fiery fountain subsided awhile, seeping into a vast gas-filled chamber whose rock roof was riven with cracks.

At last, with a great deafening roar, the mountaintop blew apart. An enormous pillar of dust and vapor climbed into the sky. Soon the sky grew dark as night. A hot snowfall of powdery pumice and stones began. On the beach, everyone swam for the ships or scrambled into boats. But they were doomed.

If Thera was the fabled Atlantis, as some modern archaeologists believe, Plato's description of what happened could be literally true: "In a single day and night of misfortune . . . the island of Atlantis disappeared in the sea." Geological evidence proves that Thera underwent a volcanic eruption of maximum violence. When the volcano had spat out all its fiery core, the hollowed-out cone collapsed in on itself, falling into its lake of lava far below sea level. This suddenly opened a pit about forty-seven miles across and a quarter mile deep—sucking in approximately fifteen cubic miles of sea water.

After the downrush came the backwash, a spreading circle of water more than a hundred feet high, probably followed by others nearly as gigantic. The wave must have overturned all ships, drowned everyone on the Cyclades Islands except people in the mountains, and destroyed Crete's coastal cities. It raced across the Aegean and the eastern Mediterranean at more than a hundred miles an hour. Less than three hours later it engulfed the Egyptian delta, 450 miles away, where the children of Israel labored as slaves at the time.

The suction in the sea and the subsequent outward wave (about twenty minutes later) might have given the Israelites their land path through the Red Sea, and might have crushed the pursuing Egyptians under the huge returning tidal wave. The iron-oxide fallout from Thera's explosion might have made the Nile run red. Certainly it blanketed the Jaffa shoreline, 562 miles away, with rosy pumice.

Egypt's Ten Plagues, as recorded in the Bible, might be explained by phenomena that accompany great volcanic eruptions. Whirlwinds, swamps, and red rain often are created by meteorological disturbances associated with eruptions, and there are aerial shock waves as destructive as those from a great bomb blast.

The Bible said that in Egypt the waters reddened, killing fish and driving frogs ashore. Darkness covered the land for three days. The wind roared. A fiery hail fell. Strong vapors destroyed what crops remained.

Egyptian documents confirmed the disaster. "The sun is veiled and shines not," said one papyrus. "O that the earth would cease from noise," lamented another.

Whether Egypt's plagues raged during the time of Moses can't yet be confirmed or denied, because no contemporary evidence has been found. The Exodus took place during Solomon's reign, the Bible said, which was from 970 to 930 B.C. But the story of Moses was told to biblical scribes many centuries afterward, and could be incorrectly placed in time. It might have coincided with Thera's explosion, which scientists date at approximately 1520 B.C.

As for Thera, some of it sank into the newly opened undersea crater, and some was buried under thick layers of volcanic ash and powdered pumice. It was a dead island for centuries. Then Greek villagers came and settled. The first suspicion that a city lay under them arose during construction of the Suez Canal in the nineteenth century. Ash from there was known to make high-quality waterproof cement, so it was mined for the Suez project. French miners found that the layer of volcanic ash was a hundred feet thick in places. This implied the biggest volcanic eruption on record.

The French crews got curious and kept digging. Under tons of ash and pumice they found signs of a then-unknown civilization. Archaeologists visited, and burrowed into underground structures that were found to contain frescoes and pottery and artwork unlike anything from classical Greece. At that stage of archaeology, their age was unguessable.

A young Greek student of archaeology, Spyridon Marinatos, grew obsessed with curiosity about what had really happened on this bleak and sinister island. In 1932 he got a university grant of $135—a princely sum then—to excavate. He unearthed a small part of the old city, including a villa with glowing floral motifs. He found bronzes of a high quality, beautiful ceramics—including one of a bull, the Minoans' sacred beast—and ornate decorations in earth colors and crushed lapis lazuli.

Marinatos theorized that a huge eruption had destroyed much of the island and all its civilization. He was ignored by most of his colleagues. But in 1937 he became a visiting professor at the State University of Utrecht, where he could delve into voluminous records of the 1883 Krakatau eruption in the Netherlands East Indies. That volcanic island burst with a roar heard 2,968 miles away. Volcanic dust hid the daylight for 275 miles around. The empty shell of the volcano slumped into a 600-foot-deep crater in the sea, making waves 120 feet high. The waves swept away entire towns and villages on the neighboring coasts of Java and Sumatra, drowned 36,380 people, and tore loose the chains of anchored ships in South America.

Colossal as it was, Krakatau's explosion was only a fraction as strong as the eruption at Thera. Eight square miles of Krakatau fell into the sea; Thera lost thirty-two square miles. Krakatau's crater was one fifth the size of Thera's. The ash that fell around Krakatau nowhere exceeded sixteen inches; the deposit on Thera was a hundred feet plus.

In 1956 an accidental discovery on the island aroused more interest among antiquaries. At the bottom of a mine shaft, Professor Angelos Galanopoulos of the Athens Seismological Institute found fire-blackened ruins of a stone house. Inside were pieces of charred wood and the teeth of a man and a woman. Radiocarbon analysis indicated that they died about 1400 B.C.—the approximate date assigned to the volcanic eruption.

So the proof began to look convincing: an island civilization had been shaken, abandoned, and submerged, much as Plato described it. Thera really could have been the center—or one of the key cities—of the fabled empire of Atlantis, since details of its death fitted Plato's story. Professor Galanopoulos propounded the Atlantis theory with deep conviction.

By 1967 enough people were interested to enable Marinatos (by then a professor emeritus and Inspector General of Antiquities for the Greek government) to take charge of systematic digging on the island. He kept at it for seven years, until he died in a fall at the site. He had estimated that a hundred years of excavation would be needed to uncover the whole city. Others carried on. Each season a house or two was uncovered, debris was sifted, tiny fragments of frescoes and pots were pieced together, streets were mapped, and structures were restored and strengthened.

"We had expected to find ruins of a prehistoric town—just foundations and fallen stones," a researcher said. "In most finds the ruins don't come up to your knees. Here we found not a ruin but a museum in three dimensions—every interior sealed under preserving ash or pumice."

The buildings weren't really intact, though. Many walls bulged outward from the force of the airblast when the volcano erupted. Frescoes were peppered with small holes, as from shotguns.

I prowled through ancient streets that the excavators had dug out. One large structure looked like a palace. In its storeroom I saw twenty man-sized vases, their insides coated with microscopic traces of old grain, oil, and wine. Elsewhere in the palace I saw a coppersmith's workshop; a sacrificial area where a blackened fireplace contained charred bones of lambs and birds; bronze roasting pans with flecks of what had been barley, flour, onions, buns, roasted snails, and sea urchins. There had been no time for dishwashing, evidently, after the Therans' last meal.

In one house I saw a commodious bathtub—but it was very short; the people were no more than five and a half feet tall. In another house was a rare find: layers of dark dust within the white volcanic ash. Researchers applied epoxy resin to harden it, and eventually drew forth a replica of a sizable basket of twigs and bark strips. Elsewhere was an impression in the dust, into which a master restorer had gently poured plaster. When the plaster hardened and the ash was scraped off, he had a plaster cast of a wooden bed so detailed that the thongs that had once bound the frame showed clearly. It was the first piece of wooden furniture recreated in an Aegean site.

I saw big wall paintings, some extending around a whole room. Bare-breasted women wore jeweled necklaces and eye makeup. Naked boys fought, wearing boxing gloves. Monkeys and antelopes cavorted; they were of species that now exist only in Africa, according to experts. A piece of one fresco showed a Negroid head. Did the empire of Atlantis stretch into Africa?

Apparently, Thera's city had taken the form of a circle, with the mountain at its center. Around it were rings of land and water, with bridges connecting the land rings, and canals big enough for ships connecting the water rings. The docks were on the outermost ring. It was a novel design—coinciding with Plato's description of the chief city of Atlantis: "fortified by a fence of alternate rings of sea and land, smaller and greater, one within another."

The harbor of Atlantis was "constantly crowded by merchant vessels and their passengers arriving from all quarters, whose vast numbers occasioned incessant shouting, clamor and general uproar day and night." Thera's harbor could have been like that, to judge from the dense neighborhoods, good-sized homes, and luxurious furnishings. The absence of gold and skeletons suggests that the ancient inhabitants had warning, as Plato said the Atlanteans had.

Professor Galanopolous said that Thera was part of the great Minoan civilization that spread through Crete and around the shores of the Aegean. All coastal cities were swept away by the wave from the dying Thera. But Knossos, where the legendary King Minos built his labyrinth for the Minotaur, was several miles inland on Crete, so it survived the tidal wave. It had been excavated.

I knew I had to see it.

3

The Heirs of Minos

BEFORE I WENT THERE, I knew that the dead palace of Knossos sometimes had an odd effect on imaginative people. Leonard Cottrell, an eminent British archaeological writer, mentioned his feelings about it several times. In one book, *Lost Worlds*, he merely hinted:

> When one descends that shadowed Knossian staircase, with its colonnades opening onto a light-well, or when one stands in the dimly lit, frescoed rooms of state, one feels nearest to those remote people.

His disquiet showed more clearly in another book, *The Bull of Minos*. At one point he wrote:

> As I followed the curator to the Central Court, a curious, faint uneasiness began. . . . I am not a superstitious man; I have no belief in the supernatural. But I have to admit that the atmosphere of the Palace depressed me. It was—there is no other word for it—sinister.

Elsewhere in the same book he remarked, "There was something which had haunted me since I entered the Palace, a sense of doom, a smell of death."

When Sir Arthur Evans, the excavator of Knossos, first landed in Crete, he felt a deep sense of the past. Homer had known and sung of this "rich and lovely land in the dark blue sea." It had ninety towns, Homer said, and "one of the ninety was a great city called

Knossos . . . [where] King Minos ruled and enjoyed the friendship of almighty Zeus." Evans could see snow-capped Mount Ida, supposed birthplace of Zeus, crowning the mountainous skyline.

Evans roamed Crete, picking up more of the old beads inscribed with what he thought might be ancient Greek or Cretan writing. He wasn't yet much interested in Homeric myths; he wanted clay tablets or carved inscriptions.

His search led him to remote parts of the 160-mile-long island. Here and there he noticed traces of a once-mighty civilization. There had been great paved highways running from coast to coast. There had been aqueducts, altars, theaters, villas, seaports—all surprisingly different from the Greek and Roman styles.

Knossos, a mere village now, still existed a few miles inland from the port of Heraklion. Heinrich Schliemann, the self-taught German archaeologist who found Troy and taught the world that Greek legends must be taken seriously after all, had been well aware of Homer's allusions to this and other places on the island. He planned to dig at Knossos, but quarreled with the owner of the land, and died soon after.

When Evans saw the piles of rubble and ruins that had fascinated Schliemann, it was enough to make up his mind. He boldly announced that he represented a "Cretan Exploration Fund" (which then existed only in his mind) and wished to buy some land on the fund's behalf. Since he had inherited two fortunes, he could easily strike a bargain with the Turkish owner.

But then the Turkish government, which ruled Crete, refused to let him touch the land. When Crete was freed in 1900 he returned, bought the remainder of the site, wangled the new government's cooperation, and hired 150 workmen to help him excavate.

He was a man of demonic energy. It took him only nine weeks to make a sensational discovery. The ruins of supposedly mythical Knossos lay only a few feet underground; unlike most buried cities, it had not been built over later. The astonished Evans found himself looking at a sprawling, complex network of walls covering at least six acres.

The cellars contained miles of storerooms—great stone-built magazines with rows of smoke-blackened jars big enough to contain two men each, rather like those in which Ali Baba found the Forty Thieves. In these cellars Evans found what he sought: a hoard of almost two thousand clay tablets and stone seals, bearing symbols like those that had first set him on the trail. Evidently fires, gutting the palace, had accidentally baked and preserved the soft tablets (which the original scribes had used only for temporary notes). Evans confidently expected to decode the pictographs and scripts, but never succeeded. They turned out to be in three separate unknown languages, one of which is still impenetrable.

Evans announced that he would need a year to find everything of interest at the site. He underestimated: Forty-one years later he was still digging there. He went to Crete to decipher a system of writing, but he discovered a civilization.

Eventually he proved that Minoan ships were crossing seas as early as 4000 B.C., before any other known maritime power. Stretching back into the ancient days of mankind, before Zeus ruled in heaven, this civilization was at least as old as the pharaohs, and perhaps much older.

To strangers it must have looked benign and peaceful as well as grand. There were no fortifications on Crete. Not only Knossos was vast. The port of Heraklion, as the Greeks called it, was bigger than Athens. Across the island on the southern shore was Phaistos, also with a majestic unfortified palace. Two other palaces were later found elsewhere on Crete. Archaeologists began to realize that Cretan (Minoan) culture had been palace-centered.

It had overtones of evil. Because Knossos was built on the slope of a hill, it was five or more stories high in some parts. On upper levels were spacious chambers. In the dim depths underneath, what a contrast! Instead of splendid halls or sunny courtyards was an intricate coil of winding stairways and dead-end storagerooms and intersecting passages, bringing to mind the "labyrinth" in which Homer said King Minos kept the monstrous Minotaur.

So this much of the myth was fact. Minos did have a Maze.

Even on the upper floors, Minoan palaces were confusing, with many rooms and corridors. This labyrinthine design made them—to modern eyes—places of terror. Probably these convolutions had a two-fold or three-fold purpose: to confuse intruders, to protect the center from intrusion, and possibly to confine someone or something.

The Maze became the Minoan trademark. We find heraldic versions of it on coins of Knossos for four centuries. Maze patterns decorated walls, found their way onto textiles, were inscribed on funerary urns and storage vats. What kind of people, I wondered, took such pride in bewildering and scaring the unwary?

And why were there no outer walls for defense? Why were there scarcely any signs of weapons or soldiers, until the very last years of the empire?

Control of the seas by a powerful navy could explain why Minoan lords felt secure against invasion from overseas. But what about attack by one lord against another? And was there no need for police protection, or compulsion, against the swarms of lower-class workers?

I recalled frightening tales about Crete in Greek mythology. The despot Minos had made a demand so wild and sinister that it might have emanated from a madhouse: he ordered Athens to send him fourteen youths and maidens each eight years (presumably to be given alive to the monster who lurked in the Maze). And Athens meekly complied.

It now appears that Minos was many men, not one. The rulers at Knossos were always called Minos, as rulers of Egypt were called Pharaoh. According to Sir James Frazer, the great expert on magic and religion, every eight years Minos traditionally climbed to the cave on Mount Ida and gave an account of his kingship to his divine father Zeus. The tradition plainly implied that without this eight-year renewal he would have to forfeit the throne.

Why eight years? Because, Frazer said, only once in eight years does the full moon coincide with the shortest or longest day of the year. Minoans must have kept exact records of the rising and setting of the sun and the moon.

This renewal of the king's power might have some secret connection with the octennial tribute of youths and maidens from Athens—another reason for suspecting that the Minotaur tale wasn't totally untrue.

But what happened to the youngsters when they arrived at Knossos? Frazer thought the youths might have been part of a terrible rite:

> Perhaps they were roasted alive in a bronze image of a bull, or of a bull-headed man, in order to renew the strength of the king. This at all events is suggested by the legend of Talos, a bronze man who clutched people and leaped with them into the fire.

> He is said to have been given by Zeus . . . to guard the island of Crete, which he patrolled thrice daily. According to one account he was a bull.

> Probably he was identical with the Minotaur, and stripped of mythical features was nothing but a bronze image. Human vic-

tims may have been sacrificed to the idol by being roasted in its hollow body.

Talos? The Greeks said he was a giant of brass who kept strangers off Crete by throwing huge rocks at approaching ships. Or he made himself red-hot and burned trespassers to death in his embrace.

If people believed this, it could account for the absence of fortifications on the island. No one would dare approach. Whatever the truth of the tales, Minos and Talos and the Minotaur in the Maze made Crete sound terribly uninviting to strangers. All the more reason to go and see.

The seas around the legend-haunted island were gray-blue almost to blackness. Crete stretched clear across the horizon long before my motor launch reached it. As we drew nearer, the view was harsh and spectacular, fit only for wild goats and bandits, today as in antiquity. Once Crete was famed for its oaks and cypresses, olives and vines, and abundant springs. But now the springs are dry, and Crete is mostly barren because of Christian and Saracen mismanagement during and after the Middle Ages.

Even at its greenest, Crete must have looked cruel to those in the tribute-ships approaching the capital, because they would see only the high shores—huge wrinkled yellow cliffs hiding the land beyond. Where the cliffs opened to a river mouth, they would sail into the big harbor at Heraklion (or Amnistos, as the Minoans seem to have called it, or Candia, as it is called in most of today's travel guides) and see houses like rows of towers, three or four stories high. The waterfront would be crowded with Minoans, small and brown and quick-eyed, watching to see the captives brought ashore.

In the Minoans' heyday, the route to Knossos was a stone highway for chariots and carts. But earthquakes and tidal waves and storms of brimstone from Thera long ago obliterated the pavement. Today there is only a rough dirt road.

I drove along it, through the port and up into a winding steep-sided valley. This too would have seemed forbidding to Theseus and other captives. But their trip was short, for the road rose and fell until, only four miles inland, it came out on a little plain with a range of stark rocky mountains beyond.

Even then, almost at their destination, captives may not have seen Knossos. I didn't, at first.

The great palace lay in a hollow, half hidden by trees and slopes. Only the northern side, the way to the sea, was open. When we got there I was still musing about why this mountainous island became the center of an empire. Other great civilizations of about the same time—Egypt, Mesopotamia, the Indus Valley—grew up along fertile river valleys. But Crete had no large rivers, and few plains. How could a highly distinctive culture arise here and flourish for two thousand years?

I forgot this riddle when I noticed, sharp against the hard blue Cretan sky, a mighty pair of sculpted horns like those of a gigantic bull. They reared over the highest roof edge of the Palace of Minos.

Such insolent horns, which Evans called horns of consecration, stood atop many Minoan palaces. Minoan religion seemed to adore the bull; its horns were the only substitute for the aspiring steeples and domes in most religious centers of other empires. The roofs of Knossos were flat, without even watchtowers or battlements.

I walked up a paved ramp into a courtyard, and saw a fresco of a great red bull charging across a wall. Beyond the threshold, past low walls, smooth pavement and crimson columns (tapering downward, strangely), I made a turn and was inside the palace.

There were bright frescoes of sportive fishes, swooping birds, children gathering flowers, crowds of classic-featured chattering ladies with painted lips and naked breasts, aglitter with ornaments, and graceful half-nude men with slim waists, black braided hair, and jeweled bracelets and bangles. There was a young prince in a gaudy feather headdress (like an Aztec?) with lilies, a symbol of royalty, beside him.

Everywhere I felt the strangeness of Knossos. We were only a few hundred miles from Egypt, to which the Minoans had sailed for two thousand years. Yet, there was nothing Egyptian—or Grecian—in the architecture, or in the faces or dress of these people. Who were they? Where had they come from? Where had they gone?

As for the Room of the Throne, it made me slightly nervous. I went in through a low-ceilinged anteroom, opened a wooden door, and stood in the wide dim room of the mysterious kings. Against the wall, in its original place, rose the oldest throne in Europe—stark and simple, but skillfully carved, with rounded seat and high curved back. On either side were guardian griffins. They were painted on a blue field of lilies, but they were ugly lionlike creatures with vulture heads. Along the walls were stone benches where priests had sat watching. The floor was hard glazed earth.

To those who had revered Minos, the room could have seemed like a cathedral chapter house. But to me it spoke of dark gods and the ghost waiting for the ferry on the sighing shore. I felt glad to stride out into the sparkling Cretan sunshine.

There is a theory that legends of Atlantis were garbled descriptions of Minoan Crete. Somewhere around 1400 B.C., when the empire was at a peak of power and prosperity, disaster came suddenly, as it supposedly did to Atlantis. The giant waves racing out from Thera engulfed Minoan cities on the coasts—but not Knossos, since it was inland and on higher ground. The palace of Knossos was leveled at least once by an earthquake, only to be rebuilt more grandly. It survived at least a half century after Thera's destruction.

Then it too was destroyed. At Knossos and at other sites on Crete are clear signs of fire: charred beams and pillars, blackened stone, clay tablets baked solid. There had been sudden panic. In one room, the excavators found a block of purple Spartan basalt half sawed through, as if abandoned in haste. In the throne room were evidences of an unfinished religious ceremony.

Evans thought an earthquake started the fire. John D. S. Pendlebury, the assistant who had helped Evans exhume Knossos, thought it was attacked and looted, probably by raiders from mainland Greece.

My own hunch was that Pendlebury was right. After all, Knossos had recovered from earlier disasters caused by earthquakes, but this time it did not. Also, in modern cities with gas mains and power lines, earthquakes often start bad fires, but this wasn't necessarily true in the ancient world. Many Minoan cities apparently burned as if put to the torch. And nothing of value was found in them (except at Zakros, which was packed in volcanic ash). Invaders would have carried off the missing valuables. So I think someone discovered that Crete was rotten-ripe for plucking. When they came, whoever they were, they may merely have hastened an inevitable doom.

Knossos was never rebuilt, although squatters occupied the ruins for a long time. But where did the Minoans (or Atlanteans?) go when fleeing their palaces? The end of their empire is a mystery as dark as the mystery of Minoan script. There are inklings that some islanders may have gone to Asia Minor and fathered the brutal Philistines, who warred on Hebrews. Others probably sailed elsewhere. Herodotus and Strabo say that Cretans founded Troy. Homer says that a grandson of Minos, Idomenus, led one of the famous contingents against Troy under Agamemnon. A scattering of finds that suggest Minoan mazes have turned up along the edges of Europe—and of America. The resemblance among these, scattered along five thousand miles of coast within a span of at most two hundred years, is so close that no expert doubts their relationship to one another. But are they Minoan? No one can say . . . yet.

Could Minoans—refugees from a fallen civilization—have sailed all the way to prehistoric America? About two hundred small ancient sites have recently been dug up in New England. They contain stone sacrificial tables and bowls similar to some at the ritual chambers of Knossos. They are certainly not Viking or Celtic or Mayan. They might be Minoan.

At Mystery Hill, New Hampshire, there is a stone labyrinth. On its walls are inscriptions that, according to Harvard epigrapher Barry Fell and others, resemble Minoan hieroglyphs. If they are, then America was discovered by Europeans more than three thousand years before Columbus sailed, more than twenty-five centuries before the Vikings came.

Elsewhere are other unexplained finds that might be links to the Minoans. On a rock at Lake Assawompsett, Massachusetts, is a carving of a ship—rather like the Minoan ships, with high bow and stern and one square sail on a central mast.

There is a stone near Fort Benning, Georgia, with markings that could be Minoan. At two places in Brazil, near the coast, are stones bearing inscriptions in a similar unreadable language.

If Minoans got to America, they probably died in lonely destitution. After the luxury of their palaces and the warmth of Crete, prehistoric North America would have been rigorous indeed. Any Minoans who were here left no permanent traces, with the possible exception of those strange stone relics.

So there was no way I could follow their faint trail any farther into the New World. But there were other sea trails I wanted to follow farther: the trails of Homeric heroes in the Aegean Sea.

We skimmed up the eastern Peloponnesian coast on the first leg of the trip. Peloponnesus is the southernmost quarter of the Greek mainland. Its name, which means "Pelops' Isle" (although it isn't really an island) commemorated a daring wanderer who won a throne there.

Pelops came from Asia Minor to seek the hand of a certain Greek princess—a perilous quest, because the king, who had been warned in a prophecy that his son-in-law would kill him, sought to prevent his daughter's marriage by challenging any suitor to a chariot race. The suitors had always lost, and their penalty was death.

But Pelops won, married the princess, and himself became king. He had bribed a groom to tamper with the royal chariot: the wheels flew off during the race, and the king was killed. When the groom demanded his reward—half of the kingdom and one night in the arms of the princess—Pelops drowned him. As he sank, the man put a curse on Pelops and all his breed.

The curse hung on for four generations. Pelops and his children came to bad ends. His grandsons Menelaus and Agamemnon ruled Sparta and Mycenae respectively, but both had faithless wives. Menelaus's beautiful wife, Helen (whose "face launched a thousand ships"), ran off to Troy with a lover, and Agamemnon mobilized an expedition to fetch her back, thus starting the siege of Troy. When Agamemnon at last came triumphantly home, his own wife and her paramour caught him unarmed and cut him to pieces. The cycle of doom took one more turn. Agamemnon's son Orestes killed the treacherous pair, then went mad. The Furies (underworld demons who avenged spilled family blood) followed him in a swarm all over the Aegean.

To see the place where this bloodstained family had lived out its fate, I landed at Argos, the natural terminus for sailing from Crete. I drove up into mountains and across the peaceful Argive plain—and suddenly beetling cliffs thrust up dead ahead. Anyone who has read of the long-ago happenings here would have felt uneasy. The cliffs were wild, naked, menacing, the scene of appalling deeds.

One more turn, then the remnants of a city spread around me. A stone gateway about eighteen feet high opened into the hillside. I knew it as the entrance to the supposed tomb of Agamemnon. Standing in the giant doorway, I peered up at its stone crosspiece, which weighed 240,000 pounds by archaeologists' estimates. It was about thirty feet long and sixteen feet wide and more than three feet thick. Carved from a single piece of limestone, the crosspiece was a larger building unit than any used in Egyptian pyramids. Yet somehow these unknown Mycenaeans had maneuvered it onto the stone uprights without cranes or jacks, and fitted it neatly into place, where it stayed for three thousand years.

The palace of Mycenae seemed almost as intricate as those on Crete. It had been decorated mostly in the Minoan manner. I walked through dozens of ruined rooms, now open to the sky and choked with weeds. Here once were painted floors, columned porticoes, grand stairways, and frescoed walls. The frescoes that remained showed that Mycenaean ladies followed the opulent fashions of the women of Knossos. Art found in some graves was unmistakably Minoan.

Either an influx from Crete or contact with it stimulated Mycenae to become more refined if not less brutal. Nobody knows how the Mycenaean civilization began or where it came from. Like most, it probably arose from an interplay of migrant breeds and heritages. If the Mycenaeans' ancestors were Minoans, they themselves became something quite different. They were taller and broader, and often bearded. (Minoan men were always clean-shaven.) They used bronze swords and armor, and gloried in deeds of hunting and war. Their fondness for hunting got into Greek myths; one of the labors of Hercules was to capture a wild boar, which he carried to the marketplace at Mycenae.

The last few lords of Mycenae had Cretan artists engrave for them, on vases and rings, a proud record of feats of banditry. Mycenae was well placed for its citizens to plunder travelers on the higher road from the Gulf of Argolis to the Isthmus of Corinth, and to set out occasionally on raids by land or by sea. So it grew rich on warfare, piracy, and trade.

Historians now call the fourteenth and thirteenth centuries B.C. the Mycenaean age. By 1300 B.C. Mycenae was far richer than any other city in Europe. In size, in the splendor of her artworks, and in the impregnable location of her fortress-palace Mycenae had no rival —except perhaps nearby Tiryns, one of her numerous vassal states. Mycenae's last king was called "lord of all Argos and many islands" by Homer, who said that Agamemnon alone contributed no less than a hundred ships to the fleet that sailed against Troy.

One morning in 1190 B.C. or thereabout, Agamemnon and his men marched out through their proud Gate of Lions for their last campaign. I too went out through the Gate of Lions, and glanced up at the two royal beasts, now worn and headless, who stood guard over a long-gone grandeur. Mycenae's riddle lay not in its end but its beginning, long before Pelops—perhaps as early as 3000 B.C.—and I found no clue to that among the silent stones.

We sailed again, winding through the Aegean past legendary Naxos and Skyros. We rounded the knife-edged peninsula where Mount Athos stood sentinel; sighted Thasos—"bare and ugly as a donkey's back," Archilochus called it—where the plentiful gold of Troy was mined; and watched Lemnos carve the sky to starboard. This was the island where Jason and his Argonauts had dallied with women who had killed all the men on Lemnos.

Ahead was the giant arrowhead of stone called Samothrace, its great dark cliffs and wooded bluffs looming straight up from the sea. It had no harbor, which kept it wild. But many a Greek had rowed ashore in a boat of ox hide, seeking dwarf gods who might give charms for protection from shipwreck (in return for sacrifices, of course).

We stayed well clear. We sped past the round hills of Imroz, and I felt the ship rolling in the current from the Dardanelles—or Hellespont, as men called it when Greek ships owned the seas and Trojan chariots ruled the plains.

I watched broad brown fields of Turkey slide past. That flat expanse had been "the ringing plains of windy Troy." Soon I saw the straits of Helle like the mouth of a great river. Shortly, had I been Agamemnon or Ulysses or Achilles, I would have been gazing across the water at a fearsome sight: Troy, sunning itself on its rock like an old proud lion.

I imagined the scene as the Greek armada drew near. A signal fire on the cliff would belch smoke. Bronze war gongs in the towers would be yammering. From Troy's four gates, columns of spearmen would be deploying. Dust clouds would rise as chariots rumbled onto the plain and turned toward the beach. From coves, Trojan guard galleys would sprint out, speeded by the surge of the Hellespont, to ram Agamemnon's first warships.

There would be hours of carnage on the water, on the beach, across four miles of plain. Eventually the Trojans would move back behind their great palisades. Greek ships would loll on the sand like sea monsters gathered to spawn. The plain would swarm with Greeks digging trenches and piling stones for breastworks.

Then, for ten years, nothing much would happen. Neither army sought battle. Troy was ringed by watchfires of the invading host—but the formidable two-man two-horse Trojan chariots, fortresses on wheels, periodically made lightning-fast onslaughts, cutting paths to the citadel for supply trains or reinforcements from its allies in eastern lands. The Greeks contented themselves by sending ships to attack distant towns.

Who were the Trojans? A proud people, now lost in time.

An Egyptian papyrus mentioned them briefly as allies of the Hittites, who controlled most of present-day Turkey from a stronghold east of Ankara. Herodotus, the studious Greek often referred to as the father of history, knew little about Trojans, since he was born centuries after them, but he thought they might have been Cretans, perhaps settling at the strait after Knossos fell. Homer depicted them as speaking Greek and worshiping Greek gods.

Digging revealed that Troy was a site of not one but nine cities. Each overlay its predecessor, as if Troy had had nine lives. The Troy against which the Greeks sailed might have been partly Minoan, partly Mycenaean, and partly Asiatic. It was large—the wall was three miles around—and prosperous.

From the lower Aegean city-states it bought copper, olive oil, wine, and pottery. From Thrace and the Danube came amber, bronze swords, and horses. From Spain came silver, from Egypt ivory, and from distant China so great a rarity as jade. In return, Troy hauled from the interior and exported timber, silver, gold, woolen fabrics, and wild asses. Its seaport must have been as thriving as the approximately contemporary Tartessus.

In the city the houses were small and closely packed together. Storage jars were sunk deeply into floors, as if to provide for a long siege. Near the base of the walls were masses of horse bones, confirming the *Iliad*'s final line, "Thus they performed the final rites for Hector, tamer of horses." There could be no doubt that the siege of Troy narrated by Homer and Virgil actually took place.

I could visualize the night. The dark teeth of the Trojan fortress were unbreakable. But the Greeks built a huge wooden horse, concealed their bravest soldiers inside, and left it outside Troy as a peace offering. They vacated their camp, and went into hiding, whereupon the Trojans dragged the horse into their towered city. In a victorious mood, they ignored their chronic doom-sayer Cassandra, who warned that a horse would ruin them. They scoffed at their priest Laocoon, who cried, "Beware of Greeks bearing gifts!" In the dead of night the Greeks emerged and opened the gates. Troy was sacked, its men slaughtered, its treasures plundered, its women and children dragged off as slaves.

There was plenty to burn: oil and grain were stored; the stone-walled houses had thatched roofs and doors and furniture and thick wooden beams. Soon the greatest pyre that men ever lit was burning. Priam's marble throne was turning black, and the blue dolphins were leaping on a sea of fire, and the Cretan reeds were crackling. Someone swept together hundreds of gold baubles in a box, and tried to

Sailing into the harbor of Santorini, one sees the walls of the collapsed volcanic crater. The explosion here is thought to have been far greater than that of Krakatau in 1883—and tidal waves from Krakatau caused destruction thousands of miles away.

Most of Santorini today is stony and barren, but once it was a rich port for a flourishing maritime civilization.

Scenes of the excavation still going on at Santorini. The people who lived here seem to have enjoyed the comfort and luxury that Plato attributed to lost Atlantis.

These animal frescoes, discovered only a few years ago, are examples of the lively and beautiful style that was widespread before a "Dark Age" closed in around the Aegean Sea.

The Hall of the Colonnade. The Minoans, like the Greeks after them, usually painted plaster and marble surfaces, even statues. The usual notion that classical statuary should be white and "pure" is mistaken.

The Queen's *Megaron*, or Great Hall, contains a
fresco of dolphins and fish.

A staircase in the many-
leveled palace. Dug
into the hillside beneath
it are long halls of
storage chambers.

The South House of the
palace at Knossos. Sir
Arthur Evans began to
undo the effects of fire,
earthquake, and centuries
of neglect.

A bas-relief of a bull, the ever-present symbol of Minos' power. Its curving horns were identified with the crescent moon and with the curved, double-bladed ceremonial axe or *labrys*.

The entrance to a burial chamber known as the Tomb of Agamemnon. Did the Mycenaean prince buried here lead his kinsmen against the walls of Troy?

Stonehenge today, time-worn and still mysterious.

Avebury Mound in Wiltshire, England. Many such burial mounds are near junctions of the raised causeway roads that were built in prehistoric times in southern England.

Why did Stonehenge builders bring some of its stones from far away in Wales? Were they in touch with others who set up the megaliths in Europe and beyond?

flee, only to be crushed by a rock falling from the palace wall. The box was buried under the debris, for Heinrich Schliemann to find three thousand years later.

When the glow climbed the night sky, other fires were lit far away. One leaped from a peak in the Rhodope Mountains. In a great curve to the west, lights flickered from Imroz and Samothrace and Thasos and Parnassus. All around the Aegean the balefires proclaimed that Troy had fallen.

A world burned itself out that night around the dark sea, and soon a tide of iron would be creeping down ravines toward Tiryns and Mycenae and Argos. The highlands had grown a crop of fighters more grim than Homer's heroes.

They battered open the lordly palaces. At Mycenae, archaeologists found evidence that defenses had been hurriedly strengthened and the water supply protected. But the city perished. It left no records. Only the mute stones stood witness to whatever happened. At Tiryns the evidence was dramatic—at the foot of the city walls, buried beneath ashes and charcoal, the skeletons of the last defenders lay where they had fallen or been thrown.

Half-civilized tribes from the north, called Dorians, were overrunning central Greece and Peloponnesus. They came with iron weapons, herds of cattle, and wagon trains carrying their women and children. They meant to stay, and they did. They put nobles to the sword and turned townspeople into serfs.

Some Greeks got away into the mountains of Arcadia, some into Attica, some to islands, some to the coasts of Asia. The invaders followed them into Attica, but were repelled at the small city of Athens; they followed to Crete, and made final the destruction of Knossos; they captured and colonized Thera and other isles.

By about 1100 B.C., high civilization was confined mainly to its earlier homes in Egypt and Mesopotamia. Asia Minor was in darkness. Greece forgot the art of writing. The history of Crete and Mycenae vanished into dim legend. Time had run out for the Bronze Age.

The Dorians practiced no arts and few crafts and trades. They squatted in burnt-out palaces but built nothing there, preferring farm and village life. Each valley had its huddle of huts, and every huddle owed fealty to a local chieftain. Sometimes one village fought another for good bottom land, but not for glory. Every man, feeling unsafe, carried arms. Life was chaos as families wandered, seeking security and peace.

This terminal catastrophe in the prehistory of civilization around the Aegean is what modern historians call "the Dorian conquest" and "the first Dark Age of Europe." The darkness lasted about four hundred years.

Through those centuries there were trickles of migration—mostly to the stronghold of Athens, which never fell to the Dorian hordes because of its natural fortress, the rocky Acropolis. Eventually the population grew too large for the limited space. So Greeks began sailing in small craft to start new settlements in the Cyclades Islands, and later along the west coast of Asia Minor. This new extension of Greece came to be called Ionia.

The refugees brought with them an ancient tradition of song. Somewhere in Ionia a blind Greek named Homer began to wander, singing lays of great deeds done long ago, set to the music of his lyre.

4

Britain's Shadow People

It was the half-dark before daybreak in June, four or five thousand years ago, in the Wiltshire uplands of England. Torches were pale in the growing light. Gazing back through time, one could get glimpses of a procession along an avenue of stone—of priests, perhaps fantastically arrayed in skins and horns and fearsome painted masks, of chiefs with necklaces of teeth, their great heads of hair held up with pins of bone, of women in skins or flaxen robes, of a great peering crowd of shock-headed men and naked children.

They had come from distant places for this one dawn alone. The plain around was dotted with encampments, but the camps were deserted; everyone had left them for the bonfires, for the winding procession with torches around the fields, and at last the climax of this annual festival of the New Year.

Now there was chanting or offering of sacrifices. The god alone stood silent, barely visible at the altar in the gloom of the shrine. Priests called invocations. Then the worshipers' eyes, sensitized by the dimness, saw the god suddenly shine between dark shadows as the sun's first beam shone straight at him down the long alley of roughhewn temple pillars.

At least this was how it seemed to me—and to students of the remarkable fact of "orientation" in the megalithic monuments of ancient civilizations and tribes.

Many temples of Egypt and Babylonia were meticulously oriented —that is, built so that all grand entries faced the same direction. In Babylon this was due east, where the sun would rise on March 21 and September 21, the equinoxes. The spring equinox, at least, was important because it was then that the Euphrates and the Tigris flooded.

The pyramids at Giza were also oriented east and west. The Sphinx faced east. However, many Egyptian temples south of the Nile delta faced the point where the sun rose on the longest day, or where the star Sirius shone on that same dawn—for in Egypt the Nile's annual rise occurred close to that date.

Greek temples and theaters were oriented for optimum light or shadow during the year. I wondered how they had accomplished this, because it was illegal to study the sun's movements (it was considered sacrilegious) in Athens at the height of the Periclean age. The Altar of Heaven in Peking was oriented to midwinter, and one of the Chinese emperor's most important duties was to spend midwinter's day in this temple, sacrificing and praying for a propitious year.

Primitive peoples also understood orientation. Far before any cities were known in northwestern Europe—even before the Egyptians built pyramids—a group known to prehistorians as the Megalithic ("Big Stone") Cult was erecting odd and varied monuments of huge rough-cut stones. In our time, many of these were discovered to be exactly oriented to the summer solstice.

These gigantic jumbles lay along the coasts of Spain and Portugal and deep into France, and in Holland, northern Germany, and much of Scandinavia. But the largest numbers were in and around the British Isles; at least six hundred massive stone shrines still dot the landscape in the uplands from the southern coast of Brittany to the north of Scotland and the Outer Hebrides.

It was 1963 when archaeologists became aware of a purpose in the stone circles of England and Brittany. Some of these circles had been planned, evidently, for the dramatic effect on whoever gathered to watch at dawn on June 24, the first day of summer (called, confusingly, Midsummer's Day in Europe). At dawn of that one day, a priest could stand at the altar in the exact center and be irradiated with glory when the rising sun shone directly at him, like a theater spotlight, through a line of stone pillars or squared portals. Who could doubt that these carefully engineered stone calendars were also meant to be places of worship?

"Midsummer" rites took place through a quarter of the world from Ireland on the west to Russia on the east, from Norway and Sweden on the north to Spain and Greece on the south. Early folk tales and written records mentioned them as having been celebrated since time immemorial.

They weren't originally celebrated in great stone rings, of course. The first festivals must have been bonfires and torch processions. Only when someone began to mark the sun's movements did the idea arise of placing big stones in certain patterns so that someone who knew how could foretell the day when the sun would make its highest and longest arc. Having invented this, designers might have thought of using the same stone reckoning-circles as temples where the ignorant could be summoned periodically to pray and be impressed.

Of all these places the largest and most awesome were in England, Scotland, Ireland, and Brittany. Greatest of all was a pattern of gigantic stone structures standing alone on the broad Salisbury Plain in southern England. Its original name is unknown, but the name that came down from post-Roman times is Stonehenge, which meant "stones hanging" in the old Anglo-Saxon.

Stonehenge was laid out in a definite but mysterious pattern. Around the site was a circular ditch a hundred yards in diameter. Inside it, great stones (some tumbled or broken in recent centuries) had stood in four series. The two outermost series formed circles. The third was a horseshoe. The innermost was an oval enclosing a central block of blue marble, sixteen feet long by four across, known as the Altar Stone.

The outermost circular colonnade consisted of upright eighteen-foot sandstone pillars, connected by horizontal slabs atop them—the "hanging" stones. These weren't merely resting on top. Someone had cut perfectly round holes in them, which fitted exactly onto projections from the flat tops of the uprights. (I had seen this same peg-and-hole plan in the great gate at Mycenae.) Moreover, the capstones were locked together laterally, with tongue-and-groove joints. Somebody had to lift them twenty feet, then fit them precisely into place like a gigantic Chinese puzzle. They were leveled so accurately that I wondered how it could have been done without instruments.

The two tallest stones (twenty-two feet) were in the middle of the horseshoe, with a fifteen-foot capstone over them. Outside the circle to the northeast stood another pair of stones—and beyond that, one great slab called the Friar's Heel. Once a year someone could stand at the Altar Stone, peer through the pillars of the two great circles and the pair of outer stones, and see the rising sun just above the heel stone.

This fact was forgotten with the passing of centuries. Natives made up more exotic explanations for Stonehenge and other huge prehistoric monuments like Avebury twenty miles to the north, Castle Rigg in Scotland, the "giants' graves" of Newgrange within the Bend of the Boyne in Ireland, and the great South Brittany monolith (now broken in three pieces), which once towered more than sixty feet high, was clearly visible ten miles across the sea, and was estimated to weigh 680,000 pounds.

Everyone agreed that these monuments had to have been of supernatural origin. No mortal could have fixed such masses in such precise symmetry. Obviously they belonged to the remote past, when giants and heroes and wizards walked the land. The Celts of Brittany, Wales, and Ireland named their prehistoric stone formations in accordance with their belief that the "little people" could lift any amount of weight. The English, harking back to tales of Druid priests, attributed Stonehenge and other stone rings to them. Or, some thought, King Arthur and his knights might be responsible.

What was England really like, I wondered, in its earliest days of human habitation? Professor R. C. Collingwood drew a detailed picture:

> Britain was backward by comparison with the Continent; primitive in its civilization, stagnant and passive in its life, receiving most of what progress it enjoyed through invasion and importation from overseas.
>
> Its people lived in isolated farms or hut-villages . . . by agriculture and livestock, augmented no doubt by hunting and fishing. They made rude pottery without a wheel, but they were visited by itinerant bronze-founders able to make swords, axes, sickles, carpenters tools, metal parts of wheeled vehicles, buckets, and cauldrons.
>
> Judging by the absence of towns, these people were little organized, and their political life was simple and undeveloped.

This late Bronze Age in the island, by all evidence, began about 1000 B.C. and lasted until about 400 B.C. But the Romans, when they came in 55 B.C. to colonize Britain, found no written language there.

But for Stonehenge the radiocarbon date estimated for the beginning of construction was between 2775 and 1900 B.C. Construction may have continued until as late as 1400 B.C. So we must assume that those who planned and built it were Stone Age types—even less skillful than their ignorant Bronze Age successors described by Professor Collingwood!

And so the most celebrated monument surviving from pre-Roman England loomed as a huge, silent contradiction to everything archaeologists and geologists had deduced about the island.

The stark fact seems to be that a large number of people, for some almost unimaginable reason, felt a compulsion to transport at least eighty stones, weighing four tons or more apiece, from Mount Prescelly in southwestern Wales (definitely identified as the source of the Stonehenge rock) to Salisbury Plain—135 miles as the crow flies.

To me, the question wasn't whether intelligent, civilized men with Stone Age tools could do the job. The question was whether Stone Age men—illiterate, hindered by superstitions, untrained—were capable first of conceiving the complex structure of Stonehenge, second of planning it in detail without drawings, and finally of organizing for the prolonged and herculean toil needed to cut and move the stones and set them up on the site.

The only imaginable answer, to me, was that some other people, much more civilized, also lived in Britain during the thousand-odd-year period when Stonehenge and other astronomically aligned megaliths were being built. In historic times, two peoples with different racial origins and different levels of culture often lived side by side. Surely it could happen in a prehistoric age too.

Wouldn't the more advanced race leave traces of itself? Perhaps it had. Recently, British archaeologists began studying what they called a "Wessex culture," which existed around 1550 B.C. The only evidence I knew about was in 130 mound graves. But all were graves of aristocrats, with fine bronze pins from central Europe; gold earrings presumably from Ireland, where the nearest gold lay; fine pottery from Brittany; amber drinking cups and magnificent necklaces with several hundred amber beads, of unknown origin. One mound in Cornwall contained a goldsmith's masterpiece: a cup hammered from a single sheet of gold, its handle attached by gold rivets and washers.

Then too, tombs were being excavated within sight of Stonehenge itself. They were comparable to those of Mycenae. For example, a man entombed in an eleven-foot-high burial mound had a solid gold breastplate as big as a dinner plate. He wore a belt with a two-piece gold clasp, beautifully worked. Three bronze daggers were with him, and the handle of one was designed in chevrons with thousands of tiny gold pins. A bronze ax was wrapped in cloth. Bronze rivets above the skull suggested a helmet.

Whoever these unknown elite were, they disappeared completely by the time the Roman Empire grew interested in Britain. Small numbers of them might have inhabited the country for one or two thousand years, building colossal stone observatories and using them, perhaps while the kings of Minoan Crete and Mycenaean Greece came and went. Then their miniature civilization quietly passed away, for uncertain reasons.

According to well-substantiated theory, Stonehenge and other megaliths were constructed as astronomical instruments, and it is believed that designers of megaliths must have understood how the cycles of eclipses were determined. But why construct them in Britain? Many eclipses weren't observable there, either because of bad weather or because of geographic location. When visible, they wouldn't be as impressive to sun worshipers or moon worshipers as they would be in brighter regions.

One of the few factors that made Britain a good place for sky study, so far as I knew, was that the horizon in northern latitudes would give a good sight line for the apparent slow weaving of the moon. This deviation, which at its maximum appeared as only about two thirds of the width of the sun, could be seen at the maximum in Britain.

Why would people on this far northern island be curious about eclipse dates and other meteorological cycles? Satisfaction of their curiosity required the immense toil of stone moving as well as elaborate record keeping and calculating.

Maybe because they were providing the information for people who badly needed it elsewhere.

In a theocracy like Egypt or Sumer, or perhaps Crete or Mycenae, priest-rulers could use such data to enhance their power. They could do much more than tell their flock when to plant and harvest, and be proven right. On the day or night that a faraway stone computer had predicted an eclipse, they might well give dire warnings, somewhat as the Connecticut Yankee did at Camelot in Mark Twain's fantasy. And when the prophesied blotting out of the heavenly body started, they could intone the magic words that enabled the sun or the moon to escape the blackness.

Maybe they couldn't build the necessary massive stone patterns in their own land, for reasons of latitude or topography, or simply because their people would have asked too many questions. Very well. Suppose they sent expeditions to England and Wales and Brittany to arrange for construction and observation. Then how did they keep in touch through the centuries? Were they capable of telepathy or teleportation, as Hindu sages were said to be?

Probably no one will ever know. But I thought I knew what eventually happened to the unknown elite.

Men armed with iron arrived and slaughtered the men of bronze. At this point we could recognize across the millennia a fellow being. A creature capable of killing someone with iron was surely, to modern eyes, a man and a brother. It took brains to know that iron was better than bronze for bashing skulls.

England's transition from Bronze Age to Iron Age took a long time. Bronze was still used widely until the last century before Christ. On this subject Professor Collingwood wrote:

> Many settlements indicate a mode of life not perceptibly different from that of their late Bronze Age background; they are farms or villages, often undefended, still using bronze and even flint implements and possessing very little iron, but indicating their date by a change in the style of their pottery.

This was about three centuries before Christ. But as the newcomers with iron weapons multiplied and developed, local wars erupted. The country grew more savage. Belgic tribes, a people of chariots and horsemen, arrived and built fortified towns. But the tramp of the Roman Legions was following them. Caesar saw the Britons as a tougher and cruder branch of the Celtics he had faced in Gaul and had never forgotten. Those whom he fought in Britain were just as fearsome. Not only did they paint themselves blue, they drove war chariots hooked with scythes at the axles.

Their religion was that of the Druids, with terrible white-robed priests who were said to drive a man mad by throwing a wisp of straw in his face. Druids had profoundly influenced the life of Germany and Gaul as well as Britain. "Those who want to study Druidism," wrote Caesar, "generally go to Britain for the purpose."

Romans (and later peoples) knew little about Druid beliefs except that they undoubtedly entailed human sacrifice. The mysterious priesthoods of the trees bound themselves and their votaries by the most deadly sacraments that men could take. Although Romans had scant respect for human life, as everyone knew from their treatment of gladiators and Christians, they drew the line at murder to please the gods. Caesar and the proconsuls worked systematically to drive Druids out of England. Some found refuge in the Welsh mountains.

There, for perhaps another thousand years, their descendants kept alive under the name Merlin (from the Celtic sky god Myrddhin) the tradition of magic that had been handed down since the unknown time when the Druids came out of nowhere—or perhaps out of Africa, as one legend said.

I talked with Gerald Hawkins, author of *Beyond Stonehenge*, and asked if he would speculate about the origin of the people who created the arches of Stonehenge. What did it take to build Stonehenge?

"I estimate one and a half million man days of work and many broken legs," he replied. "Certainly the stones couldn't be carried but they would have to be rolled or dragged. One archeologist has called them howling barbarians, but I prefer to regard them not as primitive people but simple people in their lifestyle. I believe that a lot of their thought processes exist with us today and a lot of their achievements are what we're striving for. As to what was in their minds, I have uncovered certain very hard facts, numerical relationships, an interest in precision, an interest in time patterns and this means something very fundamental to the psychological basis to their beliefs. What they were doing was a complete entity to them, and it must have been extremely satisfying. They did not do it by being driven as slaves. They did not do it for money because there was no monetary system. They did it because they wanted to, and here we have perhaps the beginning of our civilization, the essence of civilization, a community with a common purpose and a common set of ideas."

Britain was a Roman province for nearly four hundred years, most of which were tranquil and left little for history to note. The Romans built noble roads, fortresses, market cities, country houses—whose ruins the next comers contemplated with awe. But Roman law, language, and institutions disappeared when the legions left the province to sink or swim in the great convulsion of the Dark Ages.

A strange fact emerged many centuries later when scholars pored through the detailed reports by Roman officials in Britain. Nowhere did they mention Stonehenge or other strange megaliths. Surely the Romans, as great builders themselves, were puzzled by the huge stone circles. Why were they silent?

Perhaps they loathed Druids too much to mention any works, as they thought, of the occult practitioners. Stonehenge had probably become notorious as a Druid temple. By the seventeenth century all such "rude monuments" were commonly ascribed to the last pre-

Christian inhabitants of each country—in Scandinavia to the Vikings, in France to the Gauls, and in Britain to the Celts and especially their Celtic priests and judges and seers, the Druids.

Even in my own travels I had heard people damn Stonehenge as a bloody place where Druids read the omens, sacrificed humans, and who knew what else. But even if Stonehenge was used for Druid rites, it was not built by Druids. Archaeologists proved decades ago that Stonehenge was twice as old as the Druids. Even so, right up to today, members of a "Most Ancient Order of Druids" meet at Stonehenge and perform secret ceremonies that they say date back to Atlantis.

5

The Invisible Machines

LOOKING OUT over a lifeless wasteland, I thought of something Oliver Cromwell said: "No one rises so high as he who knows not whither he is going." The thought came out of memory and hit me because it applied to me at that very moment.

Not knowing where I might go, I had set out to find whatever was understandable of lost civilizations. Now, having followed a winding trail back and back through five millennia, I found myself with an unexpected overview of those vanished empires. The trail had led me to a new perspective.

The perspective was in my mind's eye, of course. My corporeal eyes were squinting at some low mounds rising from a yellow-brown plain, and a tumbled disorder of broken bricks. These were the remnants of the long-lost biblical city Ur of the Chaldees, mentioned in the eleventh chapter of the Book of Genesis as the home of the first patriarch Abraham.

An idea had dawned on me: An invisible machine had once been at work here. Almost the same machine was designed and put together by someone in the jungles of Cambodia, by someone else in the Indus Valley badlands, by others near here in this famed fertile crescent of land where so many of the earliest cities arose. The idea of the machine also gave me a little clearer understanding of the religious zeal of lost civilizations, particularly those mentioned in the Holy Scriptures.

Forty years ago nobody knew where Ur lay, if indeed it had ever existed. In those years the Old Testament was widely regarded as a poetic recounting of garbled folklore, rather than as a historical narrative of the Israelite nation. But then Ur was found, farther back in the darkness of time than even the cities of Egypt. This and other discoveries in the ancient Near East began to reverse the tide of skepticism.

Today the ruins of Ur are one of many stops on the famous Baghdad railway. I took the train at Basra, near the Persian Gulf, and went clanking through 120 miles of hot and dreary wastes. When the train let me off and the noise of the wheels died away, I was surrounded by a vast silence. I seemed to stand in the middle of an enormous brown dish bisected by the gleaming line of the railroad track. But when I turned I saw a higher mound among the low ones in the distance.

It was the ziggurat of Ur, forerunner of the Tower of Babel.

As I hiked to it my spirits soared despite the smothering heat. Ur was probably the place, from all archaeological evidence so far, where man first refined civilization itself.

It was where the machines I had postulated had begun their wondrous work. Even in ruins, Ur was a place I was eager to explore.

Here the wheel first rolled upon a gridwork of city streets. Here chieftains first created the military phalanx and the chariot, two seemingly omnipotent weapons of their day. Here writing was first scratched on clay tablets. From here, it was said, Abraham took arithmetic to Egypt.

The residents of Ur, and those who learned from them in other Sumerian cities, were self-taught architects and hydraulic engineers. They wrote epic poetry. They studied the stars. Their minds evolved basic ideas for education, philosophy, and medicine. Scientific lore that they had passed on to the Arabs would eventually help awaken medieval Europe.

It was here—not in Egypt or Babylon or Greece—that men first made systematic, rational laws to govern human behavior. They established a crude and fragmentary but recognizable democracy—as well as the brutal and now-familiar concept of empire. They built the earliest known true city.

Now, a city isn't an overgrown village. There were villages for untold centuries before the strange new machines made cities possible. We might find seeds of civilization in a primitive farmer's hut, but we could see the flowering only in a city.

As you read this, perhaps you're thinking I was heat-struck. "Machines" long before the steam engine or even the waterwheel? Where was my proof?

I would have to admit that no specimen of the machine could be found in archaeological digs. The reason it has evaded detection, despite masses of direct evidence, is that it was composed almost entirely of human parts: a disciplined assemblage of men. Its only lifeless parts, probably, were levers and inclined planes, and perhaps logs used as rollers.

Such a machine could concentrate enormous energy and accomplish previously unimaginable feats. I don't think I am playing with words when I classify a disciplined mass of people as a machine. Lewis Mumford elaborated this idea as long ago as 1934 in his book *Technics and Civilization.*

"Machine" is defined in dictionaries as "any combination of interrelated parts for using or applying energy to do work." By this definition the machine that built the walls of Ur and so many other early cities was a true machine—all the more mechanical because the human bodies that were its moving parts had become what modern technologists would call servomechanisms—virtual robots, totally obedient.

What induced a crowd of people to dehumanize themselves for months or years of preplanned labor? I think it was a powerful belief in something beyond themselves. In a word, religion.

Some genius discovered this way of establishing feelings of solidarity among thousands of persons. It was a task for an expert, a full-time specialist. Paul Wheatley of the University of Chicago, studying ancient cities, concluded that "specialized priests were among the first to be released from the daily round of subsistence labor."

These priests exhorted other people needed for the building of walls and temples. They sold the idea of enhancing the glory of high-born individuals close to the gods. Probably they also sold visions of what a city could mean to the city dwellers themselves. It could mean more abundance and more leisure someday, and could free everyone from the dull village grind.

The toilers might even see themselves as purchasing an earthly paradise; without walls there could be no paradise. (The very word *paradise*, in the original Persian, meant "walled garden.") They probably cherished hopes of order, beauty, and human fellowship. Why not? Behind walls they did create the beautiful ideas and art that comprised civilization.

But it turned out that countless workers passed their whole lifetimes in the human machine. The wall was only the beginning of their toil. Public works and public utilities were essential even for a small city like Ur. Canals had to be cut, wide fields irrigated, crops threshed, streets paved, waterworks built.

Someone planned this. Maybe committees did it in Ur and Mohenjo-Daro and Zimbabwe, but I couldn't imagine it. A supreme Big Brother was more likely. And in fact he was found to exist in every ancient city where detailed records came to light: a king revered as divine. The village's hunter-chieftain became a monarch and god when he built a city.

Minos, Theseus, the pharaohs, and countless kings and sultans and potentates acted in the name of a god when they created their cities. Each king's first act, the very key to his authority, was to put up a temple. Then he erected a wall around the temple and his followers, turning the whole area into a sacred place: a city.

A king's power to make decisions could be good for his people. A large population, acting as one, could bring about vast public improvements, far beyond the scope of villages. Unlike a village council of elders, a king could make decrees that would change the environment or the people's behavior.

But his power was precarious unless his people worshiped him.

Without this religious fervor, it seemed to me, people wouldn't have done much more than erect the city walls. But they went on to build pyramids and ziggurats and tombs—Angkor Wat and Stonehenge and Knossos and many others. I would guess that every prehistoric complex of stone buildings was the home of a supposed god.

This was the other big reason, probably, why people liked to live in cities. To inhabit the same city as a god was to be "out of this world," so to speak. It was to be a member of a supercommunity. The idea could captivate even distant villages; they made pilgrimages to the city on religious festival days.

Every society has an image of itself, its way of life. In ancient times, kings and priests shaped this image. The medieval Christian image of heaven as a place where the blessed found their highest fulfillment in beholding God and singing his praises was only a slightly etherealized version of how a city like Ur seemed to its residents. Even in the comparatively late Etruscan culture, when a new city was founded, a priest held the plow that traced the outlines of the wall to be built.

A king not only played God but provided a satisfying life for his subjects. They shared vicariously in his triumphs of hunting, warfare, amorous conquest, or whatever. He also had to keep them busy—so he decreed the building of temples, tombs, and monuments. People could get joy from such labor. The great European cathedrals were built by voluntary toil through centuries.

What kept people busy in Ur? Mostly the brick mountain rising from an ocean of dust, toward which I was walking.

It was the Ziggurat of the Moon God Nannar. Sir Leonard Woolley had excavated and partially restored it in the 1930s. He wrote:

> The ziggurat is a peculiar feature of Sumerian architecture which can now be traced back to the earliest times. . . .

> The immigrants to lower Mesopotamia found themselves on a vast level plain where there was no hill on which god could be properly worshiped. In every town which was big enough to warrant the effort the inhabitants built a "high place," a tower rising in stages, crowned by the town's principal shrine. This was the ziggurat.

> Of them all, the biggest and most famous was, in course of time, the Ziggurat of Babylon, which in Hebrew tradition became known as the Tower of Babel. It was but a repetition on a slightly larger scale of the ziggurat of Ur, and it too was built by Ur-Nammu.

Ur-Nammu was one of the last Sumerian kings. His stone mountain set a fashion among civilizations for two thousand years. It was a three-stage pyramid, each step a broad terrace, inset with a winding external stairway. I climbed to the lofty height where the city's patron divinity Nannar might dwell. His one-room sanctum was paved with blue enameled tiles and paneled with rare woods like cedar and cypress, inlaid with marble, onyx, alabaster, agate, and gold.

This temple, like so many that followed, had been more than just a monument. It was a holy place, tended and cared for every day. Hymns and prayers were composed and recited there. Rites were planned and performed. Sacred festivals were celebrated. So a specialized priesthood proliferated. The temple and its coterie naturally became the intellectual center. Writing was invented and practiced in the temples, and probably arithmetic too.

Poor as well as rich turned over to the temples whatever share of worldly goods they thought would be sufficiently pleasing. The priests couldn't personally spend or consume the wealth that flowed in, so they became the city's financiers, investing in profitable-looking ventures such as trade missions elsewhere. They also became money changers and money lenders to the citizenry. Sometimes they lent to the sick or poor without interest, merely asking a return of the principal when the gods became more beneficent. Gods weren't aloof from men; some of them lived on earth in the temples, ate heartily, and augmented the population through communion with pious women.

Building the ziggurat was the great labor to which Ur-Nammu consecrated masses of willing manpower. Earlier there had been other big jobs. The outer wall had been first and biggest. "It was colossal and must have seemed to the builder impregnable," Sir Leonard Woolley wrote. "But it was to fall in the end. Not a trace remained. . . . Just because the defenses of Ur had been so strong the victorious enemy dismantled them systematically, leaving not one brick upon another."

When there were no outside enemies, as in the Mayan and Incan and Indus Valley civilizations, at least for a while—the authoritarian system devoured itself. The great forces set in motion by Man the Organizer called for commensurately great collective enterprises. The human machines had to operate in a big way or they wouldn't work at all; no Boss, however big his bureaucratic apparatus, could govern a hundred little enterprises with their own craft skills, their own pride and quirks. Therefore, the machines were impersonal, if not dehumanized, by their very nature, and the planners developed the habit of "thinking big."

The superhuman pyramid building and dam building and palace building reduced the size and importance of the humans involved except for the central figure, the regal priestly Organizer himself. He knew he must keep the people worshiping him; once his royal power was switched off, his huge human machine either "went dead" or went wild. To keep power he had to seem able to see the future. Hence the enormous pains taken by priesthoods so that they could awe the populace by foretelling eclipses and solstices.

But even in the shadow of the pyramids the old cooperative ways and diverse thinking of the villages crept in and found niches, despite all Mr. Big could do. There had to be families and neighborhoods. There had to be a mixture of vocations, and a few independent craftsmen. There had to be a marketplace. So, even though it took centuries if not millennia, independent thinking filtered through the community. And ultimately the people went into the citadel and hacked the priests to death, or strangled them, or frightened them into fleeing.

Wherever this happened, civilization disintegrated and cities emptied. Leaderless and disorganized, the people disappeared in the mists of time.

But in a sense they had transcended themselves. They had risen above superstition and robot obedience. If only they had gone further, had learned to organize for their own good as well as that of whatever gods they revered!

Not knowing the past, they were condemned to repeat it, as George Santayana said. They had no way of knowing why other civilizations perished. Our generation was the first to know, even in dim outline.

Will our knowledge show us how to make our story a finer one? We have a great civilization to save or to lose. Those dead civilizations challenge us and we need the challenge.

Man isn't complete. Ancient brutish traits still lurk within him, but he is learning to outgrow them. However gigantic or sacred our buildings may be, we are beginning to see that true civilization must be achieved in individual hearts. Looking back at those splendid but ultimately tragic ruins in deserts and jungles, maybe we'll see how to create the sublime society for which most of us have always yearned.

Part Two

EXTRATERRESTRIALS

6

The Hunt and the Witnesses

"This is an example of a UFO ground effect," he was saying. "It's a soybean field in Iowa where a farmer found that a forty-foot circular patch of soybeans had been destroyed." I stared down at the picture Allen Hynek was describing. A hot white spot had been burned into a large patch of neatly planted rows.

"I went there and examined it," he continued. "The plants were not crushed or broken, but looked as though they had been subjected to intense radiation from the top. The circle was discovered in the morning. The night before, the daughter of the man who owned the land reported that she had seen a UFO land."

There was no pause for dramatic effect, nor any particular underlining of the letters UFO. To Allen Hynek, UFOs were commonplace subjects. A former chairman of the Department of Astronomy at Northwestern University, he is director of the Center for UFO Studies at Evanston, Illinois. He had crossed over from academe to what many of his former colleagues might consider the "wild side." I knew him, however, as a dedicated research scientist who pursues the study of UFOs from a hard-nosed nothing-is-accepted-until-it-can-be-verified basis.

Dr. Hynek had entered the field as a skeptic. Years ago, while he was teaching at Northwestern, he was asked to become a consultant for the U.S. Air Force on Project Blue Book, one of the early studies of UFOs. The conclusion reached in the Blue Book report was that there was insufficient evidence to consider the possibility that UFOs exist. Allen Hynek pursued the study long after the Air Force concluded the program. In the intervening twenty years he has moved from skeptic to expert. Allen Hynek might object to the description. He would prefer, I think, "scientist in search of an answer."

Clearly he enjoyed his labors. Behind his thick-lensed glasses, his eyes gleamed as he detailed the differences between UFOs, IFOs (Identifiable Flying Objects) and Daylight Disks (sparkling circles traveling across daylight skies). After twenty years of research, writing, and analysis, he hadn't tired of his subject, nor apparently had he let any part of his thinking become ritualized dogma. He seemed to accept his role as man-on-the-spot with amazing ease. By the very nature of his efforts he had become the bull's-eye for anyone who wanted to attack the field of UFO study. Allen Hynek was the best spokesman for a rational approach to the question.

Among its many activities, the Center for UFO Studies maintains a field staff and a twenty-four-hour hot line. The telephone ties the Center to such federal agencies as the FAA, the FBI, and virtually every civilian defense unit in the country. Reports of sightings are referred to the Center, where they are checked, cataloged, and—when warranted—investigated. In addition, the Center provides information and facilities for scientists at a number of prominent universities, among them UCLA, Johns Hopkins, and the University of London.

The most critical function of the Center is to collect a data bank, a register of every conceivable type of UFO sighting. Allen Hynek had described the Center's information pool as numbering some seventy thousand entries. For Hynek this extraordinary collection of information represents the most heavily weighted argument in favor of the existence of UFOs.

"When you ask about real evidence," he says, "the one absolutely incontrovertible fact is that UFO reports exist, and not just from the United States, but from all over the world. You may say: 'Well, so what? Reports are cheap.'

"One has to examine the caliber of the people that the reports come from, and this is what we do at the Center. The observer is our only fact-gathering instrument. We must know its caliber.

"You know, when I first started my work with the Air Force, I was convinced that the stuff was just nonsense, and I thought that, well, we in the USA are peculiarly given to silly things. Then I was surprised to find that the reports were actually coming from all parts of the world, and from credible people."

Allen Hynek has probably interviewed as many "sighters" as anyone in the world. In the course of cataloging UFO information, he constantly came into contact with policemen, pilots, scientists, and air-traffic controllers—witnesses, as he put it, of unquestionable integrity.

He listed forms of corollary evidence that helped convince him that in fact something was seen. "If reports were limited to just the sightings in the sky, I don't think the Center for UFO Studies would exist, and no scientist would be willing to take the time to look at it. But it's because you have radar evidence, photographic evidence, and even evidence of animals.

"Often people tell me that what first called their attention to something strange going on was the fact that the horses in the barn were raising a fuss. In one case, when they went out to find out what was disturbing the animals, they saw this glowing craft hovering over the barn."

I wanted something more tangible than eyewitness accounts. Dr. Hynek suggested I begin with "trace cases," those times when the UFO encounter actually left a physical trace that could be studied at a later date.

"There are hundreds of cases in the files," he said, "which list real physical evidence, such as burned patches on the ground, landing marks, broken tree branches."

For closer study of these, I contacted Ted Phillips, a field investigator for the Center. We met in Columbia, Missouri, not far from Ted's hometown of Sedalia. Ted's full-time occupation is inspector for the Missouri State Highway Department. His avocation is UFOs, an interest that dates back to his involvement in the Vanguard satellite program. He got deeply involved in 1964 when he became so intrigued by a local UFO story that he started his own on-the-spot investigation. Since then he's covered hundreds of cases. He explained to me his specialty, physical-trace events.

"The most positive type of report, the most direct avenue of approach to resolving the UFO problem, is through physical traces, because they remain long after the visual observation by the witnesses. We have something that can be photographed, studied, and analyzed for a long period of time. But investigations of physical-trace cases take money. So we are highly selective in cases that we investigate. They have to meet certain standards. A high-quality trace case must be seen by two or more credible witnesses within a hundred to two hundred and fifty feet of a UFO. It must be on the ground or extremely near the ground. The duration of observation must be no less than one minute, so the witnesses have a little bit of time to establish that they're seeing something really strange—a physical trace that has no immediate natural explanation."

There have been any number of so-called "fairy rings" that have been misidentified as landing tracks left by UFO craft. They are in fact mushroom or fungus growths in which the spores are released in the soil in a circular configuration. Sometimes, not always, the plant life around that ring will die because of the fungus growth in the soil. Poisons or defoliants occasionally cause a round "bald" spot in an otherwise normal vegetation pattern, but they too are easy to spot. The UFO trace is generally clear: an irregular burned area or a circular burned, depressed, or dehydrated area with the surrounding environment still standing unchanged. Many times plant life is swirled in a clockwise or counterclockwise position. In other cases the soil is dried, sapped of all moisture, obviously quite dead.

Ted explained his checking process. "After we've done photographic work, then we get the samples. These are generally taken in half-inch increments from the surface down to a considerable depth. These are filed away in separated containers and cataloged, showing the precise spot where they're taken. So if you're sitting five hundred miles away from the site, you know exactly where that sample came from. And then, of course, we take control samples along several given lines. I do it generally in five-foot increments to a distance of up to three hundred feet, to be sure that we're getting a very representative profile of the soil leading away from the landing site."

I asked him if the laboratory experiments gave conclusive results, thinking in particular of the Delphos, Kansas, incident. It happened on the Johnson farm at sundown on November 2, 1971. Darrell Johnson and his wife were inside the house. His son was working in the sheep pen. Suddenly flashing lights lit up the yard area. At the same moment, there was a violent reaction among the animals. The family dog went berserk. The sheep began to bellow. Darrell and Irma Johnson came out of the house in time to see the UFO take off. What was left behind was a shiny doughnut ring on the ground. To this day, water will not be absorbed by the ring.

Ted explained that lab analysis had finally determined that the ground was irradiated, that siliconelike particles had been created, which sealed out water. Stranger to me was the information that when Darrell and Irma Johnson touched the ring, their fingers went numb, and the numbing effects have lasted for five years.

When I asked Ted Phillips whether or not he's ever found out exactly what that coating was, he explained that the number of tests needed and the expense of those tests put further examination out of his reach. I was frustrated by Ted's answer. I wanted more. I wanted evidence that a rocket plume had irradiated the soil, and I wanted to know more about the process of testing. I asked Ted to introduce me to one of the men who had conducted the soil analysis for him. He suggested I contact Dr. Edward Zeller, professor of geology, astronomy, and physics at the University of Kansas.

Most of Dr. Zeller's career has been spent studying the relationship of radiation to solids. His specialty is radiation physics. He was involved in space-program operations, studying the effects of radiation in interplanetary and interstellar space. He had been at Lawrence, Kansas, for twenty years and seemed to be a likely candidate for my next set of questions.

I had done some preliminary reading about the properties of soil. It seemed to me that a scientist was going to have to look for variability in soil samples that were said to have been affected by the UFO vis-à-vis the control sample. But what is variability in soil? Are we talking about the components of soil or the structure of the soil? After some dry text reading I learned that in order to understand variability I would have to study the thermoluminescence process.

Simply put, if the soil is subjected either to radiation or to heating, a characteristic signature will be left behind in the soil. Most crystalline materials—window glass, sand, normal rocks—will show a certain amount of luminescence if you were, say, to heat them on a hot plate in a dark room. If the materials are strongly irradiated, they show much more of this luminescence than if they're just heated. So when we talk about the differences in the variability of soil samples, we are essentially talking about seeing the differences in the luminescent properties of the soil.

Over the past twenty years Dr. Zeller has run innumerable tests on soil samples taken from UFO sites. I was hoping I could pin down information that would show a high nuclear-radiation level in the samples.

"Dr. Zeller," I asked, "has a Geiger counter ever turned up an inordinate amount of radioactivity?"

"We have never found anything in the samples that I have studied that gave a particularly high radiation account." Luminescence, however, was another story. There had been a lot of unexpected results in luminescence tests.

"Which were the most interesting?" I asked.

"There are a whole bunch of Medford samples, and in the Medford samples the variability is higher than I would expect in material from a normal field. In other words, if you just start across a field and start analyzing soils, you expect a reasonable level of uniformity. In the case of the Medford site, I see such large variability that I find it unexpected."

I dived into my notes on Medford. Medford, Minnesota. The Kay home. A beautiful two-story brick-and-wood colonial. Neatly manicured lawn. Big circular driveway. Helen Kay, her daughter, Jane, and son, Jerry. Really nice people. Feet on the ground. Solid citizens. Sunday, November 2, 1975. Jane was doing her homework. Jerry and his wife had just left after an evening's visit. They all described an incoming big orange ball alighting on a nearby football field. Jane flashed on the word "UFO." Jerry thought of a huge pyrotechnic display being dropped by parachute. Helen wasn't sure. It was definitely not an airplane, she said, or any helicopter she had ever imagined.

The football field on which the Kays saw the UFO set down was the Medford field that had produced the sample for Dr. Zeller. It seemed to me that here was an opportunity to come up with at least tangible evidence of a UFO landing.

"The basic thing at the Medford site," Dr. Zeller went on, "is that some of the samples show almost ten times the amount of luminescence that others do, and that's unusual. We wouldn't expect that level of variability in soil samples that under the microscope look very similar. The Medford-site samples looked to us to be quite uniform initially, and therefore we would have expected them to have similar luminescent properties. We find large-scale variation in the glow curves, but no large-scale variation in the microscopic appearance of the samples. The only thing we can say is that these high variability conditions are unusual. Exactly what they mean, I can't tell you."

Dr. Zeller wasn't willing to commit himself to UFO speculation. He is truly a cautious scientist thoroughly disciplined in scientific method.

I tried to get him to speculate what the source of strange physical traces might be. "Does the kind of phenomenon that occurs lead you to think of some kind of flying object that exists in our world today? Something that is manmade, I mean."

"I must answer this by saying we're in the dark. First of all, unfortunately we can't reproduce these conditions. We simply can't call down a flying saucer, as it were, and ask it to hover above the soil while we watch the effects. I don't think it would be possible at all for a helicopter to produce this type of effect. There's simply nothing in the downwash from the blades that could do it. As for other types of vehicles—automobiles, trucks, or aircraft of any other sort—the answer is no, they couldn't produce that type of effect. No possibility at all."

And that was as far as Dr. Zeller would go, on or off the record. The process of wrenching answers from scientists sometimes proves to be very painful. UFOs are the stuff popular journals exploit. They seem to bear a leprous label that puts them beyond the pale of legitimate inquiry. The Viking mission to Mars and the speculation about life on other planets has the federal government's blessings and money. UFOs do not.

Dr. Zeller left me with this thought. He said, "You know, frankly, I've never seen an unidentified flying object. However, I have never seen a meteorite land, and I know they exist."

I found a need to see and hear firsthand, minute-by-minute accounts of a UFO landing. I wasn't satisfied with the reports I had read in newspapers and magazines. It seemed to me that they were edited in such a way as to reflect the bias of the reporter.

For those who share my frustration, I have decided to set down one story as I heard it, in the exact words of the individual who lived it.

Phil Baker was one of the interview subjects. His home is in Mellen, Wisconsin, about twenty miles south of Ashland. Mellen brings to life Andrew Wyeth's brown-toned view of rural northern America. Long ribbons of narrow blacktop or just plain dirt roads link one isolated farmhouse to another. Phil Baker has lived in this country all his life. He works in a wood-veneer manufacturing plant, but his heart is with the land. Each spring he anxiously awaits the last frost so that he can get out his harrow, turn his fields, and plant his summer food crop. Surrounded by his family and his land, he feels fulfilled. Fellow townsmen of Phil Baker, like newspaper editor Jasper Landry and Undersheriff George Ree, know him as a solid citizen.

Phil Baker, his wife, and four children—ages ten to seventeen—all participated in a singular event. Here is what happened, in their words, as they told it to me.

"My name is Philip Baker. I live at Mellen, Wisconsin, the northerly part of Wisconsin—that is, I work for Louisiana Pacific, Seaway Division, at Mellen, Wisconsin. I'm a machine operator. We produce high-grade veneer, which is put into the plywood. It's outside skin for the plywood.

"On March 13, 1975, in the evening, right around nine o'clock, I was sitting on the davenport. I had just gotten a box of seed that I had sent for, and opened it, when my daughter came in from outdoors. She was going to put the cats out. She came back in, and she was quite badly frightened. She said there was a UFO sitting on the town road up here. I could tell by the way she said it that she was badly frightened."

Jane Baker: "When I first saw it, I was scared. I felt like running. I didn't know where to go. I was scared. I don't know, when I watch these movies on TV, there's little green men coming out with long arms, getting the people and killing them. I got scared. I didn't know what to do. I really got scared, so I ran into the house. I didn't feel like going out, but when he went out, I went out—but I really felt like going upstairs and going under my blankets and hiding or something. I got scared."

Phil Baker: "By the time I got my shoes on and stepped out the door and stood there on the porch and looked, there it was, sitting big as life.

"What I saw was this object. It was dome-shaped and had a brilliant halo. Bluish-green lights and red lights were around the outside, and in the center it had a real brilliant yellowish-white light that appeared to be coming from inside. It was really brilliant, and when I looked at it, I kind of had to squint my eyes.

"The object was making a very loud, high-pitched whiny sound. As we watched it, the high-pitched noise died down. It was just like it ran down. The red and green lights—they dimmed, until the colored lights themselves went out completely. The halo that appeared to be over it also dimmed considerably, and then it made a noise. It was like heavy metal hammering. Not like you're hammering tin or something, but a heavy metal. It did not have a rhythm to it.

"I thought I should go a little closer and try to examine it a little. I was frightened. My wife hollered out at me that I shouldn't go no closer, that we should call somebody. And I said, 'Well, who shall we call?' because that was the problem. You read so much about people calling, and everyone thinks they're a little bit odd, or something's wrong. So I hesitated."

Mrs. Baker: "I came downstairs and waited till Jane came running in and saying that Phil's going too close, and I went out and yelled at him to come in, because I didn't know what it was and I wasn't about to leave him get too close to it. It was dark, and all we could see was these lights, and I was ascared of it more than anything, because it was something unknown. I only stood on this porch, so actually I didn't see that much of it, but I knew darn well it wasn't something that had just come out of the sky from around here. That's why I told him not to get close."

Phil Baker: "Finally I called the undersheriff. He just lived down here a couple of miles, and when I was on the telephone speaking to him, the lights on the object completely faded off, and there was a bang, and it disappeared, and that was the end of the object. It was weird. I saw this object on the road, but my mind was telling me: Now, let's not believe it, because people probably'll think you're weird or simply that you're seein' things.

"The undersheriff came, and we went up the road. I really didn't know what we were going to find. That explosion—I thought maybe we'd find some parts of metal or something, but what we were going to look for, I really didn't know."

George Ree, undersheriff of Mellen, Wisconsin: "Mr. Phil Baker called my residence. He told me there was a strange object north of his house. I could not understand him at first, so I told Mr. Baker to slow down, tell me what his problem was. So I finally got it out of Mr. Baker. I left my home. I went to Mr. Baker's. Mr. Baker and his children were standing out on that road when I came there. Mr. Baker told me, he said, I just missed this object. He said that I was about a minute too late. He was very, very excited. His children were very excited, so I didn't think too much of it. I quieted Mr. Baker down. I talked to his children and Mr. Baker, and I left. Then I came home."

Phil Baker: "I apologized when the undersheriff left me off, because I thought: Now we didn't find anything, he'll think I'm a little off. He says, 'Oh, no, just forget about it.' I said, 'Okay, let's forget about it,' and I said, 'but don't tell anybody about it, then.' Monty, my oldest boy, he was all upset. He says to my other two boys, 'Now, don't say anything, don't say anything to the kids at schools. We don't want any of this to get out.' Janie was in tears. She says, 'Well, I know what I saw. Don't try to tell me I didn't see anything 'cause,' she said, 'I know I saw it.'"

The story might be explained away in many ways. But later that evening, the strange sight on the town road outside the Baker home took another shape in the sky over Ashland County. Undersheriff Ree picks up the narrative.

Ree: "After I arrived at home, in about . . . I would say forty-five minutes, the sheriff called my residence and told me to go down into Iron County and check on these objects in the sky. When I arrived, one of my other deputies was at the scene, and there was two Iron County deputies. I pulled up behind the two squad cars, and I got outside and I asked the fellas what they was looking at. They told me there was a big, large, bright light which would have been on the outside of Highway 77. So we—my one deputy, myself, two Iron County deputies—we were watching this light. As we were watching this one object, one of the deputies says, 'Look to the right!' He said, 'There is another object!' It was about at treetop level, traveling at a high rate of speed toward that big bright light we had seen. The smaller light did not get too close to the large bright light that we were watching.

"In the meantime, there was two deputies working up on U.S. 2, west of Odena, which we call Birch Hill. We were talking back and forth on our police radio, and I told this deputy that if he would go up on the Birch Hill tower that he could probably see what we were looking at. So he drove up to Birch Hill—that's approximately six-teen miles east of Ashland—and him and another deputy got up on the tower, and from the tower he could see what we were looking at. He first saw this one that was very low—I considered it to be much lower than the two other objects. He could see that very plain. It was flashing. I say it was green and white. The deputies claim it was blue and white, so maybe I'm color-blind. I do not know. I still say it was green and white instead of blue and white. The rest of the people said it was blue and white. I'll go along with their story. There's more of them than me. In the meantime, as the deputies were up on the tower, they kept watching the one light. The first light that we saw never moved. It stayed stationary. The second light that came up—that was doing what we later considered was a jig—it was going around in a circle. It was moving from left to right and was just hav-ing a good old time up there. In the meantime, this one on the north of Highway 77 just stayed there, but the lights kept on flashing.

"After a period of time of . . . I don't know . . . fifteen, twenty minutes, half an hour—we lost track of time—the one that was north of the highway decided it was going to move. I got on the radio. I was standing by the squad car, I had the mike in my hand at all times talking to the other deputies, and I told him, I said, 'Pete, that one is coming back your way.' He said, 'I'll see.' Then he said, 'I can see it just comin' back.' Pete left the tower and went down to what they call the Madigan Road. He just started onto the Madigan Road when this object came zooming down over his squad car. At the time Pete said, 'The light is going over me!' His radio went out, and later, in about thirty seconds, forty-five seconds, his radio came back on and he told us over the radio that the light was so bright that he could have read a newspaper as this object went over his squad car."

A wild night in Ashland County, Wisconsin. A night with a light show in the sky, witnessed by six policemen.

Like the Bakers and the Kay family, George Ree has been subjected to "that look," to endless interrogation and doubts of his veracity. Wherever I went, I found similar stories.

Why is skepticism about UFOs so powerful and so widespread? Why are so many scientists reluctant to become involved with the subject? For the answers, we need to take a broader look at the whole UFO phenomenon.

7

The Scientists' Dilemma

UFOs CAME of age in the United States in the year 1976. A national poll found in its opinion sampling that 50 percent of the respondents believed UFOs exist. Despite the cavils of the scientific establishment, despite the evident skepticism of most media sources, half the people of the country apparently consider UFOs a reality. Few topics have been so consistently maligned yet managed to remain part of the public consciousness.

There are obviously liabilities that come along with a subject's tenacious ability to draw followers. The potential for misguided hoaxes is enormous. I suspected that Ted Phillips' work would be plagued by pranksters. "Surprisingly," he told me, "we get very few hoaxes, and when we do, they're very easy to spot."

Are UFOs reality or illusion? Just before his death in 1961, Carl Gustav Jung suggested that they are projections of the mind, corresponding to a deep human need. They are the result of a troubled world, an erosion of orthodox religious belief, something new that man has created to fill a deep religious void. Jung wrote that "God in his omniscience, omnipotence, and omnipresence is a totality symbol par excellence, something round, complete, and perfect."

Boston psychiatrist Benjamin Simon tends to agree that the saucers could represent "something for everybody," providing an "oceanic or cosmic feeling of immersion in the total universe, a sort of nirvana."

It was Simon's work with Barney and Betty Hill, a couple from New Hampshire, that prompted author John G. Fuller to write a best-selling chronicle of their adventures in his book *The Interrupted Journey*. Fuller tells us that under hypnosis the Hills were literally abducted by a flying saucer and medically examined by humanoids, who tested Mrs. Hill, among other things, for pregnancy, causing substantial psychological damage.

There are those who have followed their faith down what I consider very creative paths. The cults have helped to taint the study, yet I understand why they have grown up. Through the ages man has woven yarns, myths, and religions to explain the bizarre phenomena he has witnessed. The myths are the result of his frustrations. Man is a great storyteller, assigning frameworks from which he can continue to live and function amid a welter of troubling confusions. He lives with and maintains various theories until they no longer make any sense in light of his ever-ongoing experiences. I found it no surprise that in the face of the UFO mystery some nonscientists find it fulfilling to establish religions.

In the autumn of each year, not far from the Berkeley campus of the University of California, a very special group invades the premises of the gracious old Claremont Hotel. I decided I would join the truth-seekers, and began to prepare myself mentally for my journey to the annual Spacecraft Convention.

The convention was sponsored by Understanding, Inc., Borderline Science, Research Associated, and Source Unlimited. Upon entering the foyer I encountered an endless barrage of booths, display stands, UFO photos, religious symbols, and other curiosities peculiar to that group of people who opted to distinguish themselves from orthodox or establishment UFO investigations. Mounds of books, drawings, and photographs of spacecraft heaped into great imposing stacks lined the stalls and bookracks scattered about the hall. There was an authenticity in the facial expressions of many of the convention-goers. They regarded their business at the convention very seriously. I spoke to some of the exhibitors and found them to be earnest in their beliefs. Many of them honestly feel they have been in either telepathic or physical communication with our planet's intergalactic friends and foes. These people, these truth-seekers, represent the contactees who are beyond the threshold of even the new science. They claim somehow to have tangled with the Master Jesus, Firkon of Mars, Orthon of Venus, and others. Their speech is peppered and exotically accented with the mention of names like Clarion, Tythan,

Korendor, Blaau, Schara, and Foser—the earth's invisible second moon.

I walked over to a booth with a hand-scrawled sign reading "The Reorganized Church of the UFO. Listen to the Words of the Space People." I stared at the spectators around me and noticed a young man in the corner busily signing photographs of himself. He appeared to be a newly recruited celebrity in cosmic society. My neighborly bystander suddenly whispered, "He has made contact with Pollious, the grand coordinator of the Andromeda sector of the Galactic Union."

In the middle of the hall I noticed a fragile silver-haired lady sitting alone in front of an old tape recorder perched on an oak table. She looked at me, eyes twinkling. "Would you like to hear the beautiful message we have?" I nodded. With that, she flicked the button, and a stilted voice began to resound, fading in and out from moment to moment.

"I am Lelan, the head of the government of the planet Nobelia. I speak to you from across the parsecs. We have contacted the president of the United States, the pope, and all the other world leaders, but they have chosen to ignore us, so we are acting through a far wiser man. R. Spencer Jason will be your leader. We must rescue you from the evil influence of vicious inhabitants of the planet Zeno. Let me warn you that the Zenonians will stop at nothing to prevent our saving Earth. They control all government officials on your planet. . . ." The tape was still playing as I quietly slipped away.

Most groups develop because of a strong belief in specific events that have been said to have already happened or that are prophesied to occur in the near future. A number of years ago the Lake City *Herald* of Lake City, Minnesota, headlined this story: PROPHECY FROM PLANET CLARION CALL TO CITY: FLEE THAT FLOOD. IT'LL SWAMP US ON DEC. 21, 1951 OUTER SPACE TELLS SUBURBANITE. "Lake City," it reported, "will be destroyed by a flood from the Great Lake just before dawn, Dec. 21, according to suburban housewife Mrs. Marian Keech of 847 West School St., who said the prophecy is not her own. It is the purport of many messages she has received by automatic writing. The messages, according to Mrs. Keech, are sent to her by superior beings from a planet called 'Clarion.' These beings have been visiting the earth, she says, in what we call flying saucers. During their visits, she says, they have observed fault lines in the earth's crust that foretoken the deluge. Mrs. Keech reports she was told the flood will spread to form an inland sea, stretching from the

Arctic Circle to the Gulf of Mexico. At the same time, she says a cataclysm will submerge the West Coast from Seattle, Washington, to Chile in South America."

The book *When Prophecy Fails* details the events leading up to the above article. Marian Keech had become acquainted with the entities of two planets, whom she referred to as the Guardians. She received many messages from the Guardians, instructing her to share her information with only people she could trust. It was soon after this advice that she met Dr. Thomas and Daisy Armstrong, both devotees of the cult and founders of a group called the Seekers, who met weekly to discuss metaphysical subjects. Their friendship seemed to be part of a prescribed destiny. The Armstrongs and Mrs. Keech began to correspond with each other. Mrs. Keech kept them informed of new developments in the Guardians' messages.

During the subsequent months, the messages assumed a new flavor. The Clarionites, or Guardians, promised they would visit Earth and let themselves be seen. The themes of violence and warfare were repeated, and commands were issued to Mrs. Keech to "instruct the people of Earth . . . that they are rushing toward suicide."

Equipped with her new belief, Mrs. Keech, together with the Armstrongs, developed a complex rationale delineating the Seekers' credo while adding momentum to Mrs. Keech's continuing conversations with the Guardians. Their new philosophy surfaced when Dr. Armstrong released a mimeographed "Open Letter to American Editors and Publishers" explaining Mrs. Keech's prophecy. Hence, they embarked on the first voyage of a new movement.

A second dispatch followed: "The place is Lake City, and the country around. The date is December 21. As the scene opens, it is dawn but still dark. The actors are awakened to the sound of a terrible rumbling. The earth shakes, the tall buildings topple. The waters of the Great Lake rise in a terrific wave which covers the city and spreads east and west. A new river forms and flows from the Lake to the Gulf of Mexico."

Having publicly committed themselves to the message, the Seekers began actively to proselytize. Although their effect was minimal, they were able to assemble a group of believers. These followers believed in the legitimacy of the message and were convinced that the Guardians would spare them from the horrible catastrophe about to take place by whisking them away in their flying saucers. One of the Seekers made an interesting comment on her own conviction. She said, "I have to believe the Flood is coming on the twenty-first because I've spent nearly all my money. I quit my job, I quit comptometer school, and my apartment costs me one hundred dollars a month. I *have* to believe."

Publicly committed as the Seekers were, the long wait for the Clarion vessel was pure agony for most of the group. Many went into self-induced trances (one childless woman announced that she was about to give birth to the baby Jesus). As the time grew near, precautions were taken against the group's common enemies—the disbelievers, scoffers, and the unenlightened.

It was now December 17, and Dr. Armstrong explained his position. "I'll say to you that all of you who are interested in saucers are in a special category. Now, you don't know that, but you are—because it seems that the people around the world who have been having a special interest in saucers are people who have had that interest because they had something with themselves that goes back to things they have forgotten. . . . Spacemen have said that they are here for a purpose, and one of those purposes is to remove certain of their own people from the earth. . . ."

Excitement was mounting in Lake City. The newsmen were persistent. The reporting ranged from straightforward news releases to tongue-in-cheek items. Armstrong and Mrs. Keech recorded a tape for national broadcast. The Seekers were readying themselves for takeoff in the spacecraft, and time was drawing near.

On December 20 Marian Keech received the message they were waiting for: "At the hour of midnight you shall be put into parked cars and taken to a place where ye shall be put aboard a porch [saucer] and ye shall be purposed by the time you are there. At that time you shall have the fortuned ones forget the few who have not come, and at no time are they to be called for. They are but enacting a scene, and not a person who should be there will fail to be there at the time you are to say 'What is your question?' . . . and at no time are you to ask what is what, and not a plan shall go astray and for the time being be glad and be fortuned to be among the favored. And be ye ready for further instructions."

It was signed "Beleis."

The taut line of tension finally slackened, only to be drawn into a knot once again. It was true. Preparations would actually continue!

Calls continued to pour in, and the group handled them with quiet, knowing courtesy. Exhausted by lack of sleep, they carefully explained their doctrine to all who would listen, and many did. In the early afternoon, two wire services informed Mrs. Keech that earthquakes had occurred in California and in Italy. "It all ties in with what I believe," was her comment. Then more instructions came: "Be on your toes and give it to the papers at the time they come to you. . . . Give them the works and put thy furbish in."

And then nothing!

Visitors began to decline. Armstrong's sister tried to have Daisy and him declared legally insane and requested the custody of their children. But Mrs. Keech's belief persisted, although Armstrong began to hedge and in an interview delivered a series of thin, specious denials and excuses. However, the Seekers continued to contend that the invisible spacemen had, in fact, made an appearance!

The followers were satisfied. The world hadn't been destroyed. And despite the cynicism of their enemies, the Seekers—the believers —had fulfilled their need to search for the truth about the unknown. This need to believe proved paramount to the belief itself. It maintained their psychological stability. The Seekers' tale numbers just one more in man's many attempts to order his experiences in the universe in a way in which he can most comfortably comprehend the unknown horizons.

I have spent a great deal of time on the telephone interviewing various astronomers on the subject of extraterrestrial life (ETL) and the UFO connection. Their views on UFOs can be divided into three major categories. 1. All UFO sightings can be explained by natural phenomena. This view seems to be on the decline. 2. A small number of UFO sightings cannot be explained and remain a mystery. This view is increasingly being shared by both conservative and liberal scientists. 3. The unexplained UFO sightings are accountable to the presence of extraterrestrial visitors. Only the most romantic observers are willing to accept the extraterrestrial conclusion.

The famous New Mexico astronomer Clyde Tombaugh was first on my interview list. He had discovered the planet Pluto and was one of the few remaining visual astronomers who still physically peered at the celestial horizons through a telescope. He had also seen his own UFO—a sighting that has remained a classic up to the present day. In August 1949 he observed a flight of rectangles of light arranged as if they were "ports" on an elliptical object. I wanted to speak to Dr. Tombaugh and try to get an update of his views.

Dr. Tombaugh answered the phone. After I told him my business, he politely and quietly refused to make any statement whatsoever.

He was very apologetic but firm about his refusal. When I asked him why he had taken a position of silence on the matter, he told me that he had received so much backlash from previous statements that he no longer wanted to be involved with such an emotional topic. It caused him more grief than he felt it was worth. He told me that he had precious little time left to investigate those things that mattered to him and that a statement would only encourage a replay of a familiar and painful barrage of positive and negative feedback. He didn't have the time or the inclination to get involved.

His refusal to comment was statement enough. It demonstrated just how emotionally charged the entire subject has been in the past and remains at the present. It provides a clue to the inconsistencies of thought and frequent blatant lack of imagination and nerve that sometimes accompany scientific discussions on the UFO subject.

Everyone I interviewed suggested that I obtain Frank Drake's views. Dr. Drake was instrumental in initiating the search for extraterrestrial life through the use of radio telescopes. Presently the director of the National Astronomy and Ionosphere Center at Cornell University, Dr. Drake has been asked about UFOs on more occasions, perhaps, than any other astronomer in the country.

"With regard to the possibilities of there being intelligent creatures elsewhere in the universe," he said slowly, "I think that all of the information we have from astronomy, biology, and the evolution of intelligence and technology on the earth would indicate that it is certain that there is intelligent life and indeed civilizations elsewhere in space. Their numbers may be small and their manifestations on an astronomical scale very faint. Therefore, the question is not whether they are there—they are—but rather, how difficult it is to detect. My own belief is that it is indeed a very demanding enterprise to detect the manifestations of other civilizations and it will require an effort on our part which is of the same order as the largest scientific undertakings that we have so far pursued."

Dr. Drake was very familiar with his subject. He had pushed for a concentrated search for extraterrestrial life and was a convinced exponent of the exobiological thesis. He continued, "In the matter of UFOs, I have followed the subject for years and investigated personally many UFOs. I have never seen evidence that would convince me that UFOs are an indication of extraterrestrial intelligent activity. The evidence just has not been delivered, in any case." That was it. He asked me if that was all I wanted, and then cordially bid me good day. I had my statement—short and sweet.

What was it about the UFO phenomenon which placed such absolute limits on so many scientists' imaginations? Had the lunatic fringe tainted the problem that much? Conservative or establishment scientists, as well as liberals, have tried to explain the unexplained before. But the UFO problem precludes and inhibits any such attempts. Except for a relatively small handful of brave souls, most scientists shied away from any speculations; they did this almost unconsciously. When I would ask them to let their imaginations fly, they would reply that they couldn't do that, yet a moment before, they had raptured in glorious, scientific abandon about the ultimate possibilities for finding ETL. When the UFO problem emerged, though, they were at loose ends to try to explain what was going on.

Views were changing. During my survey I found that more and more "conservative" scientists as well as "liberal" scientists acknowledged the existence of UFOs as something unexplained but real. Was this the beginning of a new trend? Would this acknowledgment challenge scientists' previous dogmatic refusal to deal with the UFO subject? Would "liberal" statements on the possibilities of communication with ETL begin to accommodate or accept other "extreme" hypotheses—like the extraterrestrial origin of UFOs? Or is consistency of thought a factor at all in such an emotionally charged area?

I dug back into the history of modern UFO study, and everywhere I looked, the story was the same. It began in the rarefied air near Mount Rainier in 1947. Pilot Kenneth Arnold saw nine saucerlike objects shimmer and fly erratically across the cold, clear sky. His report of the incident did more than add the words "flying saucer" to our vocabulary. It began the modern debate: "UFOs—Yes or No?" After that time, Project Blue Book, the Air Force investigative unit, now discontinued, examined thousands of sightings. Most of the sighted objects were crossed off as birds, atmospheric phenomena, balloons, satellites, the aurora borealis, and assorted planets and stars, but 6 percent remain as absolutely unexplained or "unidentified." Add to this 6 percent the fact that Blue Book falsely attributed sightings to the Orion constellation when it was not visible, to the Goodyear blimp when it was six hundred miles away, and to military activity when none was taking place. Such discrepancies stoke the imagination of every investigator. The Pentagon, some believed, knows something we don't. In the opinion of most of those who follow the UFO problem, the Air Force is guilty of suppression of vital information.

Harassed by such a significant number of Americans continually chafing at what officially was a closed matter, the Air Force in 1966 financed a team of investigators at the University of Colorado in an attempt to unravel some of Blue Book's conclusions. The former director of the National Bureau of Standards, Edward Condon, was to head the team and tackle what could only be considered an intriguing assignment.

Concurrently with this, Allen Hynek, from the Center for UFO Studies, addressed *Science* magazine in a letter critical of his colleagues who scoffed at the saucer mystery with "buffoonery and caustic banter." He said that if he had spoken out before the Colorado team had been set up, "I would have been regarded as a nut."

After studying the material from Project Blue Book and other sources, James E. McDonald, a University of Arizona atmospheric physicist, concluded: "UFOs are the number-one problem of world science. I'm afraid that the evidence points to no other acceptable hypothesis than the extraterrestrial. The amount of evidence is overwhelmingly real."

On the other side, a colleague of McDonald's, astronomer Gerard Kuiper, states that the subject is "fanciful," and astronomer Carl Sagan of Cornell says that "at the present time there is no evidence that unambiguously connects the various flying-saucer sightings with extraterrestrial activity."

I wanted to talk to Major Donald Keyhoe, USMC, retired. He was the director of the National Investigation Committee on Aerial Phenomena (NICAP) from 1957 to 1970. Before assuming that post, he had conducted a private investigation on the UFO reports that the Air Force's Project Sign had studied (later called Project Grudge and Project Blue Book).

Major Keyhoe lives in a small town called Luray, Virginia. When I was on the phone with Major Keyhoe, he was in a quiet mood. He had been through hundreds of interviews before, and I suppose I just numbered one more on his list.

Because of his association with the military, Major Keyhoe was privy to a great deal of classified information. But there was one morsel contained in his book *Aliens from Space* that particularly interested me:

Since 1947, UFOs have maneuvered over space bases, atomic-energy centers, airports, cities, farms, obviously observing every aspect of our civilization for some highly important purpose. During the long surveillance, the Air Force has made two full-scale evaluations of the verified evidence. In both analyses, detailed and documented later, Air Force scientists and intelligence officers reached this secret conclusion: *the UFOs are spacecraft from a more advanced world engaged in an extensive survey of our world.*

"Major Keyhoe, do you still believe that the UFOs are extraterrestrial?" I asked.

"There isn't any question about it," he exclaimed. "You can go through any alternative there is, and it comes down just to one thing. I mean the idea that everybody's wrong, everybody's made mistakes."

"Is there evidence—?" I began, but he didn't let me finish my sentence.

"There's not only evidence, there's proof. Visual sightings, information—all of them sighting these things, objects flying around the formation. There's radar in two different positions picking up the things and tracking them. Photographs of the radioscopes, all showing exactly what happened. For a while the Air Force refused to release any radarscope, and then they denied there were any radar trackings. Finally they did admit they had trackings, but they said there was none of it that was significant. The only significance was that they were tracking real objects which were under intelligent control."

That brought our conversation to an end. Major Keyhoe was holding steadfast to the accusations he had made in *Aliens from Space*. According to Keyhoe:

In 1969 the Air Force announced that all UFO reports had been explained. In this same nationwide announcement the Air Force declared its UFO investigation ended. *At that very time, Air Force interceptor pilots were trying to bring down these unknown flying objects by secret orders of the Aerospace Defense Command.*

I wasn't used to such straightforward statements. Major Keyhoe didn't seem to employ disclaimers or qualifiers. It was a refreshing change of pace from the scholarly academic approach, which attempted to remain objective at all times.

Dr. Frank Salisbury is a well-known plant physiologist at Utah State University. He started researching UFOs and exobiology, the study of life in outer space, after publishing a paper in 1962 entitled

"Martian Biology." In 1968 he participated in the scientific rebuttal of the Condon Report before the House Committee on Science and Astronautics, helping to demonstrate that the report was biased and incomplete. I wondered if his views had since changed. He said, "There are five possible hypotheses sometimes used to explain UFOs, namely, that they're natural phenomena, secret weapons, hoaxes, psychological phenomena, or extraterrestrial machines. I decided that maybe they were indeed extraterrestrial machines. But as the years went on, it became more and more difficult for me to explain them simply as visitors from another world who had just discovered us and were surveying us. From the various sightings listed in history books, it seemed that they've been around for centuries, and it's difficult to imagine that they would survey us that long without some kind of formal contact. Furthermore, they seem to engage in things that just don't make sense. Whatever they were—and at the time, I was thinking of extraterrestrial machines—I thought they were putting on a display for our benefit. Why would they play with us this way? Why would they manipulate us?"

He paused. The ideas he was about to articulate were complex matters, and he approached them gingerly. "I think that they really do try to manipulate us. I think there is an intelligence behind it. At least, that's my feeling right now. There is an intelligence of some kind behind it, and they're trying to manipulate us in various ways for reasons that I haven't the faintest idea about. I don't know. I think that we need to broaden our way of thinking about such things; we have to consider not only the idea that they are extraterrestrial machines, but maybe they're something more subtle and more scary in a lot of ways."

I stopped him. "What do you mean?" I asked.

"Well," he said, "maybe you can start talking about devils and angels, if you want to. These are beings in a different dimension that are able at will to manifest themselves for their own purposes, be they good or bad. So how about that?"

Having entered the realm of gross speculation, Dr. Salisbury seemed relieved that he had finally been able to air this growing conviction. He continued. "I think that becomes an extremely unscientific sort of a way to think about things, but I've kind of been forced into it in the last two or three years. And I don't know what to do about it anymore from the standpoint of the objective scientific investigation that I've tried to pursue for these many years."

"It must be quite a dilemma for you, in view of your training," I said.

"Yes," he replied, "I find it a dilemma, except that I must state that I'm an active member of the Mormon Church, and it's becoming easier to think about it in terms of my theology than it is my science."

As I left his office, I realized that it *would* be easier for him in view of his religion. Didn't the Mormons believe that they were the descendants of the spirit children of God, that they came from someplace other than the earth? I understood the problem he faced in trying to reconcile his new beliefs with classic scientific methods. He had begun to stretch far beyond the limits of acceptable scientific speculation. Alternative explanations are the launch pads from which old mysteries may be explored and perhaps solved, but they are treacherous swamps to scientists.

8

The Prospects Out There

SPACE IS vast and awesome. Earth is a rather small planet consisting of rock and metal. The sun, our star, is also relatively small, and is one of some two hundred billion suns that make up our Milky Way galaxy. Furthermore, the Milky Way galaxy is only one of billions of galaxies that are also strewn with billions of suns or stars. We aren't even in the center of our galaxy; it takes light traveling at 186,000 miles a second 30,000 years to reach us. Planet earth and the life that arose are products of an endless series of evolutionary events. Therefore, it should come as no surprise that earth is probably not the first, last, or best habitable planet around. Considering that there are approximately 10^{11} (100 billion) stars in our galaxy and 10^{11} other galaxies, there are at least 10^{20} stars in the universe. Most of these stars, according to scientists, may be accompanied by solar systems or planets.

Scientists I. S. Sjklovskii and Carl Sagan, in their book *Intelligent Life in the Universe*, have computed that a million solar systems are formed in the universe each hour. This fact in itself is a sobering thought for any of us still imagining that we are the only solar system to have evolved life.

Two thousand years ago, Lucretius, the Roman poet, wrote, "Nature is not unique to the visible world. We must have faith that in other regions of space there exist other earths, inhabited by other people and animals."

Anaxagoras, an early believer in the heliocentric theory, believed the moon to be inhabited. He also proposed that invisible life seeds, from which all living things came, were dispersed throughout the universe. Similar concepts of "panspermia" are still proposed today.

The Epicureans or materialists believed that many worlds, other than our earth, were suitable for life and existed out in space. Metrodoros, a famous Epicurean, wrote: "To consider the earth the only populated world in infinite space is as absurd as to assert that in an entire field sown with millet, only one grain will grow."

After the birth of Jesus Christ, Christianity, influenced by Ptolemaic theories, taught that earth was the center of the universe, making the concept of life elsewhere totally incompatible and incredible.

Nicolaus Copernicus, the Polish astronomer, rejected the Ptolemaic system. He placed earth in its proper perspective as only one planet among many others revolving around the sun. The idea demoted the earth from a central, unique position and suggested the possibility of other inhabited planets.

Konstantin E. Tsiolkovski, the Russian founder of astronautics, believed in the plurality of worlds. He states, "All the phases of the development of life may be found on the various planets. Did man exist several thousand years ago, and will he be extinct in several million years? This entire process may be found on other planets. . . ." That extraterrestrial civilizations might exist at various developmental levels has not been proved. The question still remains.

But let's begin to answer the question with a survey of current facts and near-fact speculations about other suns and other planets. What evidence is there that planets similar to ours (a planet that can support life) exist? Since the sun—a star—is our source of life-giving energy, then the first thing we need to know is that other stars like our sun do exist.

Knowing that there are more than one hundred billion stars in our galaxy, the next question is whether there are planets around those stars. Because of recent findings, most astronomers believe that planets accompanying stars are probably the rule rather than the exception.

Stephen Dole and Isaac Asimov, in *Planets for Man*, classified planets into three types: 1. Planets without a measurable atmosphere. The small gravitational fields on these planets can't hold even those gases with massive molecules. Since there are probably more small planets than larger ones, most fall into this class, Mercury and the moon being two examples. 2. Planets with light atmospheres. The gravitational fields here are large enough to retain moderately heavy gases, such as nitrogen, which have been produced by volcanic

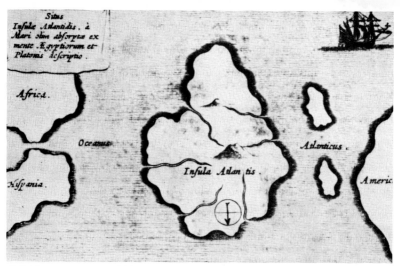

A 17th-century map following Plato's description of Atlantis.

The Bimini Wall might be a deserted city. An Atlantis theory could explain these well-engineered stone structures under 35 feet of water.

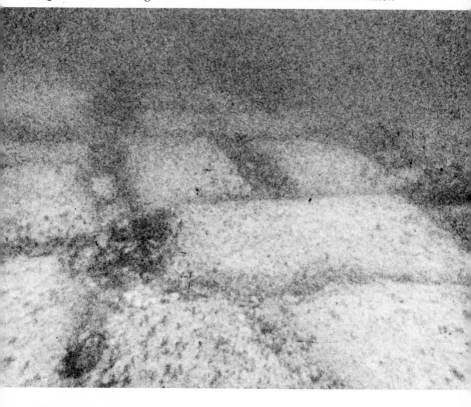

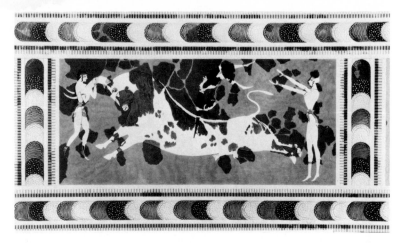

The Minoan spectacle known as the Bull Dance seems to have combined ritual, sport, and remnants of a tradition of animal sacrifice.

Archaeological Collection, Townhall, Crete, Greece.

Part of a stone labyrinth at Mystery Hill, N. H. Some believe that Minoan sailors or refugees may have reached the New World.

The Lion Gate of Mycenae. Some of the stone blocks are so large that later Greeks called these walls "Cyclopean," believing they had been built by mythical giants, the Cyclopes.

The "Serpent Goddess," an ivory statuette discovered on Crete. Does it represent an actual rite of Minoan religion—or memories of a maternal deity even older than Minoan times?

The brick step-pyramid of Ur-Nammu, one of the places where priest-kings created an "invisible machine" that transformed human history.

A model reconstruction of Stonehenge. Archaeologists and astronomers have shown that it was a celestial computer, its stones aligned with the courses of the sun, moon, and stars.

The giant radio telescope at Arecibo. A natural bowl in
the hills of Puerto Rico was prepared and covered with reflective
material to focus impulses from far out in space.

*The Arecibo Observatory is part of
the National Astronomy and Ionosphere Center
which is operated by Cornell University under
contract with the National Science Foundation.*

The 1679-bit Arecibo Message, written in only
two characters and transmitted sequentially
by switching the transmitter frequency between
two specific radio frequencies, would tell
extra-terrestrial listeners something about us.

The Arecibo Observatory

Ted Phillips, an investigator of physical traces
that might be linked to UFO landings.

action. Earth, the one habitable planet in our solar system, and Venus are members of this type. 3. Planets with massive atmospheres composed largely of helium and hydrogen. Jupiter, Saturn, Uranus, and Neptune are members of the third type.

According to Ronald Bracewell in *The Galactic Club*, around each star there exists what he calls a habitable zone, an area containing the most likely planetary candidates. Obviously planets too close to a star would be too hot for life to arise, and those too far away would be too cold. The ideal temperature limits are thought to be within that temperature range where water is liquid. Scientists believe that the first organic molecule was created in the oceans. Hence water would be another requirement. The period of rotation should be less than ninety-six hours in order to prevent either extremely high daytime temperatures or excessively low temperatures at night. The planet should be more than three billion years old, the estimated period of time needed both to produce a breathable atmosphere and to allow for the evolution of complex life forms.

Dole and Asimov discovered that roughly six hundred million habitable planets might exist in our galaxy alone. This figure represents only the planets with conditions suitable for life as we know it, places where we of earth could live comfortably, not needing extreme protection from the natural environment and without dependence on material imported from other planets.

But there's still another field to explore. The second form of life. What about the planets with atmospheric and temperature conditions which spawn "life as we don't know it"? If life on other planets is totally unlike life on earth—not based on carbon—it would prove that life could take multiple forms on the most basic levels. Yet how would we recognize life as we don't know it?

A clear definition generalizing all life—carbon-based, silicon-based, or otherwise—seems to be necessary. Carl Sagan in *The Cosmic Connection* states, "A molecular system—capable of replication, mutation and replication of its mutations—can be called alive." So perhaps life is generally defined as something that isn't static. It evolves.

Sagan labels as chauvinism the assumption that life elsewhere has to be, in a major sense, like life here. There are oxygen chauvinists; they ignore the fact that life first arose on earth in the absence of oxygen. In fact, there are many organisms on earth today that live without oxygen and are poisoned by it.

Some people rule out life in the freezing temperatures of Jupiter. But according to Sagan, "It is now quite firmly established, both from theory and from radio observations of these planets, that as we penetrate below the visible clouds, the temperatures increase. There is always a region in the atmospheres of Jupiter, Saturn, Uranus, and Neptune that is at quite comfortable temperatures by terrestrial standards."

All of us are at the mercy of our experiences. We have an unconscious bias as to what is possible in the universe. We think that all conceivable life must conform to the preconceptions for which our experiences have programmed us. But perhaps we are just one possibility—one level of development. Maybe we should realize that there is planetary chauvinism too. Does intelligent life have to develop and reside on planets? Couldn't it inhabit interstellar space in exotic cosmic monuments? Sagan muses, "Just as we are organisms completely at home only on dry land, although we evolved from the sea, the universe may be populated with societies that arose on planets but that are comfortable only in the depths of interstellar space."

Each spring I make a trek into the southern California deserts to camp out for a weekend. One night in particular stands out. We retired to our sleeping bags. The evening was moonless and inky-black and as I lay gazing at the star-dusted sky, a strange feeling of utter loneliness crept over me. Those who live in cities never see the sky as it was that evening. It was like an enormous intergalactic fireworks display—here and there a shooting star, whole whorls of many solar systems, distant suns and galaxies sparkling across the vast ice reaches of outer space.

The words of J. B. S. Haldane came to my mind: "Now, my suspicion is that the universe is not only queerer than we suppose, but queerer than we *can* suppose. I suspect that there are more things in heaven and earth than are dreamed of in *any* philosophy. That is the reason why I have no philosophy myself, and must be my excuse for dreaming."

The past fifteen years have reversed the thinking of the scientific community regarding extraterrestrial intelligence, known as ETI. And while speculation about ETI has always been a heated one, today large segments of the scientific establishment are examining the hard probabilities that the universe is populated and that our galaxy is teeming with life.

Astronomers have embarked on vast listening programs. The United States has the largest radio telescope in the world at Arecibo Observatory in Puerto Rico. The thousand-foot diameter dish at

Arecibo enables us to gather a wide spectrum of signals. The National Radio Astronomy Observatory in Green Bank, West Virginia has an eighty-five-foot-dish antenna. It was there that the first attempt to listen to signals from another world was made.

The real stimulus for present-day eavesdropping programs came from Giuseppe Cocconi and Phillip Morrison, both professors at Cornell University. Shortly before their concentrated efforts to organize an eavesdropping program, scientist Hendrick Christoffel Van de Hulst made an important discovery. His work removed the major roadblock to using the radio's spectrum to intercept extraterrestrial signals. Unlike light, radio lacked the sharp emission or absorption lines that had proved so useful in astronomy. These lines were used to detect relative motion toward and away from the observer. Van de Hulst proposed that the clouds of individual hydrogen atoms should emit radio noise waves at a 21-centimeter wavelength. Since these clouds exist everywhere inside space there should be a sharp increase of cosmic radio noise at the magic 21-centimenter wavelength. He was proved correct. Suddenly the dust that formerly closed much of the universe to our telescopes became transparent by using 21-centimeter emissions as a guidepost.

The 21-centimeter discovery sparked a flurry of activity. Large antennae were put under construction or planned; radio waves from space now opened up myriad lines of investigation. Cocconi and Morrison jumped at the possibility of looking for signals from ETI. They wrote an article in *Nature*, hoping to publicize their ideas among reputable scientists who were interested in searching for signals. "We shall assume," they wrote, "that long ago the ETI established a channel of communication that would one day become known to us, and that they look forward patiently to the answering signals from the sun which would make known to them that a new society has entered the community of intelligence."

Almost in tandem with the suggestion of Morrison and Cocconi a plan was being prepared to search for intelligent life. Directed by Frank Drake, it was called Project Ozma, in memory of the princess of the imaginary land of OZ—a place far in the distance inhabited by exotic beings. Drake selected two targets: Tau Ceti and Epsilon Eridani. They were eleven light-years away, observable with an eighty-five-foot dish generated by a million-watt transmitter operating through a six-hundred-foot antenna.

The National Radio Astronomy Observatory at Green Bank, West Virginia was the site of Project Ozma. Listening began on April 3,

1960. In a very short time, strong signals were heard. It seemed as if they had come from the control room. Everyone began looking for quirks in the circuitry that might account for the strange pulses, but nothing was found. Apparently, or so the public was told later, the signals were due to secret military experiments in radar countermeasures. Yet a strange thing happened after the first signals were reported. The Ozma search was abruptly suspended. No further explanation was given except that the telescope was needed in other projects. Whether the "secret military experiment" was indeed the source of the signals will never be known. But as Major Keyhoe notes, "If this had been true, Project Ozma could have continued with no excitement. It could not possibly explain the incredible actions which followed."

In 1971, twenty-four scientists and engineers in the Stanford/NASA-Ames Summer Faculty Fellowship Program gathered to devise a system for detecting extraterrestrial life. Dr. Bernard M. Oliver and Dr. John Billingham directed the group, and investigated the different aspects involved in making radio contact. They studied the design and cost of large antenna structures, electrical transmission and control, signal processing and sensitive radio receivers. The culmination of the study was a 243-page volume entitled *Project Cyclops*. The Cyclops scientists established that radio is the superior means of contact, particularly into the microwave range of wavelengths from about 10 to 30 centimeters.

The entire proposed Cyclops system would comprise one thousand or more large radio telescope dishes spread over an area of up to ten miles across. I called Dr. Billingham to find out what the projected cost of such an "orchard" system of telescopes would be. He emphasized that there could be neither a fixed cost nor a fixed size. The size would be the size that it takes to detect signals. Cyclops, if it were to be built, would start very small and increase its size gradually.

Project Cyclops officially ended when the report was finished. But each summer since 1971, Ames Research Center scientists assemble to discuss certain aspects of eventual radio contact. In the summer of 1976 they studied the requirements needed to build a telescope that would photograph stars outside our solar system. The scientists at Cyclops feel that if funding were to materialize, and a sufficient amount of equipment could be built, there might be a good chance of detecting life on other planets.

The present lack of funds and state of technology in the area of radio contact severely limits the possibility of new discoveries. Nonetheless, attempts are being made. The persistent and adamant belief in life on other planets and our ability to contact it has spurred the U.S. space program. In November 1974, at the Arecibo Observatory in Puerto Rico, Frank Drake sent the first and only intentional signal from earth to M-13. I called Dr. Drake's assistant and asked her why M-13 was the target. Apparently it was the globular cluster of stars which happened to be in the right position at the time. It will take 24,000 years for our signal to reach M-13 and another 24,000 years for an answer to return to earth. It's easy to understand why we are more intrigued with listening programs than making ourselves heard.

Scientists interested in using the Arecibo radio telescope for interstellar communication searches are severely limited. They can listen for signals only every three months for a thirty-hour period. So far, there are no questionable echoes. Until the time devoted to listening to signals increases, practical results will be few and far between.

In September 1971 a symposium was held at the Byurakan Astrophysical Observatory in Soviet Armenia under the auspices of the Soviet and U.S. academies of science. The symposium was attended by distinguished scientists—including two Nobel laureates. The question was raised: Should mankind try to listen in on extraterrestrial communications between life forms in other planetary systems, in other galaxies? A proposal was issued: "It seems to us appropriate that the search for extraterrestrial intelligence should be made by the representatives of mankind."

But why bother searching? For one thing, the sheer excitement of the search for another civilization could be invigorating for all of us.

It seems that civilization has all but forgotten the excitement and cultural stimulation brought to societies by the discoveries of the fifteenth, sixteenth, and seventeenth centuries. Man discovered new worlds. He traveled around the globe, exposing himself to cultures that were new and different. From these new worlds he learned alien languages, alien customs, and alien philosophies, and he ate alien foods. How different were the stone pyramids of the Yucatán from the manicured lawns of Buckingham Palace. How different were the religions of the Chinese from the beliefs dictated by the Vatican. From this contact there evolved a period of cultural enrichment, growth, revolution, and the inevitable rise of a high technology.

Although the tradition of cultural exploration and expansion is deeply rooted within us, new geographic or cultural frontiers have all but vanished. Does this leave mankind with a frustration that has not yet surfaced and now lies barely submerged in our own consciousness?

At the beginning of the space race, the hopes were high that not only would we put a man on the moon before the Russians, but also that our interplanetary probes would bring us some confirmation that a primitive form of life existed somewhere in our solar system.

But many illusions were shattered when space probes gave us a closer look. Venus was found too hot to support life. The moon was barren and lifeless. Mars was a bleak, pockmarked rock, and the great canals of Giovanni Schiaparelli were nothing but illusions. Earth, as seen from space, was an incredibly breathtaking sight—so unlike the scarred landscapes of neighborhood satellites and planets. Hanging in space like a shimmering turquoise globe was man's home. Fragile, delicate, and in danger. Then, with that perspective, the clamor for ecology grew and the support for the exploration of space withered.

Let us suppose that man and his technology are able to restore a proper ecological balance to earth. Let us suppose that man's inventions can recycle our wastes, develop new sources of energy, and control our birth rate. Then what? Will we accept forever a status of zero population growth? Will we be satisfied to wait alone in the universe, knowing only ourselves?

Of course, there are many things we can do. Continue to probe the universe, the atom, and ourselves. But as long as we limit ourselves to earth-based life alone, many enormously exciting and very fundamental questions will remain unanswered—perhaps forever. It is most likely we will find the answers not in ourselves, but in the stars.

As we have seen, the foremost and overriding question is simply: Are we alone? Is earth singular in the solar system, the galaxy, the universe? Has some cosmic miracle caused just one speck of dust to bear life? Are billions of other stars and their planets without any form of biological intelligence?

We have mentioned that only very recently have we signaled our presence in the universe because electromagnetic communication has been with us less than a century. But we too are able to detect such signals, so any race we contact will be at least as technologically sophisticated as ourselves. Indeed, it is likely that they are more so.

There are some immediately valuable benefits to science and technology from contact with other cultures. However, such an exchange could not be in the form of a dialogue, for the distances are much too great, with delay times likely to be a century or more. So most likely there will be no question-and-answer transmissions, but a series of simultaneous transmissions, each a documentary about the society involved—its planetary data, its life forms, its age, its history, and its religious beliefs. And so, over a period of a century or so, we might receive a tremendous amount of information that would enable us to build a model of the other race. It is not impossible that we could even gain access to an alien data bank.

If we do succeed in establishing interstellar contact, it is also highly possible that we are not the first civilization to have done so. In fact, it may well be that such communication has been taking place ever since the first civilization evolved four or five billion years ago.

We would literally be given an enormous body of knowledge, knowledge handed down from race to race, from culture to culture, from planet to planet. In this galactic heritage we may find the total histories of countless unknown planets and their inhabitants. We could receive astronomical data dating back aeons, perhaps pictures of our own and neighboring galaxies taken by races that have long since vanished. We would have at our disposal a sort of cosmic archaeological record of a galaxy.

If such a heritage exists—and it almost certainly does—then it can only serve to illuminate our past, present, and future. It could serve to give us the social forms and structures most suitable for self-preservation, genetic evolution, and ecological repairs. It could give us access to new art forms, artistic achievements and other endeavors. It could give us answers to those branches of science, technology, and medicine that still elude us. It could mean the end of the cultural isolation of the human race.

What are the possible dangers of such a venture? What risks would result from contact with extraterrestrial intelligences? If we expose our existence to an alien civilization more advanced and therefore more powerful than ours, are we placing ourselves in even greater danger?

Although the invasion of the earth by hostile aliens has been a cloying theme in science fiction, it seems that this possibility is extremely remote. The annihilation or colonization of the earth by hordes of superior beings would be a very impractical venture for any advanced culture. Interstellar travel is enormously expensive, and only the most extreme crisis would ever justify a mass interstellar exodus. In fact, if a culture did need, say, additional living space, it is more likely that a civilization capable of interstellar travel could well have solved its population problems by internal means long ago. Or if not, such a race, to avoid extinction by means of a mass exodus, would almost certainly seek an uninhabited world rather than face the additional problems that invasion would bring. And to such an advanced race, likely worlds would most probably have been cataloged far in advance of any planned departure date.

Or perhaps an alien culture would attempt to subvert us, under the guise of benevolence. But there is no logical reason to believe that this would aid an intelligent culture in any way. Giving the imagination full run, there is no limit to the kinds of treachery that could confront us, and our only defense would be appropriate security measures and a high degree of suspicion.

So it seems that the greatest threat that contact with an extraterrestrial civilization could bring to bear is not to man's body and environment, but to his psyche. The concept, of course, is anathema to many religions, and man, with his long heritage of Judeo-Christian culture, may not be able to cope with a reexamination of God-created universes. Also, as sociologists are quick to point out, contact between two different cultures has always resulted in the domination of the weaker by the stronger.

On the other hand, there is no precedent of such a contact being made by radio alone. Physical contact has always been the case in point, and without aggression on the part of the more advanced cultures, the lesser cultures have often benefited and prospered.

While it is true that interstellar communication is not totally devoid of risk, I am quick to suggest that the benefits far surpass those risks. We cannot logically conclude that our civilization would be placed in danger by radio contact alone, although the subject should be debated and resolved at a national level.

In the case of interstellar contact, the long delays required and the remoteness of the contact should allow most of us to readily adapt to the realization that we are not alone in the universe. Generations would be required for a dialogue. But the knowledge derived from a civilization that has solved its problems could be of great help to mankind.

9

The Visitors

MANY EXAMPLES of visitations to earth by strange beings from strange worlds are given in the Scriptures. Genesis 28:12 gives a description of an unexplained contact. Regarding a vision he had in the desert, Jacob saw a ladder directly from heaven to earth, certainly a good example of early space transportation. "And he began to dream, and, look! There was a ladder stationed upon the earth and its top reaching up to the heavens; and look! There were God's angels ascending and descending on it." In debating UFOs scientifically, Carl Sagan (*The Cosmic Connection*) uses Jacob's vision as an example of explainable phenomena—a full-scale display of the aurora borealis. However, as convincing as Sagan's explanation is, the aurora borealis is generally confined to arctic and antarctic regions, although a major display of lights was recorded in Rome in 464 B.C. But for some, Jacob's ladder will always be Jacob's ladder.

Various people have suggested that the vision of Ezekiel around 600 B.C. might have been a sighting of a spacecraft landing and some UFO-nauts coming out of it. Now, suppose that Ezekiel really saw an actual event and not just a vision inside his head. Then what was it that he saw?

Arthur Orton produced an interesting analysis in *Analog Science Fact/Fiction* in which he suggested that beings seen by Ezekiel might have been wearing individual helicopter backpacks.

The vision begins, "And I looked, and, behold, a whirlwind came out of the north, a great cloud, and a fire. . . ." And Ezekiel continues, "Also out of the midst thereof came the likeness of four living creatures. . . . Their wings were joined one to another; they turned not when they went; they went every one straight forward. . . . Whithersoever the spirit was to go, they went, thither was their spirit to go; and the wheels were lifted over against them: for the spirit of the living creatures was in the wheels. . . . And when they went I heard the noise of their wings like the noise of great waters."

Arthur Orton's summary presents the vision of Ezekiel:

We have a description of four spacesuited and helicopter-equipped men getting off of or out of something that landed in a cloud of dust or smoke. The four men start their helicopters, take off and fly to some height. On returning to the ground, they remove their flying gear and wait. (*Analog Science Fact/ Fiction*)

Orton concludes that the nature of Ezekiel's description reads like a deposition. He states, "It [the vision] is the presentation of a tableau that makes no sense to the man who witnessed it or to those to whom he is describing it."

On our own continent we find an eighteenth-century Indian legend that mentions luminous humanoid beings who paralyzed people with a small tube. The touch was described as being like a bombardment of cactus needles. Most Indian legends have been passed down from generation to generation and tribe to tribe, with little success on the part of folklorists to pin down dates and sources. However, the popular Star Husband Tale indicates a strong belief on the part of early Indians that extraterrestrials did exist and were able to transcend to earth. In this particular tale, two Indian girls sleeping in the open at night gaze at two stars—one bright, the other dim. They both wish to be married to these stars, and upon awakening, find that each is married to a star, one to a young man (the bright star), and the other to an old man (the dim one). They live with these men in the upper world, above the sky that can be seen from earth.

Although many Indian legends, like Greek myths, personified the sun, moon, and visible stars and looked to them as gods of sorts, there is an underlying theme to the tales that indicates a knowledge and willingness on the part of the Indians to accept the concept of life outside of what they could see and communicate with. A Paiute chief, Mezzaluma, recounted an ancient tale for a Canadian journal, *Topside*. When asked where the North American Indians came from, Chief Mezzaluma answered, "The Indians were created in the sky by Gitchie Manitou, the Great Spirit, who sent down here a big thunderbird to find a place for his children to live. He discovered this land . . . and brought Indians to settle on it. They were taught to use the land wisely and never abuse its natural resources."

Gordon Lore and Harold Deneault, Jr., in their book *Mysteries of the Skies*, have cited an interesting piece of testimony offered in the late summer of 1917 by John Boback, a storekeeper in Youngstown, Pennsylvania. While he was walking on the railroad ties, an eerie "swishing sound" on his left jolted him. On the north side of the tracks he noticed an elliptical object as large as an automobile sitting in a pasture about a hundred feet away. The outer shell was smooth; it had no fins or propellers. The structure lay flat on its underside. An interior light from portholes on the upper portion of the object reminded Boback of automobile headlights. Moments later it lifted off into a smooth, gradual climb. The altitude and acceleration seemed to make the interior become increasingly brighter. It seems that one aspect of the sighting puzzled Boback. At takeoff the UFO had not nosed upward, as he had expected. It had risen from the ground and remained parallel with the surface. At no time did it hover, spin, or revolve during the two minutes he observed it.

The movement and physical description are consistent with reports gathered by NICAP, and the Center for UFO Studies. Granted, many accounts drawn from ancient sources could probably be explained as other than UFOs, but the number of explainable phenomena cited in the past is constant with the number of explainable phenomena cited today. Most investigators agree that at least 20 percent of today's reported cases are totally unexplained. Strange aerial objects have been seen and recorded frequently prior to recent times, by people from all walks of life, including a substantial number of reputable astronomers and other scientists. These reports preceded the era of heavier-than-air flight. The very antiquity of the sightings makes it hard to write them off as a by-product of imaginations enriched by twentieth-century technology.

Turning to possible extensions of that technology, I queried Dr. Robert Wood of the McDonnell Douglas Corporation: How would you design the best space vehicles and excursion modules? What would they do? How would they differ from what we already have? "Well," Dr. Wood began, "the answer to those questions all depends on the assumptions you are willing to make. If you assume that they are inventable, then you get an updated model of the Viking system. The updated system would have a better specific impulse on the propellants. It would orbit the planet, slow down using atmospheric drag to reduce its velocity, and so forth. In short, it would operate the same way Viking does, but with more efficient components, so it could carry a larger payload for less fuel weight."

He paused, then continued. "If you invoke a new assumption about science which is as yet unprovable and try to design the best deep-space vehicles and landers possible, then you come up with a UFO. That is the best model we have, for a perfect interstellar craft. Either you assume something completely new or you play it safe and go with only what we already know. In the latter case, you come up with what we essentially already have.

"UFOs are stunningly different from our present landers. Their apparent antigravity allows them to accelerate and decelerate in an instant. They can do this without causing the occupants physical harm they would otherwise encounter without such gravity-interaction devices. UFOs seem to operate on a principle other than $F = MA$ [Force = Mass times Acceleration]. Their circular shape denotes a conductive wire around the vehicle. The currents of this hypothetical wire flow around the disk and might somehow relate to controlling gravity."

Dr. Wood and I talked for a long time. He explained how the changing colors often observed with the UFO could be technically explained. They might be due to ordinary interaction of the vehicle with the atmosphere. Ionized air becomes red, or there might be a massive magnetic field in the vicinity of the object, which would cause excited molecules to manifest themselves in different wavelengths. He assured me that all this was speculation on his part.

Needless to say, Dr. Wood did not intimate that this was an easy task, but he did point out one very worthwhile analogy. "If we make the assumption that it can be done—that it's possible—then we can try getting experiments done to test that assumption. We can direct these experiments toward discovering the principles behind the way these machines behave. Remember, as soon as the Russians knew it was possible to make the atom bomb, they made one in two years. The big gamble, then, is in the speculation that it's possible. The USA took the gamble, and we succeeded in producing the bomb. The key, then, is that if people know that it can be done, they will figure out how to do it. But for the most part, technological people have not been willing to make that assumption. They assume that gravity-interaction systems cannot be made. Hence they aren't working on them."

I wondered how far we were away from designing something like this without any new assumptions in science. Had anybody been working on that possibility? Stanton T. Friedman is a nuclear physicist who had been working on such questions for fifteen years. He got involved in the UFO problem from an engineering perspective, and was primarily interested in understanding how UFO maneuver and design could relate to our present knowledge of physics and energetics. In 1968 he submitted a paper before the House Committee on Science and Astronautics. I read Friedman's paper and decided to contact him to see if his views had changed substantially in the interim.

During our interview Friedman reiterated time and time again that designers should be looking at UFOs to find out how to design fast, efficient interstellar spacecraft. He was an experienced lecturer and clearly delineated the technical possibilities within our grasp. He was optimistic about our ability to soon duplicate the engineering expertise UFOs seem to manifest.

"Don't UFOs do things that scientists know are impossible?" I asked. He had answered this question before. He didn't hesitate. "No laws of physics have been violated. The UFOs need great maneuverability. They have to be able to get home again."

Then Friedman began to recount all of the craft's physical characteristics, backing each with a technical-design reason for their appearance. The saucer-shaped symmetric craft allows them to move in any direction. They don't have wings like our airplanes because wings would prevent them from such unidirectional maneuvers. Their glow suggests a plasma-ionized atmosphere. Their reported color changes suggest an electromagnetic field capable of interacting with that plasma. They land in football fields or large empty spaces in the Midwest; they have no use or need for metropolitan airfields bustling with people.

His conclusion is that interstellar travel is indeed possible, with round-trip times shorter than a man's lifetime if fission or fusion propulsion systems are refined. But he also pointed out that these already envisioned methods of flight aren't the only possibilities, and explained how engineers accelerate things to high velocities: "Physicists for years have been pushing particles of one sort or another to velocities close to that of light. We don't do this by physically or mechanically pushing the particles; we do this by electrically and magnetically controlling the acceleration, taking into account the relativistic change of mass of the particles. Perhaps it's time we started thinking of new methods for aircraft acceleration."

Another group, in France, led by Claude Poher, is working on a different part of the problem: they are trying to duplicate the UFO power system. Furthermore, the French government is supposedly funding part of their experiments.

The Poher group is working in magnetohydrodynamics. They are trying to send a plasma current or electromagnetic field around a disk-shaped object to see if it can move around the object without causing shock waves. The experimenters might be able to duplicate in theory, the UFO power system. Needless to say, more work needs to be done before any conclusive results can turn up.

Some physicists believe that a better understanding of plasma will explain the mysterious behavior of ball lightning. But would even that account for what happened in Meadowview, Virginia on January 18, 1976?

At approximately eight P.M. a brilliant ball of light was sighted about two hundred feet off the ground. It landed in rolling fields. The incident was witnessed or heard by a number of people. The fire department was called out to investigate, because an explosion and a fire accompanied the landing. No trace of anything was found. The terrain where the object landed is mostly cornfields. The Langley and Seymour Johnson Air Force Base said they knew of no military operations in or around the area.

I started my quest in Meadowview with Betty Barrett, a housewife who first saw the object.

"It was a real light night, the full moon was out," she said. "I had just got settled with the kids, and I saw a car going by the house, and it was going real slow, so it kinda got my curiosity up. I went to the kitchen window and looked out to see if it had pulled in, and it went on up above the curve, and that's when I saw a great old big shining light, it would hurt your eyes to look at it. I went outside. I didn't hear a bit of sound or nothin'. I took off to my neighbor's house. I rung the doorbell and asked her to come and look. I felt foolish, but I mean if I hadn't saw it, I guess I wouldn't have believed it either, but it was the brightest thing that I'd ever saw."

Helen Counts continued the story for me.

"Mrs. Barrett rang my doorbell and asked me to come out, that she'd seen this thing that she's scared of, and it landed over in the field, and I went outside, and when I looked I couldn't see anything.

And she turned to go back to her house, and about that time something exploded, and it sounded like a dynamite, and fire just flew up everywhere. I called Central Dispatch. They're the County Sheriff, the Fire Department. I thought it was an airplane."

The story was then continued for me by Dan Ryan, assistant chief of the Meadowview Volunteer Fire Department.

"Around eight-ten I got a call which said there were fires on the top of the hill; by eight-thirty we was on the scene in the area where this plane was supposed to have crashed. I'd say twenty-five of us with three vehicles. And we searched the area with those trucks and lights and then the chief and about four or five men walked the area that night and that was just about it."

And Jim Booth, a free-lance photographer, filled in other details.

"I got to the scene about an hour and a half or so after the explosion. It was extremely cold that night, so I thought rather than just going out and freezing to death, we'd just let them do the search. I would estimate that there were at least . . . there were between twenty and thirty people involved in the search. They finally decided to end the search—that was sometime after midnight—and resume it again the next morning. We searched just about every square inch, unless it was in a wooded area that was just so dense that we couldn't see through it with the tremendous spotlights. The next day, several ground-search parties went out and went back over the areas they'd searched. They didn't go back over the fields, because they were relatively clear, good visibility, and they just went around the perimeter of the field, and could find nothing. No debris, no sign of any explosion or any fire."

A hoax, perhaps? A fraud? A flight of fancy? I didn't know. From all the interviews I conducted, this is the story: A fireball landed, then disappeared. It left no trace of its passing except in the minds of those who saw it. It is real. It fits Dr. Hynek's description. "Remember," he said, "the U in UFO simply means 'unidentified.' "

Have we been visited from outer space? Is that great void the origin of UFOs? I don't know. I will accept Allen Hynek's summary: "Maybe the whole phenomenon is as mysterious as . . . asking Ben Franklin, 'What makes the sun shine?' How could Ben have known that the sun was a nuclear reactor? In other words, it could be that the UFO phenomenon is so strange that it may signal a domain of nature that we have not yet explored—in the same sense that a hundred years ago we knew nothing about nuclear energy, for instance.

Most people like this idea of visitation from outer space, and that may yet turn out to be the answer. But as I tell my students at Northwestern: if you know the answer in advance, it's not research."

For my part, I have marked the UFO story in my files "open," to be continued.

Part Three

MAGIC
and WITCHCRAFT

10

What Is Magic?

ALL EARLY human development was surrounded by a secondary force called magic. But what does the word "magic" mean? Today, people relate magic or magicians to vaudeville entertainment: magic is a trick with a perfectly logical explanation behind it that the viewer does not know but only suspects. Since the gullible are deceived by sleight-of-hand, magic is generally accepted as a phony, artificial, clever game that was designed to relax and entertain. A modern magician can indeed be the greatest of all skeptics when it comes to accepting extrasensory perception or anything transcending the five senses.

The magic I'm talking about is quite different. I'm speaking of magic as it was known to the ancients. To "make magic" even in today's society means *to set forces in motion.* "Good medicine" to the American Indian was a positive influence. What we might call positive magic was used by the Stone Age people. This use of psychic energy later became "white magic," as opposed to "black magic."

Whether used for constructive or destructive purposes there is really no difference among the techniques of magic. Magic is merely a force. It does not differentiate between good and evil. It is the person who knows and uses this force to get certain results who determines the qualitative shading of the process.

Rollo Ahmed, the British researcher described by peer Dennis Wheatley as "a master who has devoted a lifetime to acquiring a first-hand knowledge of that grim 'other world' " points out that the black arts differ from the "white" not in method but in purpose. After all, what is magic ritual but an attempt to extend man's powers beyond the ordinary, beyond the limits imposed on "ordinary" people by education and circumstances? Only the magician knows how to break through this barrier.

Of course, what is considered magic at one point in history may be commonplace at a later date. Certainly anyone able to produce electricity during the early eighteenth century would have been suspected of supernatural powers—because he would have had knowledge of *natural* law which the rest of humanity lacked. Likewise, today's magic practitioner performs feats that are unusual only because humanity does not share his more extensive knowledge of what is possible in nature. The line between religion and magic is so hard to define, whereas science as an experience is clearly defined; an idea accepted through common reason becomes a law. A law is likely to deal with something you can see and *repeat*. But anyone who feels that science organizes all, should remember that today's improbability can be tomorrow's common occurrence.

A priest or shaman in primitive society was a person believed to have psychic abilities who served as go-between for his people and the deities. They could accept his position if they wished, and those who did benefited from it, of course. Even in those early days there was "establishment." The outsider practicing magic on his own was considered a poor security risk. A Stone Age magician had no love for amateurs. A strong belief in magic made it a potent force, and this force could not be haphazardly dealt with. It worked better when the forces in the minds of the tribe were directed to *one* person among them. Any other practitioner of magic would only split the force and make it less effective; therefore, the "official" magician prospered.

Does *belief* in magic make it work? One day I watched an Indian fakir perform the well-known rope trick. I promised myself not to be hypnotized into believing that the rope would rise of its own volition. I wasn't. But this particular magician used physical means to deceive his audience. There was that very thin, *nearly* invisible thread that pulled the rope into an upright position. Yet, all around me in the audience, people gasped and took the performance at face value.

Mundus vult decipi, decipimur is the magicians' professional motto. It means, "The world wants to be fooled, so let us fool it."

Magic is a volatile thing: it cannot be used to solve everyday problems and matters that a person is able to resolve in other ways.

Magic can be the way when *other* methods fail. But can it be the force one can turn to under heavy stress? Does man need a psychologically motivated "out"?

It's human nature to look for a shortcut. Whenever a person strives for the important, the desirable, or the difficult, he tries to eliminate all or most of the obstacles and to make the results perfect in every detail. "Honesty is the best policy," but primitive instincts in man always look for a better, quicker way to the goal.

The gap between the potency of the word *magic* and the actual accomplishment may be quite wide. The belief that magic can be applied is the first step to working the natural law. Usually, before the process even starts, the mind of the believer jumps ahead to the accomplished feat. Because of this state of anticipation, believers in magic are looked upon as dreamers living in an unreal world. But do not confuse this state of happy expectation with some *very real* accomplishments in the field of magic.

History is filled with man's attempts to harness his world and to understand the omnipotent power around him. Both magician and scientist seek to transform the world by man-made techniques. Old books on alchemy call to mind the modern chemist; as Eliphas Levi, the nineteenth-century seer, declared in *Transcendental Magic*: "Magic is the science of the secrets of nature."

The scientist uses material methods to obtain results, and accepts only that which he can test at will under conditions he controls. The magician, on the other hand, uses the powers of mind and imagination to obtain tangible results. But his system is as well organized and specific as the scientist's—only his values differ. Where the scientist is limited to demonstrated facts for his knowledge, the magician regards ideas, thought forms, verbalizations, etc. as equally tangible and therefore powerful. Religion argues that the magician is seeking to acquire power over nature and wrongly tramples on territorial rights of the priest—and to the church this is heresy.

Primitive people all over the world still use and continue to develop the basic techniques of magic. Many of these people believe that objects react upon one another by a kind of sympathy or affinity, the rules of which were defined by Sir James Frazer (1854–1941) in his famous work *The Golden Bough:* "Things that have once been in contact with each other continue to act upon one another at a distance after the physical contact has been severed": and, furthermore, "Like produces like and an effect resembles its cause." For example, a sorcerer can use a person's nail clipping or a lock of hair to "bewitch" a person from a distance.

While prayer is total supplication, with the recipient unable to influence the decision in any manner, magic is a process of active participation by the supplicant in the process of making something occur: thus, there is incentive. Of course, there is this difference: anyone can pray, no previous experience is necessary. But not everyone is a good magician. One has to have studied nature's laws and understood their workings before one can apply them to the situation at hand. If the application of magic fails nevertheless, it is not magic that is at fault, but the one applying it—he simply did not know his techniques well enough!

The tighter the wording of the incantation, the more potent the magic is likely to be. Instead of saying, "Please, my little grain stocks, my little bearded friends, won't you try so hard to grow higher no matter how bad the weather is, because we all need the grain of life," primitive man would say, "Grain grow tall." He repeated this often because he believed, just as most of our parents believed, that repetition strengthens effectiveness. Carefully choosing the words was not enough. One had to be careful that the phrases weren't too easily understood by outsiders, because then the magic would lose its potency. So this brought about formulas that were known only to insiders.

In his book *The Human Dynamo*, Professor Hans Holzer says:

To incant merely means to implore in a rhythmical, orderly pattern. The superficial difference between prayer and incantation is that prayer may be uttered in any fashion, rhythmical or disorganized, since the meaning of the words and presumably the feeling behind them is paramount. The incantation, on the other hand, requires a specific way of speaking the words. Incantations . . . consist of frequent repetition of words in monotonous tones or in sharply accented rhythms, coupled with definite physical movements. Some incantations are set to music and are sung. A typical Wicca (or Witchcraft) incantation addresses itself to the mother goddess, or to Diana, describing her beauty and wisdom, and then asking her to help the supplicant in such-and-such a way.

Invocations and evocations are closely related to incantations. All three are directed toward a specific deity, or, with some pagan religions, "demon." An incantation is a simple prayer for help, but an invocation resembles an order more than a prayer. An invocation uses polite language, contains praise of the invoked power, and at the same time commands the invoked power to perform the requested service without fail. In Judaism and Christianity invocations serve primarily as instruments of revenge or punishment. The wrath of God or of one of the saints may be called down upon someone who has wronged the supplicant. Neither Hebrew nor Christian religion invokes the deity for positive purposes; they prefer to use prayer. This may be due to the Judeo-Christian God being essentially a terrifying father figure with whom one does not toy. Invocations are used primarily in pagan religions and magic cults because the pagan gods are viewed as friends and familiars and can be *made* to serve, whether willing or not.

The term *invocation* means to call down upon oneself, to call in; *evocation* means to call out, to call from within to the outside, to bring forth.

Evocation is used in magical practices primarily to *bring out* from within the slumbering magical qualities of the *app*licant, who is now no longer a *supp*licant. The magician—not the stage magician, but the esoteric magician—is fully aware of his superior powers. When he evokes a diety or demon, he does so from a position of equality. He knows the magic formulas, he knows what must be done to make such and such a power obey the call.

The term *ritual* derives from the Latin word *ritus*, meaning the proper way, the *right* way. At all times in all cultures, great importance has been attached to the proper way of performing religious ceremonies. If even one of the necessary elements is not attended to, the ritual may fail. In the opinion of priests performing rituals, only the *entire* range of elements assures proper results.

Time is of the utmost importance. Christians insist on feast days, rather than feast hours or minutes. Pagan religions work only if they observe time to the nearest minute.

Place is second. With pagans, the outdoors or a pagan temple is preferred, although in modern times pagan rituals have been performed in living rooms as well as in the great outdoors. With Christians, Hebrews, Buddhists, and others, a church or temple is the preferred place of worship.

Costume of the officiating priest or priestess is next. There are deep symbolic reasons behind every piece of clothing worn by a priest or priestess. In Christianity, the robe worn by priests is carefully prescribed by Church law. In the pagan religions, the priest's body adornment is dominated by symbolic representations of nature and of the deities expressing that oneness with nature. The colors of the robe are carefully chosen to coincide with the particular ritual and the time of the year in which it is performed.

Tools, or the instruments used in the performance of a ritual, come next. In the Hebrew faith, candles and leather strips wound around the wrists, known as phylacteries, are used by the Orthodox. In Christianity, the Bible, the crucifix, the chalice, the bell, the fisherman's ring, and the stole are the chief tools of the officiating priest. In pagan religions, various simple tools are used, such as the knife called *athame*, the whip, the wand and the sword, the chalice, and the cord or girdle.

Next come *aromatics*, including incense. They set the emotional climate of the place of worship and influence the mood of the worshipers. Aromatics used in religious rituals are never strong enough to cause inebriation or other forms of altered consciousness, but they help relax the worshipers and create a receptive atmosphere. Among the best-known aromatics used are myrrh, frankincense, jasmine, and sandalwood.

Oils, symbolic of life eternal, are used by most religions both for burning in specially designed lamps and for anointing. The thought behind the use of oils for anointing seems to be that oil sticks to whatever one puts it upon. In addition, it was thought that the oil, pressed from plants and the life juice of those plants, would represent the life force in man and thus the act of anointing would become one of sanctifying or consecrating the recipient with part of a sacred life force.

The use of *foods*, such as wine and bread, is also common to most religions for communion. It is purely symbolic, as neither wine nor bread has any inherent magical qualities. However, in African voodoo, there are feasts in honor of the deity as part of the African religious ritual. Most of these African meals are heavily spiced and have mild psychedelic effects.

Sounds are also important to many rituals. Sacred music in church is one of the pillars of the ritual; it creates a mood of solemnity. Drums and guns are used in Eastern religions to start and end a ritual, and also to summon the deities. Haitian voodoo is unthinkable without continuous use of small drums, even during the ceremony itself and while the priest performs verbal magic. Only intellectually oriented Protestants do without the use of music in their rituals, except for fundamentalist offshoots.

Movements, including dance, are part of the rituals of many religions. In the Christian religion, the movement of the priest is carefully prescribed by the scriptures and by the interpretations of Christian doctrine. Only in very recent times have such elements as contemporary music and ritual dance been introduced into the service to win back some of the young people who have wandered away from the Church.

In some Hebraic sects, such as the Chassidic, joyous dancing is part of the ritual. In Hinduism, dance is so much an integral part of the ritual that temple dancers are trained in large schools adjacent to the temples themselves. The movement of the temple dancers is as carefully prescribed as all other parts of the ritual. Islam, considered the most intellectual of all religions, frowns upon joyous expression of human desires, but there are sects that practice ritual dancing, such as the Dervishes. In Wicca, ritual dancing is used as a means of increasing the outpour of psychic energies. In the Sabaean pagan religion, extended periods of fast dancing are also used. Dancing gives a feeling of abandonment and detachment necessary for the performance of the ritual, but it also creates energies that the officiating priest or priestess can use as a power reserve.

Last but not least, the *words* make the ritual work. They may be spoken or sung, but they are very carefully put together. Not only are the words chosen for specific effects, but the timing and placement of the words in relation to the other nine elements is very important.

11

What Is Witchcraft?

AT A COCKTAIL PARTY recently I decided to test some of my friends to see how they felt about witchcraft.

"Do you believe in witchcraft?" I asked a prominent director who had done a number of science fiction movies.

"*Believe?*" he shot back. "Of course not. But I am interested in it."

A few seasons back, television talk shows all over the country were host to a rather substantial-looking lady from England by the name of Sybil Leek.

"I'm a witch," Miss Leek declared calmly, as if centuries of witch burnings had never occurred. Miss Leek, an author of books on the occult, is a practicing witch who once lived in the fabled New Forest of southern England, traditional haunt of witches. Miss Leek did not perform any feats of magic on the air, she did not turn anyone into a frog (although in some cases her patience was being tried severely), and she came across as an altogether engaging personality with great knowledge of the occult, herbology, and, of course, magical practices.

Witches walk the streets of Los Angeles, New York, London. Like ordinary people, which they are. Today they can do so with immunity, for at least legally witchcraft is free to be practiced. It is not yet fully socially acceptable, and even witchcraft cannot change that overnight. But I wondered: where did it all begin? Where *did* witches originate?

Apparently, the prehistoric people of France and Spain used various caves for certain rituals. Half a mile or more from the entrances, archaeologists have found campfire sites that had been circled by stones. There were pictures of animals painted on flat stones carefully placed face downward inside them. Perhaps magical rites were performed inside the circles to affect the animals depicted upon the stones, which had been placed face-downward to prevent the power raised from being dissipated! In other places, clay figures of animals were found which had been pierced with spears. Archaeologists were puzzled as to their meaning, but the local people said, "It's just hunting magic. We do that every year when we want to kill wolves. They're clever; you must gain power over them, or they will get away." The research of Abbé Bruile and others show that some of these old cave paintings were used for magic, and it is safe to assume that the painting was done especially for that purpose. Undoubtedly, the beginnings of Witchcraft go back to very early times. Caves such as these prove that it was flourishing when Europe was still in the throes of the Stone Age.

We know that very early civilizations were set up along matriarchal lines. The dominant figure was the woman because she gave birth and took care of the necessities of life, the home, and the sick, and mainly because her skills were more varied and sophisticated than those of the male, whose main purpose was to provide food and shelter and defend the community against attack from the outside. The "finer things of life," then as now, were the domain of the woman. The matriarch developed into the priestess. The "old religion" of western and northern Europe was a nature religion. Unexplained forces around man were considered part of divine power. In this respect, early religion was pantheistic in that all nature was considered an expression of the deity.

After the advent of Christianity witchcraft became officially known as "the Old Religion." This was to emphasize the contrast. Even today, a person who is a witch does not refer to his or her faith as witchcraft, but prefers the term "Old Religion" or simply "the Craft." Originally, the Craft, or the Old Religion, was nothing more sinister than a form of medicine based on an intimate knowledge of herbs, drugs, the workings of nature, ESP, and simple psychology through the clever magic of poetry and the use of words to bring about certain reactions in people. These "earth people" seemed more interested in doing things for their community than in doing things in the service of any gods as such. Of course, one always must keep on good terms with the forces of energy they are working with, but the way in which these divine obligations were fulfilled merely suggests a rather down-to-earth attitude toward the religious element in their faith.

The Mother Goddess of prehistoric times has many names, but in antiquity she was usually identified with Diana, Dione, Arriarod, or Carridwen, even with the mystical Kybele of Asia Minor. In essence she was the "female principle," both the mother and the temptress, both young and old, but always feminine and always desirable—be it through physical charms, wisdom, or magical powers. Underneath, of course, was the dominating factor of fertility—physical fertility, but also creative fertility in the wider sense.

Even as with priests of other religions, the priestesses of the Old Religion often identified with their goddess, in the sense that the goddess would "descend" into them, inspiring them to act, and thus become temporarily incarnate within them.

But a priestess needed a more concrete focal point for the people she led. The image of the Mother Goddess was given a companion, the Horned God, who represented the male principle. The Horned God was not the devil; he was merely a male counterpart to the image of the Mother Goddess.

He had a costume with a headpiece made from the horns of a bull or antlers of a stag. There was a Stone Age tradition that by identifying with and disguising yourself as a strong animal you would acquire the properties and virtues of that animal.

So now we have the man in a rugged, subordinate role to the priestess. The man took care of the group during the winter cold, and the woman was in charge for the summer.

Man's symbol of his rugged role—his horns—was later used as proof that the Old Religion worshiped the devil. Actually, the Old Religion had no use for the devil. It was and is one of the main tenets of the Old Religion that man is born innocent and whatever sin or guilt a person acquires by the end of his life is really his own fault and nobody else's.

This came as a complete surprise to me. I had always associated witches with the devil, believed, as I am sure millions still do, that witchcraft practices included the worship of Satan. But as I delved into authentic accounts of modern witchcraft practices, I began to realize that I had followed a "line" strung by the medieval, Church-inspired tradition that lumped all pagans into one lot—namely, that of evil antagonists of Christianity.

The more I looked into the existing material on witchcraft, the more I realized that Satanism is not only not part of witchcraft but its very opposite—and when I got to talking to some followers of "white" (i.e., benign) witchcraft around Los Angeles, I realized that they disliked no group more than the Satanic ones. To witches, Satanists represent an embarrassment, apparently, and to Satanists, I was told, witches are simply people who don't have the guts to do things "right"—use magic for selfish purposes without regard for others.

The Old Religion was a cult "of the wise"; the Celtic language calls it "Wicca" and the word *witch* is derived from this. A witch is a wise woman who has knowledge superior to that of the average person. The male counterpart was the "wizard," not "warlock." The priestess and priest of the Old Religion were referred to by just those names, and the members of the coven were simply called that. The term *coven* comes from the same root as "covenant" or "convention" and simply means brotherhood, community, congregation.

The Old Religion, which was later called witchcraft, celebrates four main holidays, on April 30, July 31, October 31, and February 2. They are May Eve, which marks the coming of spring; Lamas, marking the incoming summer; Hallowe'en, or All Hallows' Eve, honoring the incoming autumn; and Candlemas or Brigid's Day, the winter festival. Hallowe'en is the harvest festival and perhaps the most important of the feasts. On that night, followers of the Old Religion look back on the past year and its accomplishments. With hope for the future, they celebrate a year of hard work. Incidentally, "fertility" signified the desire to produce more from the fields and farms, not erotic activities per se.

Practical tools of daily existence were used for ritual symbolism in the rites. The Old Religion has taken ordinary working tools of the household as symbols of domestic and general well-being. A common symbolic tool is the broom, which denotes domestic order and cleanliness. A straw broom was always in the corner of a clean house. In the harvest ceremony brooms were used to show how high they would like the crops to grow, if it was all right with the deity. By the action of raising the broom, witches showed how high, and thus implored the deity to grant them good crops. There is no other reason for witches to use brooms: They did not fly around on broomsticks. Persecutors neither understood nor cared to understand. There is nothing magic about a broom. When you use a broom as a symbol you are only trying to communicate the fact that your subject in some way bears a resemblance to the characteristic movement of a broom in use.

Each new moon is the beginning of a time period, for the Old Religion recognizes the division of the month, in addition to the four main holidays. In the old days it was unthinkable to meet when it was not a full moon; today, some covens will meet when it's convenient for their members, even if it's not on a full moon, so long as it is near one. The Old Religion explores the "hidden powers" in man, hence the connection with the moon. There is also a link to Diana, the ancient moon goddess, in her manifestation as Tanith, mistress of psychic powers. People instinctively knew that their energy had increased, because they had watched the moon increase its energy. A full moon greatly increases man's extrasensory perception.

For nine centuries Christianity existed peacefully side by side with the Old Religion. But when Christianity became a world power through the state, it insisted on being the only accepted religion. This position was taken against all other religions as well, even though some of them, such as Judaism, had moral codes just as valid as the Christian way.

The Old Religion felt it best to exist in many small groups and it was not looking for mass converts as the Church was. Because the poor and oppressed, who had originally embraced Christianity in the Roman days when it was the religion for them and championed their cause, were by the eleventh century disillusioned, they turned in increasing numbers to the Old Religion, which had survived from ancient times. Thus the poor, the "country bumpkins," the pagans, (Latin, *pagani*), became the main supporters of the Old Religion and continued to practice it in their homes, sometimes in the seclusion of the forests and mountains—always in fear that the Church would eventually turn against them.

It was only when I talked to experts on the subject that I learned of the real reasons why the Church persecuted witches: not for religious causes, but as a matter of doctrine. Even the word *devil*, it was explained to me, meant nothing more than "stranger" in the Romany language. There was nothing evil in the traditional Celtic Horned God of the Hunt (Cernaunos), but to the Church the horns of the stag became the insidious marks of Satan.

Many superstitions of the eleventh and twelfth centuries are still alive today. In some Roman Catholic areas, demonic theology is still taken seriously. The Church was determined and used fear to organize: the concept of the devil was used to destroy *any* enemy of the Church.

In 1364, Europe was torn by the Peasants' War. At that time the Roman Catholic Church agreed with the feudal lords that it was heresy to demand better working conditions. The Old Religion welcomed these peasants because in Wicca all people are equal.

In *The Philosophy of Witchcraft,* Ian Ferguson tells us that Joan of Arc was the symbol of rebellion against occupying England and against the collaborating Church of France. Joan was considered by some authorities a Roman Catholic saint *and* a priestess of the Old Religion.

The Church did not permit sexual equality, sexual freedom, or free expression of loving nature. It was claimed that these ideas, all parts of the Old Religion, were against Church doctrine. The position of women was way below that of men and the only place women could elevate themselves was in poetry and song. Even then, to write a romantic poem and have it talked of by neighbors was to risk some consequences. At this point, the possible ESP of witches was not under attack. But as the Church developed the devil image more fully, it became convenient to attribute all unusual talents or powers to the devil.

The Bible has been used as proof in condemning witchcraft, even though there are only passages in it that describe psychic phenomena. But to take anything out of context is to jeopardize its intended meaning. Some translations of the Bible *seem* to condemn the occult arts; the Church used quotes to justify the persecution of the members of Old Religion.

Two passages especially were used over again to accuse witches. In Exodus 22:18 we read: "Thou shalt not suffer a witch to live." This refers to a situation that existed then in the Holy land. Two types of soothsayers practiced their craft: the official and easily controlled prophets, and the psychics who dealt with ordinary people and could not be counted on to support the policies of the state. Moses wanted to protect his people, and hence the passage means "unauthorized prophecy is forbidden under penalty of death." The Hebrews did consult psychic sources. Moses, a diplomat, knew that government control in this difficult political situation was necessary for survival amid hostile people. Adapting this situation to different circumstances makes it false. The second passage is Samuel 29:6. This refers to King Saul, who asked his servants to get a woman who had a "familiar spirit," so that he could see her about his future. "Familiar spirit" is a direct term that means what it says. "Familiar" is common to a family or household or to a universe perhaps. The spirit that Saul refers to is in today's parapsychology vocabulary called a control. Saul was merely seeking a sitting with a medium. The adaptation of the Scriptures preferred to use the term *witch* instead.

When witches were condemned at trials, a "compact" with Satan was mentioned. Some of these incredible forgeries still exist. I visited the witchcraft museum at Salem, Massachusetts, and saw some documents there that accuse totally innocent women of things they knew nothing about. At the trial of the accused witches of Loudun, an actual signature of the devil was produced by the court, and duly acknowledged by the accused, too wretched from torture to contest anything. Sixteenth-century books displayed at the British Museum, which I inspected with great interest, even show exact drawings of the devil and all his "lesser" helpers, presumably drawn from testimony of the accused (and condemned) witches.

As the Old Religion became a secret, or underground, cult, its followers were careful not to be caught. The code of behavior became more secretive. Except for those born into witch families, others were admitted with much caution.

Their meetings, called Sabbaths, were held at night, usually on witchcraft holidays or nights of the full moon. This communal form of worship goes back to primitive man and was more like a folk-dance festival than a sinister ritual. (During the Reformation, Calvin burned people for the "crime" of dancing or singing.) Presiding at these Sabbaths were a priestess and priest, farm people usually known to everybody, who asked the Mother Goddess to bless their crops.

To feel freer in the open, the witches took off their clothes and danced in the nude. This custom particularly upset the Church, and later the Puritans, and even today it is a feature that makes it hard to explain the Craft to a lot of otherwise broad-minded people. But the Old Religion also had a practical reason for its nudity. Witches believed that a person's body contained energy that could be collected and directed and put to use by the community. Clothes hampered this "power field," and therefore witches felt that they must work naked. Eroticism did not necessarily help with the cone of power, or business at hand, although spontaneous lovemaking was left to the conscience of the individual. So the witches danced naked until it was time to put their clothes on and go home, until the next festival came around to let off a little more steam. They felt one with nature and they harmed no one.

The reasons why people become witches, or seek to join a coven, are many: dissatisfaction with other faiths, a need to have some sort of religious expression, and the desire to become part of a nature-oriented form of worship—with all the "unconventional" trappings this implies, such as practice of magic, the occult, psychic phenomena, and perhaps even erotic liberation.

Neither covens nor individual practicing witches ever did, or do now, solicit converts the way nearly all other religions do. In fact they discourage them, but are bound by their own codes to consider in good faith those who come to them who have the proper qualifications.

Mary is a direct descendant of a known Salem witch. At family gatherings, she celebrates her unusual ancestry with stories of the persecution her ancestor had to suffer. But this does not make Mary herself a witch. Although she has ESP and an interest in psychic research, she is not an initiate of witchcraft and therefore not automatically a "real" witch, despite her ancestry. Only when the Craft is handed down from generation to generation does the religion come with birth.

Arthur is an artist who lives in Texas. His interest in the occult does not go beyond the use of crystal balls and meditation. ESP runs in Arthur's family. He has the unusual ability to carry on conversations with deceased family members, and through these experiences he knows that his psychic talent has great possibilities. In an earlier age, his talent would have qualified him as a witch.

And what about C. James? His first interest in the occult came at the age of *four*. Mr. James was raised as a Methodist and found it to be a passive religion. Witchcraft involves the ability to say prayers and perform rites and have what is intended in those rites happen. He, as many, felt frustrated and helpless when saying prayers. Mr. James feels that there just isn't enough power generated in the Christian religions and believes that the energy that makes things happen in the Old Religion is present in all of us, and in all things.

Harrietta N. feels a particular attraction to Egyptian and Greek history. She was raised a Catholic, but at age fourteen she wanted to leave the Church. She no longer believed in God as people accepted Him to be, but in a "force of nature." She was in her early twenties when she read the book *Witches, U.S.A.* The mention of a self-blessing ritual frightened her, and it wasn't until she read of a self-blessing in *The New Pagans* that she thought it was witchcraft she was looking for. She liked the fact that her profession—she was a pharmacist—could be enhanced through the Wicca practice of healing.

Many people who possess clairvoyance think they are witches because the occult reveals itself to them. Naïvely, they think they *caused* something to happen, when in reality they were witnessing a natural phenomenon! I've heard of people who think they've made people die because they had a premonition of the event. This is the result of fear and superstition. No wonder some people actually believed the accusations of witchcraft when their only "crime" was their psychic talent.

The avenue to finding a coven is as obscure as finding a life partner through computer dating. It's difficult to know where an established coven exists, unless you happen to run into someone who knows. Secrecy is a part of *true* witchcraft.

12

The Witchcraft Scene
Today

WICCA IS divided into four groups: hereditary, traditional, Gardnerian, and Alexandrian. Hereditary witchcraft has kept the Craft alive by passing belief through the family tree. Traditionals wear robes for their rites. Gardnerians stem from Dr. Gerald B. Gardner, initiated by a hereditary witch in the New Forest, England. The late Dr. Gardner was a writer who founded a witchcraft museum on the Isle of Man. The Alexandrians are those whose initiation beliefs have in some way to do with Alexander and Maxine Sanders. Whether or not a coven should be public caused heated debate. The Alexandrian view was that the tip of the iceberg should be visible. The Bible says, "He that hath ears to listen, let him hear." There is so much for a witch to say, yet in telling *all*, he may reveal nothing.

As in anything, to have a direct experience with a group, a person must be *initiated in some way*. It is only when the individual becomes initiated by an existing group that he or she is truly a part of Wicca; without initiation, he or she remains an outsider.

I discovered that a coven of Gardnerian witches practiced in Long Island. Ray Buckland, who headed this group originally, now maintains a witchcraft museum in Weirs Beach, New Hampshire, based on the more famous one on the Isle of Man. Mr. Buckland was educated and initiated in England and follows in the footsteps of Gardner. His rituals are always performed in the nude, with Buckland as priest and his wife as high priestess.

Buckland has posed for photos in full regalia, which consists of not much more than a helmet with antlers and a G-string. His museum welcomes all, but the coven remains sheltered. The priest and priestess of this group are very selective and turn away many who are not ready.

Meanwhile, Buckland's successor, Phoenix, continues to expand the Long Island coven, while Buckland is on a tangent of his own, called Saxon Wicca. The Long Island coven is a tangible group, even though some members are also quietly establishing their own covens.

Herman Slater runs an occult shop called The Warlock Shop in Manhattan. That is his *business*; his religious pursuit is witchcraft in the Welsh tradition. Herman is not of Welsh background, and yet he feels it's perfectly normal to practice in this way, and he even lectures on it publicly. In addition, Herman Slater publishes a spectacular journal called the *Earth Religion News*, in which other witches announce their doings, and when one follows the lively exchange of opinions in the letters-to-the-editor column, one gets the feeling that witches aren't much different from other religious people, after all—they have their petty differences just like everyone else.

The Gardnerian tradition differs from the Welsh tradition in that it has three degrees, while the Welsh has four degrees. The third degree is being an elder and the fourth is being a high priest or priestess. In Slater's words:

Our high priestess wears a moon crown composed of a copper band surmounted by a silver crescent. When she trains a high priestess who splits off to form her own coven, she becomes a witch queen and wears an all-silver moon crown. Her high priest then becomes the king of the woods, which is the same as the Gardnerian Magus, and receives a copper or bronze crown surmounted by a gold sun disc. Upon initiation we take two names, a public name for outside the circle, and a name for within the circle which is held very secret. My own public name is Hermes. Our name as a high priest cannot be disclosed publicly. Our rituals are very beautiful and very simple. They are a celebration of life and contain no ceremonial magic. We are the children and the friends of the gods, and laugh and love with them. We are not solemn within the circle but freely laugh and enjoy ourselves. Unlike the Gardnerians and others, all of us have an active part in the rituals and the high priest is basically co-equal with the high priestess. At every Sabbath the high priestess draws down the horned god into the high priest. We wear robes and do not use the scourge. The circle is normally cast with a rod. It is opened with appeals to earth, air, and water, and is closed with fire. We possess the original "Great

Rite" ritual and when it is used it is used by husband and wife or lovers privately and in sacredness and respect. We do not discriminate against those who within their private lives have found love with those of their own sex. However, we work female to male within the circle. Such sexual discrimination has never been a part of paganism as we see it. There is an inner court coven for the more advanced witches, and an outer court coven for the first-degree witches.

As Eudora Welty's Southern short-story character Leota says, "Lord, yes, she's from New Orleans. Ever'body in New Orleans believes ever'thing's spooky." New Orleans is traditionally a seat of magic, the occult, and of course witchcraft. High priestess Mary Oneida Toups has been granted a charter from the state of Louisiana to conduct the religious order of witchcraft. She is a black woman of great powers who conducts a witchcraft shop where supplies, books, and information can be obtained. She explains: "I operate this occult-and-voodoo-supply witchcraft shop so that anyone interested in witchcraft may acquire the proper equipment. I am not in business for the sole and selfish purpose of gaining financial benefits from the profits of my shop. Naturally, there results monetary compensation by the virtue of my commerce: but selling the merchandise is not the end result. I am titled as Oneida, the Queen Witch of New Orleans—this being in that I guide, advise, and admonish other priests and priestesses as witches what is the established order of our religion. I possess a charter issued by the secretary of state of Louisiana and my covens and other witches seek godliness through the refinement of our being so as to qualify for the admission into the kingdom of God."

A quarterly magazine called *The New Broom* represents the work of Mark Roberts and Morgan McFarland—the two leaders of a group practicing Dianic witchcraft in the Celtic-Greek tradition. It is true that all covens stress the great Mother Goddess, but she is not necessarily identified as Diana. The Dallas group also puts people in touch with each other, although it does not hand out names of witches. The articles in *The New Broom* are varied and highly instructive. This Dallas group considers itself monotheistic, as their goddess represents the essential and primary creative force. They are pantheistic in the sense that they consider every creation in nature a child of the goddess. They separate those in tune with the nature of the universe from those who are not. One aspect of Dianic belief allows for virgin birth. This Dianic coven considers itself "her children who strive always to retain the qualities of love, learning, giving and receiving, and delighting."

Chicago is a hub of occult activities. There are established information centers, such as the Occult Book Store, the Bell, Book and Candle, and El Sabarum. El Sabarum is the home of Frederico de Arechaga, a young Spanish nobleman, a hereditary witch and spiritual head of a religious community called the Sabaeans.

One festival observed by this group is the Venus Festival, honoring that famous lady who portrays love. This is an ancient Babylonian-Sumerian festival, whose purpose was to create polarity between man and the universe. There are several parts to the rituals. First the convocation, or gathering together of people. Then the invocation, dancing and song in which the gods are invited. One incantation especially goes to Ishtar (Venus) and one is to Mana, the moon god.

It is believed that what you put into a ritual determines the results. God is a disc with two sides, both good and evil, male and female. Interestingly, this is part of achieving perfection. The incantations call up the old gods, and dancing between each step of the ritual is used to work up the power.

Another part of the ritual is the communion, in which the people feast in the presence of the gods, and here the spiritual essence of food is used. The last part, the evocation, closes the festival.

The Sabaeans also celebrate the White Goddess, the goddess of birth without delivery. Thus she is similar to the Virgin Mother. Her pregnant appearance is used as a symbolic gesture to remind us that she is the goddess of reincarnation or karma. In the Egyptian Book of the Dead she sits in judgment of the heart against the feather of truth. For it was said that if the person's heart was outweighed by the double truth of the gods, he was committed to reincarnate. In other words, if you fail the test of balance, you must be brought back to Earth through the great discomfort of birth! Frederico de Arechaga says: "A truly wise person does not have to convince or argue a truth: he just lives it."

Most people believe that California has the most fertile soil not only for all sorts of occult practices, but especially for witchcraft. Somehow, the warm climate and the extreme liberties of lifestyle for which the West is famous suggest that California abounds in unusual people . . . including witches.

Well, they're right.

Take the city of Pasadena, for instance. Deceptively demure, even dull in appearance, Pasadena nevertheless houses four major occult groups. There is for instance Fred McLaurin Adams, the great pagan leader, archaeologist, and poet (not to mention artist), whose Fera-feria group practices a unique blend of Celtic and Minoan ritual. Adams himself has adapted the ancient Greek texts for modern use, has written about them profusely in various esoteric journals, but is generally not known to the outside world. "The calendar is the back-bone of life," says Fred Adams, who also practices a special kind of esoteric astrology for those who seek his counsel.

Adams is trained not only as an artist and graphics illustrator but also as an cinematographer. Adams' home is no ordinary suburban house. The front porch is full of signs and symbols from out of the misty paths—wreaths, crossed sticks, painted stones. In the back yard, trees have been planted and named and there is a henge, a circle of nine forked sticks oriented to the pole star and the rising sun, like Stonehenge.

The main deities of the Feraferia rites are Kore and her consort, Kouros, Greek equivalents of Mother Goddess and Horned God. The Mother Goddess is frequently referred to here as the Magic Maiden, and she is of course ageless.

Feraferia is far more than witchcraft and does not even use that term to describe itself. Where Wicca and male-oriented witchcraft groups worship in rites to express their desires symbolically and, through incantations, try to change things for themselves or for others, Feraferia goes beyond the ritual: it enacts what it stands for in actual nature. Weather permitting, there are side trips into the wilderness where the group communes with nature. There are at-tempts at restoring neglected areas to their natural appearance, and, as a consequence, even the ritual is far more realistic and vital than the rituals of many intellectually inclined pagan groups.

Fred Adams has written about principles of this group:

> Wilderness is the elusive quick of all spontaneous delicately urg-ing life. The only way to re-unite mankind is to re-unite man-kind with nature. Man will become humane toward man only when he becomes humane toward all nature. The inner nature of man has been disastrously severed from the all-enveloping na-ture of wilderness. The vital link between visionary nature within and ecological nature without is poetry.

Adams later explained, "The Feraferian vision includes new inspi-rations and new combinations from the most ancient well-springs of the goddess. Innovations there are, but always in continuity with those ancient sources. You will find in the Feraferian vision no slavish archaeological reconstructions, because the new paganism must accommodate all the new developments in human knowledge and awareness that have occurred since the old paganism quite deservedly lost its congregations and crumbled to ruin."

Naturally, Feraferia is not for *everyone;* not everyone should think that Feraferia is for him or that he will be accepted for membership. All ancient cults were selective in their admission of new members. This must be so to preserve the power, integrity, and purpose of the cult. Thinning the blood makes it weaker; spreading the sacred truths too far afield lessens their impact where they are most needed.

A second Mediterranean cult in modern America is also located in California. The Church of the Eternal Source observes its own formalities as a religious group. There are nine degrees of initiate in this congregation, from the lowly aspirant, brother or sister, neophyte, zelator, novitiate, proselyte, initiate, priest, to the ninth and highest, the high priest. On the first Wednesday of each month there is a ritual of Thoth. On the second Wednesday of each month the ritual of Osiris is performed. The third Wednesday is dedicated to the gods in general while the fourth Wednesday belongs to Horus. The latter is presided over by Harold Moss. The calendar of the church even lists a fifth Wednesday, apparently during months when there are five Wednesdays in a given thirty-one-day period. The latter belongs to all the gods together. The church provides the services of its priesthood for personal counseling, counseling through divinations, marriages, funerals, blessings of infants, and other sundries ordinarily performed by the Servants of God.

Harold Moss and his Egyptian temple, better known as the Church of the Eternal Source, have recently moved to Los Angeles proper, where they maintain a sanctuary practicing the ancient Egyptian Osiris cult precisely the way it existed in pre-Christian times. The priests even make their own ritual tools and the language of the service is partly Egyptian. Although the ancient Egyptian cult is not a witchcraft form per se, much of present-day witchcraft draws on Egyptian material and concepts.

If it strikes you as strange that the gods of ancient Egypt, Greece, and Rome should be resurrected by worshipers in the 1970s in sophisticated America, stop for a moment and think: Isn't Christianity based upon the philosophy and life of a man who lived in ancient Judaea two thousand years ago? Doesn't much of the Far East look to a deified prophet who trod the earth six hundred years before the Christian era? What is time to the gods? Spiritual truth is timeless.

13

Talismans, Amulets, Potions, and Herbs

LET'S SUPPOSE that there's nothing inherently wrong or foolish about worshiping man-made objects as *symbols* of the deity. After all, it is in man's nature to admire, even worship, that which is outstanding or pleasurable. When an art collector swoons over some particularly fetching painting or a fine piece of sculpture, he is in fact worshiping the *expression* of artistic talent embodied in the work of art before him. He is not worshiping the artist as a deity, but pays indirect tribute to the artist as the creator. The artist creates the work of art, perhaps inspired by a higher power; the work of art finds its way into the hands of the collector, who admires it and thereby transfers his admiration to the one who created the work, thus closing the circle. Everyone concerned benefits: the artist has found a buyer for his output, and derives artistic satisfaction from being appreciated; the owner, because he has acquired something of meaning and value.

So it is with holy objects: man creates them, inspired by religious thought. This inspiration may be paired with worldly aims or at times may have some commercial considerations: in the Renaissance, religious sentiment was secondary to a religious painter's fame.

There is great similarity in the way holy objects are treated by all religions. Roughly, they fall into two major categories: natural and man-made. Natural holy objects include strange stones, meteorites, shells, and other formations seemingly out of the ordinary.

In my own research, I discovered that the people of the Congo, the Baluba people, believe that certain cruciform stones found in the forests have miraculous powers, and they worship them as such. The fact that these are natural crystallizations is not important to them. They feel that the unusual shape of the stones signifies the presence of the benevolent spirit and they want this spirit to serve them. In Ethiopia, some consider the teeth of wild animals fertility talismans and for that purpose carry them on their persons. The teeth of elks, hounds, wolves, and other wild animals are considered potent talismans in various other parts of the world. Certain shells are believed to be the abode of the gods in the South Seas; in India, very large or unusually colored pearls are sacred. The North American Indians believe that extremely large gold nuggets bring the finder particularly great power. Man-shaped roots or wood formations were held to be gnomes in disguise and worshiped as such in Europe; in particular, the man-shaped root called the alraun is part of witchcraft. The mandrake plant also is said to possess wondrous powers; it must be pulled from the soil at certain times and even screams when it is. Animals, dead or alive, have been worshiped at various times as sacred objects. Some Egyptian gods had animal shapes or heads. Since the people of Egypt believed in transmigration of the soul, the animals were not worshiped as animals but rather as *animal-shaped deities*. A true case of animal worship is the sacred stag of St. Hubert. When this sacred white stag appears to a hunter, he must not kill any more that day.

When it comes to man-made objects, the ability to create the object exactly as required is important, if it is to become the vessel for a superior power. Man-made holy objects fall into two categories: those that were not originally created as such and became, due to circumstances, holy, and those that were deliberately created to become holy objects and that were then consecrated as such.

An example of an "accidental" holy object is perhaps an object associated with those considered holy or in some way extraordinary by their contemporaries. An ordinary knife, consecrated for religious purposes, such as the athame of witchcraft, is a ritual object presumed to have superior power. To pagans, this or a vessel used in ceremonies in honor of the deity is a holy object. To the Christian, nothing could be holier than a nail from the "true cross" of Christ, or perhaps the shroud into which his body was placed. As for the nails of the "true cross," if all the alleged nails from that cross were counted, one could crucify an entire army. Obviously, proof is very difficult to come by.

Man-made objects actually *intended* as talismans or amulets are meant to give the owner protection and power. A talisman is an object into which supernormal power has been conjured by the one making it. An amulet has similar use, but it is worn around the neck or wrist and is generally quite small. Both talismans and amulets serve their purpose best if the power of their manufacturer is great. They are either made in the shape of a sacred person or object, or inscribed with a symbol representing them. Each object must be clearly designed as to purpose, but there are also "general purpose" talismans and amulets to ward off evil. The most efficient talisman or amulet seems to be one that is directed toward a specific purpose or a specific deity. The more the purpose of the amulet is channeled, the greater chance it has of hitting home. The fact that the owner believes in the efficiency of the talisman or amulet has much less to do with the results than generally believed.

With the Christian amulet, usually a religious medal, crucifix, pendant, or perhaps prayer beads, the appeal is made to God/Father, Jesus Christ, the Madonna, or one of the saints. In the case of gnostic amulets, objects thought to possess intellectual or spiritual knowledge, the proper demon is selected from the list of possible demons, and the appeal carefully inscribed. In this way, the individual connects with the superior power.

In the sense that thought energies enter the unconscious mind, talismans can indeed influence people. There is also the belief that the object is powerful and will help, but the belief and the implied psychological lift *alone* can't do it. The owner sets into motion within himself certain processes that would not otherwise be activated, and the energies freed within the owner are added to those obtained from the touch of the object. Together, they represent a powerful energy source and when directed by the conscious will of the owner, they will protect him. If all conditions are right, talismans can be effective. Of course, we must remember that many objects offered as alleged talismans are in fact nothing of the sort: in order to work, they can be neither mass-produced nor created for strangers without specific contact between creator and prospective owner.

Talismans are found among all peoples in all periods of history; no occult formula is more universal. Whether Egypt, Chaldea, Persia, Greece, or Rome—when excavations are made, talismans are among the first objects to be found. Certain Egyptian papyruses give the details of ceremonies for preparing the "ring of Hermes" and scarabs. Ancient authors have preserved the descriptions of a considerable number of talismans, of which it is impossible to give even an abridged enumeration.

There were talismans of all kinds—rings, engraved and sculptured stones, jewels, inscribed pieces of parchment and paper, worn on the person or hung up in houses, to which magic properties were attributed. The talisman might sometimes even be a living animal—lizard, snake, chameleon, or cat—of which the greatest possible care was taken; black cats especially have always retained a talismanic reputation for bringing good luck (or bad luck).

According to historian Émile Grillot de Givry, "Talismans may be summarily divided into maleficent and beneficent. Maleficent talismans are offensive and intended to produce harm. . . . Beneficial talismans are essentially defensive; their end is the protection of the individual against evil forces and the attraction of beneficent forces. The majority of talismans still employed belong to this latter category."

An example of natural talismans is the precious stone. By their hardness and density, precious stones show that they were formed by extremely powerful forces of affinity and cohesion. They represent matter in its highest state of coagulation and compression; consequently, the radioactive influences that they emit must be considerable. Great care was taken to assign a special curative virtue to every precious stone. Precious stones are still more active if they are employed according to their astrological affinities and combined with metals of the same nature.

"Solomon's seal" is one of the most famous talismans. It is composed of two interlaced, equilateral triangles, one of which stands on its base and the other on its apex; six points are thus produced, which are set, hexagon-fashion, in a circle. *Tetragramaton*, the divine name in four letters, must be placed in the middle.

Our knowledge of the mysterious mandrake plant is still vague, even though many strange stories have been told about it. Biblical commentators regard it as the supreme plant of Venus, which confers fruitfulness upon barren women. St. Hildegard in her work *Physica* (libre 1, "De Plantis") devotes much space to the mandrake. She says, "It is hot, something watery, and formed of the moistened earth wherewith Adam was created; hence is it that this herb, being made in man's likeness, ministers much more than other plants to the suggestion of the Devil; according to man's desire good or evil may be aroused at will, as was done aforetime with idols."

The word mandrake (middle English "drake," "dragon") is applied to all very strong plant roots thought to resemble the human body. A kind of narcotic can be produced from the root, and it was believed that small, "familiar" demons took up their abode in these plants. Mandrakes revealed knowledge of the future by shaking their heads when questions were put to them. They were once widely distributed in Germany, and were even utilized in medicine.

The philtre, or love potion, is frequently mentioned in medieval literature. The name is applied to a liquid composed of wine as a base, with the addition of expertly mixed herbs or drugs to give it the property of inspiring in the man or woman who drinks it irresistible love for some specified person. In heroic epics and plays, it is a powerful dramatic motive force, easy to set to work and of the greatest utility in "difficult" situations.

In the romance of Tristan and Iseult, a philtre intended by Iseult's mother for King Mark is drunk by Iseult and Tristan together, and it fills them with the passion that was to be fatal to them in the end. Richard Wagner, in the *Götterdämmerung,* made use of another philtre to turn Siegfried from Brynhilde and fire him with love for Gutrune, although this incident is not mentioned in the Scandinavian sagas from which he drew the elements of his musical tragedy.

This recipe, from Émile Grillot de Givry's work, sounds especially complicated:

To make oneself beloved there shall be taken, to wit, the heart of a dove, the liver of a sparrow, the womb of a swallow, the kidney of a hare, and they shall be reduced to impalpable powder. Then the person who shall compound the philtre shall add an equal part of his own blood, dried and in the same way powdered. If the person whom it is desired to draw into love is caused to swallow this powder in a dose of 2 or 3 drachms, marvelous success will follow.

Of course, witches have been the chief suppliers of love potions and philtres throughout the ages. LaVoisin, in Louis XIV's time, often employed revolting ingredients in his concoctions, like powdered moles with a pinch of the poisonous cantharides, or Spanish fly. This was, and still is, a sure giveaway of the inefficient witch. The bludgeoning effect of drugs is the last resort of the ineffectual spellbinder. Witchcraft is effected by *magical* art, not by chemical means.

For at least five hundred years, witches have also made extensive use of herbs, often for their powerful chemical properties, but equally often for properties not as well known.

It was in the Far East that our first detailed reference to herbs was made in what was an advanced civilization even in those early days. Shen-Nung, the "Red Emperor"—so called because of the "fiery" quality of his personality—used himself as a guinea pig to study the effects of various herbs upon the human constitution. He concluded that the ginseng plant was the king of all herbs and a genuine promoter of longevity, and even today the Chinese think of it as just that. Shen-Nung's own long life seems to have given eloquent support to his observations, for he died at the age of 123.

In 1500 B.C., the Egyptian pharaoh Thutmose III sent an expedition to Syria in search of new and useful medicinal plants, among other things. Relief of some of the plants they found can be seen today carved upon the walls of Thutmose's own temple in Karnak. Among the plants are many recognizable irises, sunflowers, lotuses, pomegranates, and arum lilies, all of them once highly valued botanical medicines. From the books of the Old Testament we know that a large variety of herbs and spices besides these were also raised in ancient Mesopotamia. For example, the prophet Jeremiah alludes to the balm of Gilead, a rare aromatic gum that the historian Josephus tells us was presented as a gift to King Solomon by none other than the Queen of Sheba! The Song of Solomon mentions frankincense, myrrh, camphor, saffron, cinnamon, spikenard, calamus, and aloe— all still considered valuable items in the herbal pharmacopoeia.

Between 500 and 400 B.C. the Greeks made the first serious attempt in the West to systematize their herbal lore in writing. A number of herbalist books began to appear, all of them attributed to the famous physician Hippocrates, the Father of Medicine. They catalog and describe nearly four hundred useful plants. Although their actual authorship is debatable, Hippocrates' name helped to earn them lasting respect through the centuries. Around 400 B.C., the lists were improved upon by a botanist from Euboea, Diocles of Carystus, whose book is now recognized as the first complete Western herbal.

Throughout the Middle Ages, most monasteries followed the example of Italy's Monte Cassino and studied herbalism. Dispensing Christian charity, which included healing the sick, was one of their primary duties. Each monastery owned a private herb garden and every library had copies of Apuleius and Dioscorides, now lavishly il-

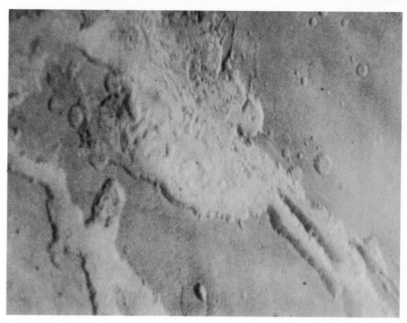

Two photographs of Mars taken from the Viking orbiter. Scientists are not certain how much water Mars may have had in its early days, but many surface features seem to indicate streambeds and erosion by water.

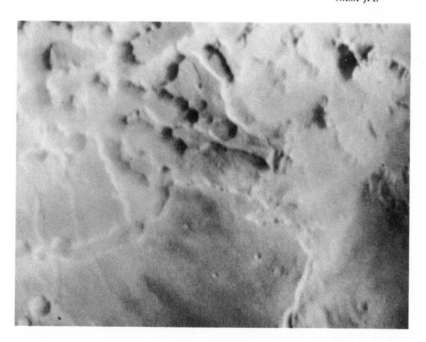

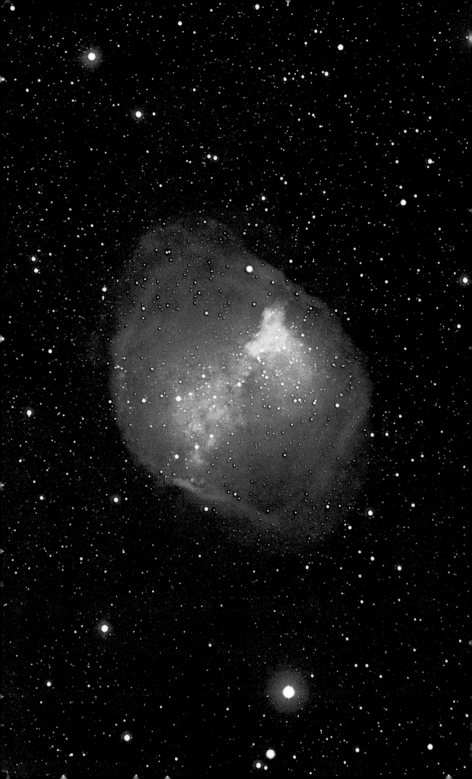

Two nebulae, sites where astronomers believe stars have exploded as novas and where new stars (with attendant planets) are being born.

An artist's interpretation of Ezekiel's vision in the Bible. Was Ezekiel really recording an extra terrestrial visitor's unfamiliar appearance?

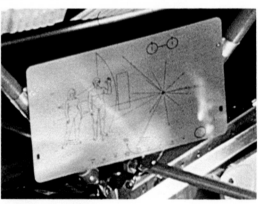

This metal plaque, prepared by Carl and Linda Sagan, was mounted on Pioneer 10. Still traveling out from the sun, the space probe is farther from home than any work of human hands has ever been. A billion years from now the plaque will still be legible.

Dr. Zeller, a soil analyst at the University of Kansas, whose thermoluminescence tests revealed peculiar properties at one spot where a UFO was seen.

lustrated in color and gold leaf. Even today, monastery ruins frequently contained old medicinal herbs growing among the weeds.

Paracelsus, a German physician born in 1493, complicated herbalism's evolution as a science with his *Doctrine of Signatures*. In brief, it claimed that every plant was "signed" or associated by a mysterious spiritual bond to a particular disease. The clue to which disease it was could be found in the shape, scent, color, or even habitat of the herb itself. For example, lungwort, whose spotted leaves were thought to resemble lungs, remedied bronchial complaints. Euphrasia officinalis, whose flowers hold a resemblance to bright eyes, was considered a good remedy for sore eyes and ophthalmia.

The next great turning point in herbal history was the appearance of John Gerard's *Herball* of 1597 which benefited greatly from Christopher Columbus' trip to the Western world in 1492. Gerard's famous herbal showed Europe hitherto unknown plants from "The New Land called America" among which were the potato, the tomato (called by him the Apple of Love), and tobacco.

During the twentieth century, official interest in herbs revived in a dramatic and quite unforeseen manner, strangely enough due to the outbreak of the two world wars. Interest in herbs has grown steadily over the past four years. During the last decade, it has, of course, received a considerable boost from books such as Aldous Huxley's *Doors of Perception* and the interest they have sparked in botanical psychoactive agents such as cannabis and peyote. But the wave of interest in plants and herbs that is sweeping the Western world is far more general, and cannot be said to be limited to those who are simply exploring the plant world for its potential psychoactive properties.

14

Spells and Curses

THE BELIEF that magic works miracles does not by itself create miracles. Like prayer, belief merely sets up energy patterns that the operator can mold into a definite shape or direction. It is the intensity and form of the prayer, not so much the real content, that make it a powerful and very real force in magic as well as in conventional religion.

Now we come to a much-quoted and often-maligned part of magic: destruction of the enemy. I don't think mere knowledge that a curse has been leveled against one or that a sorcerer is out to kill one in itself induces death.

How does a magician kill another person long-distance? First, there is the African voodoo doll, the effigy of the one who is about to die. Making an image of the victim is helpful to the deed only *because it helps the sorcerer* to have visual concentration. If he can obtain some sample of the victim's hair or nails, this will help even more. The belief among primitive peoples that such samples from the body of the intended victim are powerful magic and make his destruction easier is not entirely based on fear and superstition. Hair and nails do carry the "psychometric image" of the owner, and allow the magician to "tune in" more easily to his victim's vibrations. Thus, they are additional links between the executioner and his victim.

It seems that in modern times a photograph will do the trick. Remarkably, there are still tribes among the desert people of the Arab countries and India who won't let you photograph them for that very reason: an image of a person is *part* of that person. Proof of this concept can be obtained under somewhat less adventurous conditions. For example, Professor Hans Holzer has frequently submitted photos of a person to psychometry mediums who have then come up with amazing details of that person's life, even with information concerning secondary personalities linked with the subject of the photograph. In one of his recent investigations in which he cooperated with the police, a potential murderer was pinpointed by the medium as a result of holding a photograph of the victim!

Then there is the evil eye. Remarkably, it is still prevalent today among backward people in rural Italy and southern Europe. The idea is that the human eye has occult powers that may cause evil to a person by the mere act of looking at that person. Much of medieval superstition was built around the evil eye, and the accusation of possessing it cropped up in many of the witchcraft trials during the worst persecutions. To those who believe in the evil eye, a mere glance from it is enough to cause a variety of calamities, ranging from sickness and poverty to death.

All sorts of countermagic have been used to ward off the evil eye. Two interesting ones I've found were raising your hands with the fingers covering one another and putting the hands in front of your eyes, and the wearing of specific amulets. Also, the protective methods must be used *instantly* in order to work. Some amulets consist of a human hand, with an index finger or thumb sticking out, or a phallic symbol, since masculine sex "magic" is supposed to be a potent deterrent against the evil eye.

I doubt that the evil eye is something people cultivate at will. Some perfectly decent people had one—the king of Spain, the late Alphonso XIII, and even a renowned pope. When a person with the evil eye looks at you, something happens *inside*. This "something" may be nothing more than a strong and compelling interest in meeting the person with the fascinating eyes, or it may be something more sinister.

In India some forty years ago, a Hindu holy man looked with fierce eyes at a Moslem. Many Indians have dark, piercing eyes as part of their racial makeup. But this Moslem immediately fell ill, was unable to eat, and blamed it all on the evil eye. A minor religious war ensued and people got hurt and even killed. Is it all fantasy? Something did travel from eyeball to eyeball and somehow did cause a reaction in the recipient, a reaction over which he had no control.

In verbalizing a spell, especially when it is done with emotional force, the spell-caster sends out an action-tinged thought or phrase that reaches his victim. In *huna*, the ancient Hawaiian form of magic, there is a whole set of rules on spell-casting, and also ways to break spells. In a series of books, especially *The Secret Science Behind the Miracles*, Dr. Max Freedom Long describes the practices, which still exist today. Hawaiian magic is essentially the same as its European counterparts, only the terms are different.

To cast a spell, one need not adhere to medieval gibberish, concoct awful-smelling drinks, burn incense, or do strange things. That much is pure theatrical effect and works only to the extent that the onlooker needs it to work. But the mental discipline involved is very real indeed, and conforms rather closely to what we already know is possible within the existing framework of the effects of ESP.

According to Émile Grillot de Givry, "two kinds of spell must be distinguished—the harmful and the useful. The distinction enables us to get a clear idea of what may properly be called the 'double life' of the sorcerer; a personage all-powerful in the countryside, hated and feared in his one aspect on account of the misfortune he could bring upon a household or family, but resorted to in his other when it was a matter of avoiding misfortune or assuring success."

Certain spells were profitable only to sorcerers themselves, and gave them advantages much envied by the common run of mortals. Those who wished to make themselves invisible need only speak the following incantation, according to a manuscript entitled *The Secret of Secrets*, kept at the Bibliothèque de l'Arsenal, Paris.

O thou, Pontation! Master of invisibility, with thy masters [here follow the names of the masters], I conjure thee, Pontation, and these same masters of invisibility by Him Who makes the universe tremble, by Heaven and Earth, Cherubim and Seraphim, and by Him who made the Virgin conceive and Who is God and Man, that I may accomplish this experiment in perfectability, in such sort that at any hour I desire I may be invisible; again I conjure thee and thy ministers also, by Stabuches and Mechaerom, Esey, Enitgiga, Bellis, and Semonei, that thou come straightaway with thy said ministers and that thou perform this work as you all know how, and that this experiment may make me invisible, in such wise that no one may see me. Amen.

There are two basic groups of curses. The one uttering the malediction can formulate his curse in general terms or it can be exactly tailored to one individual whom the cursor wishes to reach. In the case of the former, general group of curses, anyone coming into contact with the accursed person, persons, places, or objects will be affected by it. In some cases, general curses are merely protection against unauthorized interference such as with the Egyptian royal tombs.

But there is a third group of curses that is even more powerful than the other two. That is when the one originating the curse is not satisfied with drawing the utmost of his own energies of hatred and anger from the depth of his self and formulating them into words but invokes the powers of darkness as well to support him in his negative quest. This is done by following certain ritual magical formulas and can be understood or undertaken only by those well versed in the black arts. By combining his own forces with outside energies derived from the psychic world around him, the magician then forges a thunderbolt of hatred that is both extremely effective and difficult to discover. It is even more difficult to counteract.

On the surface at least, the result of successful curses seems to be within the natural law and could perhaps be explained by a chain of misfortunes not necessarily connected with one another. Taken in the context of a known curse, however, they become part and parcel of a deliberate attempt to take revenge on those who have perpetrated a crime in the past, and frequently on their descendants. Curses can occur among the rich and the poor, the powerful and the humble. Just as the motivation for uttering a curse can differ widely among individuals, so the incidence of curses is spread among every culture, every type of social background.

Professor Hans Holzer, in *The Habsburg Curse*, traces the curse leveled against one of Europe's most distinguished royal dynasties back to its origin in the eleventh century. He examines the many branches of the Habsburg dynasty; explores, with the aid of well-known sensitivities, the castles and battlegrounds where ill-fated dramas were enacted; and pursues the malediction down through successive generations to its apparent demise in the twentieth century. Murder, suicide, mysterious disappearances, and madness—all were manifestations of what Professor Holzer demonstrates to be the result of a magnetic, evil force: the original Habsburg Curse.

To this day, juju, a system of magical threats and sanctions, works very smoothly in the deepest jungles of Africa. The record shows that many people have died as a result of direct intervention by a magician, without ever realizing that this was taking place.

Much more so than in the Western world, African curses depend on elements of fear and ostracism for added effectiveness. Nearly always, the victim is informed that a curse has been uttered, usually in a roundabout way to increase the uncertainty of the matter and to prevent the victim from arguing the originator of the curse out of his anger. But associating with an accursed person is equally undesirable, consequently it is customary to let the community know as well that so-and-so has been cursed. The victim will find himself isolated, and sometimes the curse takes effect in a manner not relying on magic but on brutal force, when someone in the community does away with the accursed person to protect the other from the effect of the curse.

Astrologer-historian Arthur Gatti, in *The Kennedy Curse*, analyzes thirty individual Kennedy charts and concludes that no evil witch crashed any of the christenings, but a kind of curse does haunt the Kennedy family fortunes, bringing with it extraordinarily bad luck. Besides indications of great personal gifts, ambition, wealth, and power, the charts show signs of confusion, hard choices, self-sacrifice, illness, disaster, grief, guilt, enemies, and *hidden conspiracies!*

15

Witchcraft, Sex, and the Devil

MUCH HAS BEEN written, and even more rumored, about the connection between sex and witchcraft, very little of it corresponding to fact. There is, first of all, the notion that witchcraft rites are predominantly sexy, and it is this idea that both attracts some people and repels others. Those who are attracted to witchcraft rites because they expect an orgy had better stay away to begin with, for if it is anything at all, witchcraft is a spiritual-intellectual "thing," not a flesh concourse.

Anyone even slightly familiar with the teachings of the Old Religion will recognize its insistence on "perfect couples" in the rites and its reluctance to admit single people on their own. This is not out of false prudery but because the witches know how much better people work when they work in unison and with both spiritual and physical closeness. Witches are concerned with results, not with morals. Promiscuity and *overemphasis* of the sexual aspects would hinder rather than help the results of the circle, so naturally they do not care for it. The tensions engendered by one person about the sexual aspect of another to whom he or she is not yet close are bound to detract from the overall effort put forth by the group, and consequently are usually discouraged.

The impression that witchcraft has sex as its preeminent feature persists. In 1969 the *News of the World*, a London newspaper, published a series of articles that lumped together witchcraft, ritual magic, the Black Mass, and the desecration of church yards by vandals. During the course of this series the paper uncovered the fact that a schoolteacher-priest had planned to hold Black Masses using virgins as an altar, that a couple in the Isle of Man exposed their young daughter to the danger of moral corruption by allowing her to attend naked coven meetings, and that a West London housewife had been the prime mover at similar coven meetings for years without the knowledge of her husband. If the first two allegations were true, of course, the *News of the World* performed a public service by exposing them. But by and large the articles tended to overdo the sexual aspects.

Modern witchcraft, like any other emotive concern, has been exploited by the unscrupulous. So-called black magic groups that persuade newcomers to undress and indulge in all kinds of grotesque sexual activity, secretly photograph them, and then use the photographs for blackmail, are not unknown in most large cities. Also, overt or covert prostitution is sometimes the purpose of magic-cum-witchcraft circles. Because the great advantage of ritual is that it can take many forms, any perverted but imaginative mind could invent ceremonies cloaked in a quasi-mystical veil of mumbo-jumbo that would make most witch cults look rather tame.

The greatest psychic power imaginable is raised in sexual intercourse between two fully attuned partners. This, of course, is the crux: the partners must be truly in tune, one with the other; they must be psychically, physically, and spiritually aware of their purpose and never lose sight of the reasons for their sexual union. If sex is the excuse for practicing witchcraft, it is perversion; but if sex is used for ritual purposes by properly prepared people, it can contribute to the overall results of the ritual far beyond anything that purely intellectual efforts or ritualistic movements may furnish.

We must remember that erotic elements were not objectionable to the ancients, who saw in the performance of sexual intercourse during a religious ritual a symbolic act encouraging the forces of nature to commit union likewise and thus make things grow. Every primitive religion contains such elements whether expressed symbolically or in actuality. Only by the fusion of the male and female element in nature, and thus also in man, does nature move forward. Ultimately, the polarity of things is the essential element. Through the interaction of male and female polarity, power results; or, if you prefer, by the union of the male and female polarities in a single effort, the original purpose of the power structure is fulfilled: for at the beginning there was neither male nor female, but one single force. Having been split into the female and male half, the two polarities have been trying to *rejoin* each other ever since.

Hans Holzer quotes a "very ancient" Anglo-Saxon spell, which illustrates the feeling of erotic-ecstatic union with the Goddess:

In love I come to Thee, O Mother Goddess, to fill me with the joys of life. Let there be union between thine own self and me and between my companion and me and let the union be so complete as to enshrine our trinity within and without; let the force of thy love permeate our bodies and minds, let the power raised from that union rise up to Thee so that thy works may be accomplished. I join hands with my companion in sacred union of body, mind and spirit, through which the power be raised; may the power thus raised be directed to———[predetermined purpose of ritual] and in token thereof, O Mother Goddess, instill into us your greatness, your splendor and your eternal wisdom, for the force of love is a force of life. As we come together and are one, the force within us is joined into a still greater force by the touch of your hands, O Mother Goddess, Protector of love. So mote it be.

Nowadays, it is no longer illegal to worship the devil. Probably the best known Satanic leader in America is Anton Sandor La Vey. Hans Holzer, in *The Truth About Witchcraft*, describes vividly how he met the quixotic Satanist at his San Francisco temple:

Paintings of traditional representations of hell, haunted houses, and devils adorned the walls. They were remarkably fine paintings, and the works of the high priest himself. The table was a marble slab which used to be a tombstone and still bore the inscription of the late gentleman whose earthly remains it once guarded. A skeleton leered at us from a glass cabinet in the corner and stuffed owls completed the atmospheric feeling. Soon the high priest himself arrived, wearing black pants and a black leather jacket. His face was deliberately made to appear devilish by the removal or cropping of all hair on top and the addition of a small beard. La Vey did indeed look the part.

Later that day, the amiable artist-high-priest was a totally different person. The house also seemed different . . . the decorations no longer looked like whimsical touches of a tongue-in-cheek devil worshipper, but as authentic relics closely tied to the ritual about to be performed.

By midnight, the room was filled with fifteen or sixteen congregation members. They were young and old and looked like a good cross-section of San Franciscans. Mainly men had come that night, and a goodly number of them wore small beards, perhaps in honor of their high priest. The small number of women present were average type. They all sat on folding chairs toward the rear of the room. In front of them was an altar occupied by the stretched-out body of a young woman covered by a leopardskin. A man completely covered with a black hooded robe with slits for the eyes entered the room. He was followed by four or five other men similarly dressed, who stayed a little behind. With one quick gesture, the man in the black hood yanked the leopardskin off the girl on the altar. She was, of course, nude. Her head rested comfortably on a specially built neck rest while her feet dangled somewhat over the other end of the altar. The light, provided by candles only, was sufficiently bright to highlight her body even to those seated in the rear of the room.

Now one of the other black-robed fellows handed the leader a small cup. Someone played the organ all during this opening ceremony, but it was not, of course, La Vey himself, who had not yet appeared among his flock. The music was properly atmospheric and reminded one of the old background music for Hiss the Villain in an old-time music hall. The cup, it developed, contained a mixture of semen and urine, the Satanists' answer to holy water. With a dispenser in the shape of a human phallus, the man in the black hood then sprinkled the congregation with this mixture, while a bell rang in short intervals to announce the opening of the service. The stage was set for the entrance of the high priest, Anton Sandor La Vey.

After the appropriate organ music cue, he strode in with showmanly stance, dressed in a tight-fitting black headpiece with red horns and wearing a black robe over black leotards. Taking the sword from the high priestess, he addressed the four corners of the room. "In nomine dei Satanas, Lucifer excelsi! In the name of our great god, Satan Lucifer, the ruler of the Stygian pits, I command thee to come forth out of the black realms. Come forth, in the name of the four dark princes of hell, Satan! Lucifer! Belial! Leviathan! Satan, take the chalice of ecstasy . . . which is filled with the elixir of life . . . and instill it with the power of the Black Magic . . . which diffuses and supports the universe. . . ." With that, the high priest was handed a chalice from which he drank a toast to the Prince of Darkness. He then placed the chalice right on top of the pubic area of the girl on the altar, where it rested comfortably for the rest of the service.

La Vey took pains to point out that the First Satanist Church of San Francisco should not be confused with medieval superstitions or worse. No unbaptized babies are killed in the rites, no ritual murder takes place, and no Black Mass. This is a cult dedicated to the enjoyment of worldly pleasures free from all restrictions, guilt feelings, or, hell forbid, original sin. Satanists do not believe in a personal devil as a living individual. Their devil is the *devil within* every man, that part of his nature that longs for full enjoyment of worldly pleasures. By invoking Satan, his congregation was merely calling upon its own unconscious desires to encourage their fulfillment.

As for the sacrifice of *adult* human beings, they do not do this either, although La Vey admits they have many candidates for this practice. But they do it symbolically through "the hex."

Ever since Pope Paul declared publicly that the devil was a real person *to him,* and, of course, the antagonist of the Roman Catholic Church, clergymen all over the world and laymen with religious orientation have looked into the matter of the devil and whether or not he is in fact still among us. Gregory Peck, after doing the current movie *The Omen,* says he cannot believe the devil is a person. In fact, anyone seriously suggesting that there was such a thing as the devil as a person a scant ten years ago would have been looked at with horror, or a smile, depending upon the viewpoint of the onlooker. Today, austere publications have devoted many pages to this matter; the *New York Times Magazine*'s article by Andrew M. Greeley, entitled "The Devil, You Say," rehashes much from the past, most of it false, some of it correct, to come to the conclusion that evil in man is really the kind of devil one should worry about. The author leaves unresolved the question of a personal devil, but points to the continued existence of evil in this world as certain proof that the forces of darkness do prevail at times.

According to Sigmund Freud, the devil is a father substitute for those who have no luck, are too poorly gifted, or are too ineffective to make a living. William Blatty's novel *The Exorcist,* allegedly based upon a real case in St. Louis in 1959, has given new impetus to the whole business of the reality of the devil. Catholic priests are divided between the acceptance of the reality of a personal devil and consider the business of demonic possession more properly treated by the psychiatrist. Pope Paul VI, in his address about evil and the devil, assured his listeners that he was convinced of "an intervention in us and in our world of an obscure agent, the devil. Evil is not merely a lack of something, but an effective agent, a living, spiritual being, perverted and perverting. A terrible reality. Mysterious and frightening." Is the devil a real person or a principle? In either case, the point is that the devil represents "the negative force."

The people who call themselves Satanists today are "anti-witches"; that is, they use certain elements of witchcraft but pervert them to their own point of view, which is frequently diametrically opposed to that of witchcraft. Those who are truly devilworshipers in the worst sense of the term might lead a furtive existence in secret meeting places, indulging sick impulses that have very little to do with a true cult. They do not number many, either, but, unfortunately, their actions invite negative comment in the press. Whenever word is received that an animal has been sacrificed, or that murders have occurred, in which the perpetrators claimed Satanic impulses, the public is quick to lump all pagans into the same pot. There is a certain shock value in being able to say you're a devilworshiper or Satanist just as there is undoubtedly shock value in being a witch, but the impact of those words is based upon largely erroneous images. In the mind of the average person, witches and Satanists are evil, and practically the same. Only to those who understand the vast differences between a follower of the Old Religion and a Satanist, the images become separate and distinct.

When Anton La Vey became more and more successful, he founded subdivisions or "grottos" in various cities around the country. Eventually, as is the unfortunate habit of all religious groups, dissension arose in some of these groups and they split, one portion staying under the aegis of High Priest Anton, the other going their own way. Thus it was in the case of the grotto at Dayton, Ohio. The group in Dayton is composed primarily of young people between the ages of eighteen and thirty. They are simple people; their everyday ways are no different from those of any Midwestern working person. John De Haven, a student and radio broadcaster, is their spiritual leader or "Magister Sacrorum." The group changed its name when it left the La Vey fold and became known as the Church of Satanic Brotherhood. The Dayton group publishes a newsletter in which articles pertaining to Satanic worship and excerpts from *The True Grimoire* are published, the latter being the medieval handbook of spell-casting and demonology.

John De Haven explained:

The Church of the Satanic Brotherhood is a religious association of Satanists founded by members and former members of the Church of Satan who were attracted by the idea of a national fellowship of Satanists, but who felt that the Church of Satan did not serve this purpose. Our church is governed by a council, whose authority is balanced by the ceremonial head of our church, the high priest, the executive head of our church, the Magister Sacrorum, and the general council of all members.

The major element of Satanism is the Black Mass, a blasphemous ceremony copying the Christian High Mass in every respect, except that everything is reversed. The crucifix is hung upside down, the altar is covered in black instead of white, candles are black, hymns are sung backward, the rite is performed by a defrocked priest, if possible, and whenever the name of the Lord or Christ is to be praised, it is spat upon in the Black Mass.

Ironically, devil worshipers were also victims of the Church's fantasies. Accepting the idea that there was indeed a devil, they merely switched sides. Instead of fearing him, they joined and worshiped him. Perversity was the key to their actions. All that Church and society considered good, they were to shun, while all evil deeds were stepping stones on their road to salvation in His image. Only when considered in this light do the acts of devil worshipers make some sense. They were and are not criminals as such, but misguided individuals following a belief that in itself is a program of destruction, and therefore a harmful force in our world.

16

Possession, Exorcism, and Voodoo

Perhaps no other phenomenon within psychic research has attracted so many divided opinions as possession, because it crosses over into the field of religion, and even into the area of psychiatry. Thus, it invites destructive criticism of those to whom these other fields are the only truths. Even today, very few psychiatrists are willing to accept nonphysical explanations for paranormal experiences. Even fewer religious individuals, firmly rooted in their particular beliefs, are willing to accept the psychic research view concerning possession.

In a *medical* sense, the verdict about the victim of possession is likely to be schizophrenia or some other form of mental derangement. The possibility of one person being possessed by another against his will is entirely inconceivable, with the sole marginal exception of hypnosis, of course, or some other form of undue but direct influence. When a person shows marked personality changes and acts in a way contrary to previous habits, the medical doctor will look for personality defects rather than the presence of a new or outside personality.

Possession in terms of the *religious establishment* is nothing but the entrance into the individual's soul of an outside force, generally evil. Whether or not the term demonic possession is used, the implication is that a living entity has entered the body of the victim in order to express his own will and frustrations. To the Church, this is always evil and must be dealt with through exorcists. Not every religious community accepts this version, but the orthodox faiths do believe in the existence of possession and the need for exorcism. To this day, the Roman Catholic Church retains the rite of exorcism. In an offshoot of Orthodox Judaism called the Hasidic cult, belief in the dybbuk, or possessing spirit, is still extant and is dealt with similarly as in the Roman Catholic exorcism. In both cases, the possessing spirit is asked to leave, and when it refuses, it is forced out of the body of the victim by various means. In earlier days these means included everything from torture to bizarre threats and incantations believed to be effective by the sheer power of the arrangement of phrases.

The Church believed that the death of a possessed individual in the process of trying to free that person from his possessor was unavoidable if the evil spirit was stronger than the victim. The Church felt that it was better to destroy both than permit the victim to exist under the spell of his possessor and possibly harm others. The number of unfortunate people who were thus tortured to death by seemingly well-meaning exorcists of religious background is considerable.

The popular attitude toward possession combines certain elements of the religious and medical approaches, but adds another dimension —that of fear and superstition. Both physicians and Churchmen knew very well that touching the body of a possessed individual could have no dire consequences for them, since the body belonged to the victim and not to the possessor. But in the popular view, the very touch of the possessed was poisonous and had to be avoided at all costs. Being in the presence of a possessed person or even being looked at by such an individual could have terrible consequences.

Fear, along with total misconception regarding *what* possession was, helped create a false image in the public mind. Ever since the established Church had made it into the work of the devil during the twelfth and thirteenth centuries, the popular version of what happened to the victim included some form of diabolical influence. Whether it was a demon or underling of the devil, or the Great One himself, inevitably there was at work some hellish play that created the dismal state of possession in the victim. It never occurred to the general public that possession could be the result of benevolent interference or anything less than devilish machinations.

In Spiritualism, which is considered a religion by some and an adjunct to their own religions by others, the facts of possession are fully accepted. Spiritualists do not believe in the devil, but treat the possessor as an erring spirit somehow gone astray but worthy of salvation, rather than as a servant of the devil, or the devil himself, as the Church does. The Spiritualist is imbued with his belief in the reality of "summerland," the spirit world, and the orderly way of life in it in which there is essentially only good and no evil; "spirit" controls everything on earth, including people.

The Spiritualistic approach involves clearly uncritical elements of belief and assumption, while at the same time utilizing factual material from the realms of parapsychology. Unquestionably, the Spiritualist approach to possession is the most useful, short of psychical research, because it is more likely to yield positive results than religious exorcism or purely medical treatment. In defense of religious exorcists and medical practitioners, however, it should be stated that there are individuals among them who are also aware of parapsychology and its findings and who have incorporated some of these findings into their own parochial work. They are just as likely to be successful in their endeavors as the parapsychologist might be.

When any would-be exorcist is called upon to help an unfortunate victim of possession, the first thing the exorcist should realize is that he is dealing with *two* individuals—the possessor and the possessed. No matter what has to be done to separate the two, the life and well-being of the possessed individual comes first. In past days this was not always done, and frequently altogether neglected. Since possession is a very real and very serious phenomenon and many past victims have died as a result of overzealous exorcists, every care should be taken to observe the following rules:

1. Do not use force, especially not physical force, to separate possessed and possessor. Possession is an emotional state and can only be resolved through emotional responses.

2. The exorcist must not permit himself to become party to the case. In other words, emotional involvement on the part of the operator would only be harmful.

3. Belief in one's powers and success are an integral and important part of the exorcism.

4. In most cases of possession, the possessing entity is more in need of psychiatric care than the possessed. Any notion that the victim's own characteristics, moral standards, and usual behavior will apply to the actions of the possessor is an illusion—and a dangerous

one. By the same token, the victim must in no way be made to feel guilty for being possessed or blamed for the extraordinary actions undertaken by the possessor. Clear distinctions must always be drawn between the two separate individuals.

5. Fear and hesitation on the part of the exorcist are completely incompatible with the task at hand. Not only would the possessor notice such weaknesses immediately and capitalize on them, but the exorcist himself might be endangering, by exhibiting doubts, the success of his mission. Firm in mind and body, the exorcist must presume to be superior to whatever force he may encounter in the body and mind of the victim.

Possession is central to Voodoo (or Vodun), the complex of African and Catholic belief and ritual that governs in large measure the religious life of the Haitian peasantry. If the underlying philosophy of the universe held by the Haitians is summarized, this philosophy might be phrased as follows: the ruler of the universe is God, its Creator, who shares this task with His son Jesus, the saints of the Church, and the Holy Ghost. Man has been endowed with a soul, and the soul, which has come from God, returns to God for judgment and, if necessary, for punishment at the end of its sojourn on earth.

From Africa, especially Guinea and Dahomey, the Blacks brought other deities, termed variously *loa, mysteres,* or *saints,* and these deities have been inherited through succeeding generations by the descendants of those who brought them to Haiti. The specific function of the African spirits in the Haitian system was given in the following terms by one of their devotees: "The loa are occupied with men, their task is to cure. They can make a person work better than he otherwise would. When the loa possess people, they give helpful advice. But they cannot do the things that God does. They can protect a garden, but they cannot make a garden grow, for streams, rain, and thunder come from God." Another statement clearly shows the same concept: "God made the loa, but did not make them so they might do evil. When a man purchases a loa for money, that spirit will do evil as well as good, but God becomes angry and will not accept these bad spirits into the sky, and He drives them away."

The most striking element in the Vodun cult is the manner in which the gods are said to "possess" their devotees. Despite the fact that this is the aspect of Haitian religion that seems to the casual observer its least restrained and least disciplined, possession occurs according to well-defined rules and under specifically defined circumstances.

When a person is possessed for the first time, the spirit that is said to animate him is known as a *loa bossal*, an "untamed" god. In the early days the word *bossal* was contemptuously applied to newly arrived Africans. Even today, the same feeling-tone is continued through the belief that since all things in the universe are subject to observable regulation, and animals and plants and human beings must all live according to these rules, the loa, as members of society, may not manifest the unrestrained and often dangerous traits of unpredictable behavior which characterize men before they have been "baptized" and thus brought under proper control.

In native idiom, a person when possessed is "mounted" by his god, and therefore becomes his *ch'wal*, or "horse." A devotee may come under the influence of a number of spirits during a single ceremony or dance, one loa succeeding another. The first deity that ever came to a person, however, for him constitutes the chief of his gods—his *mait'tête*—and the leader of any deities that may subsequently possess him. It is this loa alone that is "baptized" and this one alone "taken from his head" at his death; and, as far as he is concerned, all his other gods are under the control of this *mait'tête*, so that any agreement that he may enter into with this principal spirit must be respected by all others.

In capsule, the Haitian peasant thinks that being possessed by a loa means that an individual's spirit is literally dispossessed by that of the god. Personalities undergo radical change in accordance with the nature of the deity, and even the sex of the one possessed is disregarded if it differs from that of the god, so that, for example, a woman "mounted" by Ogun is always addressed as Papa Ogun. One wears the colors of the god and the ornaments he likes, eating and drinking those things he prefers, and otherwise manifesting his peculiar characteristics—rolling on the earth, if possessed by Damballa, or chattering incessantly if by Gede.

Worship of the loa is directed by priests of the cult. However, I discovered that the terms *papaloi* and *mamaloi* as designations for male and female priests, almost universally employed by non-Haitian writers, are practically unknown in Haiti, where a priest is called a *hungan*, a priestess a *mambu*.

An important function of the *hungan* or *mambu* is to foretell the future, and it is as a diviner that the Vodun priest or priestess is most

often employed. No major rite would be considered by a family unless divination was resorted to, but consultation is made for a far
wider range of affairs than those of a purely religious nature. No
proposed undertaking of any importance is begun without visiting a
diviner. When divining, the priest is usually under possession by his
gods, but other methods, such as gazing into a crystal ball or basin of
water, may also be employed. In reading about Haiti, I found that a
weird, diabolical legend has been created around the Vodun religion.
Writers portrayed Haiti as a magic island bursting with phantoms,
zombies, and devils; and their themes obscured the true spirit of
Vodun.

This was the situation until the science of ethnography took a
hand in the question: as facts fell into place, and found their rightful
meaning, it was realized that there was a strong, distinctive culture;
and with this realization came an effort to recover the essence of this
culture.

The cultivated people of Haiti were ashamed of this primitive
religion, and the writers as a rule ignored it. But in 1928, a Haitian
scientist, Dr. Jean Price-Mars, published a book called *Ainsi Parla
l'Oncle: Essais d'Ethnographie*, which proved to be a literary land-
mark. Dr. Price-Mars urged upon Haitians the importance of coming to terms with the culture of the Black lower classes, pointing out
that their superstitions played a much more considerable role in the
psychology of the educated people than they were generally willing
to admit, and made a plea for the native writers to address themselves to the presentation of Haitian life in all its aspects.

*I have witnessed the petro, the blood and fire of the dark Voodoo
ritual. My tradition and heritage are vastly different from that of the
people who bank their lives on the outcome of the ceremony. Yet as
I examine the world of magic and witchcraft, I will never be a nay-
sayer to its effects, for by the dawn's early light on a Haitian hilltop
I felt the flush of primitive passion that for all time has made me
say, "I believe."*

Part Four

STRANGE
PHENOMENA

17

ESP

In a world where the specialist is king and science is considered the guardian of reason, anything that smacks of the extraordinary is automatically suspect. In order to deal with it we must first try to fit it into one of many categories of *known* occurrences or theories. If it does not conform to our current view of the universe, we, as the average public, have one of two avenues open to us: either we can prove satisfactorily that the phenomenon does not, after all, exist—our earlier findings having been due to error or other significant factors, or we must learn to live with the notion that there are things out there (or within us) that transcend our known laws of science.

People have been wondering if there is such a thing as extrasensory perception ever since Dr. Joseph B. Rhine coined the term ESP. The three letters have since become fairly well known even among laymen, considered roughly the equivalent of the term "sixth sense" or having psychic abilities. ESP stands for extrasensory perception and refers to the ability of a person to perceive beyond the limits of the ordinary five senses as we know them.

There is no such thing as a sixth sense, actually, operating separately from the ordinary five senses. There are, however, instances in which the so-called ordinary five senses do not suffice to explain certain phenomena in the mind of a subject or between two or more subjects. What we have come to call ESP, then, is not a separate sense at all, but an extension of the ordinary five senses beyond what we used to consider their limitations. It may turn out that the various forms of unusual abilities that are responsible for many of the special phenomena reported and discussed here are in reality only different aspects of the same complex underlying force, and that we are perhaps close to a breakthrough where we can actually manipulate this force to our benefit.

According to Evelyn de Wolfe, *Los Angeles Times* staff writer, "The phenomenon of ESP remains inconclusive, ephemeral and mystifying, but for the first time in the realm of science, no one is ashamed to say they believe there is such a thing."

The technical/economic magazine *Nation's Business* of April 1971 states: "Dollars May Flow from the Sixth Sense. Is there a link between business success and extrasensory perception? We think the role of precognition deserves special consideration in sales forecasting. Wittingly or unwittingly, it is probably already used there. Much more research needs to be done on the presence and use of precognition among executives, but the evidence we have obtained indicates that such research will be well worthwhile."

The Russians have delved fully into the subject of ESP phenomena: at this time there are at least eight major universities in the Soviet Union with full-time, fully staffed research centers in parapsychology. What is more, there are no restrictions placed upon those working in this field, and they are free to publish anything they like, whether or not it conforms to dialectical Marxism. In the United States, bickering between those who accept and those who categorically reject the reality of ESP phenomena still hampers funding.

It is *not* the job of the parapsychologist to find a so-called normal, logical explanation for phenomena that we know exist. It is his job to find the truth, whatever it may be, and whatever it requires of us in the way of adjusting our thinking. Having ESP, or being psychic, is not a gift of God to a few chosen individuals. It is a *natural part of human personality*. Those who do not have any ESP are lacking it because they have either disregarded or suppressed this natural, human ability. ESP is in conflict with the *conventional* views of the limitations of time and space and of cause and effect. In a work titled A-*Causal Synchronicity, or The Law of Meaningful Coincidence*, Carl Jung explains the *new* laws.

Briefly, it means this. Let us assume you wake up in the morning and think of your uncle Charlie, whom you haven't seen in five years. You don't know where he is or what he's doing at the present time. An hour later the telephone rings; it is someone who asks you whether you have heard anything about your uncle Charlie lately. Then you go to your job. And on your way home there is Uncle

Charlie crossing the street. This is not just coincidence, according to Professor Jung, but a *meaningful* coincidence, and he shows us that there are scientifically valid connections between your impression of your uncle Charlie on arising, the questions of your caller, and the fact that you ran into your uncle Charlie shortly thereafter. This may be "illogical," but it is also quite common.

Perhaps more difficult to comprehend and more far-reaching in its consequences is the question of time and space and how the facts, as we find them in parapsychology, defy the conventional rules.

The majority of *precognitive* experiences occur spontaneously and unsought. Precognition is the ability to foretell, to have accurate information about events, situations, and people before the time that we become consciously aware of them. Some people may have a hint that a precognitive situation is about to occur: they may feel odd, experience giddiness or a sensation of tingling in various parts of the body, or simply have a vague foreboding that a psychic experience is about to take place.

Long before Jeane Dixon came into the limelight, she startled Washington friends with uncanny predictions that, often unfortunately, came true. On the morning after the assassination of President Kennedy, the New York *Journal-American* carried a brief account of Mrs. Dixon's role in the great tragedy:

The tragic death of President John F. Kennedy was forecast in 1956 and reiterated twice in the past week by Jeane Dixon, a Washington, D.C., socialite and seer.

For years she has electrified Capitol Hill with a succession of eerie and accurate predictions of things to come.

"As for the 1960 election, it will be dominated by labor and won by a Democrat. But he will be assassinated or die in office, not necessarily in his first term."

In 1934 Thomas Menes, a Spanish seer known for his frequently accurate prophecies, announced that Chancellor Dollfuss of Austria would die violently within three months. The date was May 23.

During the summer, when the Nazis tried to seize power in Austria, a group of them came upon Dollfuss in a cabinet meeting and assassinated him. This was on July 25, only two months and two days after the Madrid prophet's prediction was made. Thomas Menes became famous overnight.

Nostradamus, a sixteenth-century French physician, spoke of "a government of England from America" that would exist in the future, after another disastrous war. At that time the word *America* did not exist. Amerigo Vespucci had not yet made his voyage. Nostradamus also clearly described the murder of the French king Henry II. He named the man who would commit the murder, a schoolteacher, and the location of the deed. This was sixty-five years before the event—in fact, before the murderer had been born, and before the king in question had come to the throne.

A related experience is *premonition*, usually *feelings* about events to come, rather than sharp flashes of actual scenes. Premonitions occur more frequently than the more complex forms of precognitive experiences. In an article titled "Can Some People See into the Future?" published in *Family Weekly*, Theodore Irwin reported on a London piano teacher's strong premonition concerning the fate of Senator Robert Kennedy. Nine months before his assassination, Mrs. Lorna Middleton felt a strong premonition that he would be murdered. On March 15 of the year in which Kennedy died, she actually saw the assassination take place, and felt that it would happen while the senator was on tour in the West. This impression was followed by another one, on April 5, and again on April 11, when she had a foreboding of death connected with the Kennedy family. The actual murder took place on June 5.

As a result of people's premonitions frequently reported in the press, psychiatrist R. D. Barker set up a Central Premonitions Registry where people could register their feelings, toward the day when their impressions might become reality.

Telepathy refers to communication from mind to mind *without* the use of sensory perception. For all practical purposes, we can say that telepathy is an instant transmission of thoughts. It works best in times of stress and when the usual means of communication aren't functioning. It is particularly strong between people who have an emotional bond. The instances of mothers feeling the distress of their children, at a distance, of course, are numerous; cases where someone just has got to get through to another person, and uses his mind to send forth a message, are equally numerous and well attested to in the files of most reputable psychical research bodies, such as the American Society for Psychical Research. To a degree, telepathy can be induced experimentally. In experimental telepathy, sender and receiver should know each other in order to make the contact more possible.

Explorer Sir Hubert Wilkins and psychic Harold Sherman conducted some classic experiments in telepathy. It was agreed that Sir Hubert would mentally transmit information about himself daily from the North Pole, while Sherman was taking down whatever he received so that the material could be compared after Sir Hubert came back to New York. A team of researchers stood by Sherman in his New York hotel room, and, under test conditions, recorded the telepathic messages he received. One time, Harold Sherman insisted that he telepathically saw Sir Hubert Wilkins dancing in his evening clothes. This seemed improbable, because at the time the explorer was on an Arctic expedition. When Sir Hubert returned to New York, he was able to confirm the following: En route north, his plane had been forced to land at Calgary, Alberta, Canada, during a snowstorm. The lieutenant governor of the province happened to be in town for a ball being given in honor of a new governor general in Ottawa. He invited Sir Hubert to attend, but the explorer lacked evening clothes. Under the circumstances, the lieutenant governor loaned him a suit of tails—so what Harold Sherman had seen telepathically was indeed correct.

Psychometry is the ability to touch an object and derive from it information about its owner. This is possible because emotional experiences leave an imprint upon the outer layer of the aura, or the electromagnetic field constituting the human personality. This imprint is permanent. If a "sensitive" person touches it, he will then re-create or tune in on whatever happened to the owner of the object. He will get flashes of the past, present, and even future of that person. Psychometry, or "measuring psychically," is probably the most common form of mental mediumship.

On the whole, the press has been, and still is, hostile to the very notion of ESP. Occasionally there are exceptions, when an individual editor or writer knows how to overcome editorial policies, which are usually against the subject.

However, some well-documented accounts of ESP studies have been published in some magazines and weeklies. It is interesting to note that "alternate explanations" are offered in such articles, but at least the facts are fully presented.

According to Martin Ebon, well-known editor and researcher, belief and skepticism rival each other in the lives of many outstanding men who have recorded psychic experiences or shown unusual fascination with the so-called occult. Experiences such as telepathic impressions or prophetic dreams seem to be part of everyday life. Although they happen to just about everybody, most of us do not remember them; our culture has conditioned us to ignore the uncanny as unhealthy or fear-inspiring, although it seems to permeate the civilization of our day just as much as it did earlier cultures. Some psychic events are unique in their dramatic impact. They may change a man's whole outlook on life; they may frighten him into retreat from everything that is inexplicable; or they may arouse his curiosity toward deeper understanding of his extrasensory capacities.

18

Spiritual Survival and Reincarnation

THE DESIRE to communicate with the dead is as old as man himself. As soon as primitive man realized that death could separate him from a loved one and that he could not prevent that person's departure, he tried to find a way to contact the dead person.

Let us assume for a moment that the dead do exist, that they live on in a world beyond our physical world. It would then be of the greatest interest to learn all about the nature of that other world and the laws that govern it. It would be important also to come to a better understanding of the nature of this transition called death, to understand the "art of dying" as the medieval esoterics called it.

Having postulated that a nonphysical world populated by the dead does exist, we next examine the contacts between the two worlds. We find there are two kinds of communication between them: those initiated by the living, and those initiated by the dead. There is, it would appear, two-way traffic between the two worlds. Observation of so-called spontaneous phenomena that have occurred unexpectedly to actual people are just as important as induced experiments or attempts at contact. In all this we must keep an eye open for misinterpretation, deceit, or self-delusion.

It seems farfetched, however, to take for granted that thousands of people in all sorts of circumstances and under varying conditions hallucinate communications with the dead. It is more logical to assume that an extraordinary ESP experience does indeed occur to these people, even if this is contrary to orthodox scientific belief at the time.

Why does a dead person want his family or friends to know that death is not the end, and that he or she is in fact very much alive in another dimension? There are two strong and compelling reasons: one is the continuing ego-consciousness of the dead person. He wants to let those closest to him know that he continues to exist as an entity and consequently that he wishes to be considered a continuing factor in their lives. This is for his own sake. The second reason for this need to let the living know that life after death exists is for *their* sake. They too will eventually die. Why not give them the benefit of the dead person's experience? Why not do them the favor of letting them in on the world's greatest and most important secret: that man does not end at the grave?

Rosemary Brown is an English lady who claims to be the continuing channel of expression for some of the recent past's greatest composers. The evidence is substantial and worthy of further study. Stewart Robb, the investigator of the Brown case, is not only a qualified psychic researcher but an expert musicologist. This combination of talents makes him a particularly qualified man in this instance. Why Brahms, Liszt, and others should choose a middle-class English housewife to continue writing their music for them is not as much a puzzle as one might think at first. Rosemary Brown's lack of musical training might render her a more convincing medium. Conversely, the music of great composers such as Beethoven is openly available and the mere fact that an untutored person can write in their style is not sufficiently convincing. What is lacking, perhaps, are the intimate personal details of the composers' lives, transmitted by them to Rosemary Brown and checked out independently. If some of these personal data were unpublished but could subsequently be corroborated by a researcher through letters or other existing but inaccessible documents, we would then have a near-foolproof case for the contact between the composers and Rosemary Brown. Until this happens, the case remains open.

A particularly impressive case of after-death communication was experienced in Pennsylvania. Sandra R. lives with her family in a small town southwest of Pittsburgh. Her brother, Neal, twenty-two, had been working as a bank teller for three years. Neal often said that he had a feeling that if he went into the Army he'd be killed. Consequently, his mother and sister, to whom Neal was quite close, persuaded him to join the National Guard for a six-month tour of duty. Since he was of age and would probably be drafted, he might thus shorten his length of service. Neal finally agreed that this was the best thing to do under the circumstances. He quit his position at the bank, joined the National Guard, and tried to make the best of the situation. In April 1963 he got his orders to report to basic training a week from the following Monday. Several times during those last days at home, he mentioned the fact that he was to leave at 5:00 A.M. Sunday, as if this was something important and final. On the Monday preceding his departure, he visited friends to say goodbye. When he left home, he had the usual kiss on the cheek for his mother, and he gaily said, "I'll see you," and went out. He never returned. Early the following morning, the family was notified that he had been found dead in his parked car on a lonely country road about two miles away from his home. He had committed suicide by inhaling carbon monoxide. The family was shocked. At first they could not believe the news, for they were sure he would leave some sort of note for them. But nothing was ever found, even though they searched the house from top to bottom. All of Neal's affairs were in order. He had left no debts or commitments, but also no message of any kind for anyone. He was buried in his home town, and the family tried to adjust to their great loss. His sister, Sandra, was three years younger, but the two had been close enough to have had many telepathic experiences in which they would read each other's thoughts. She could not understand why her brother had not confided in her before taking his life.

In the house, both Sandra's room and Neal's were upstairs. After the young man's death, Sandra could not think of sleeping so near to her late brother's room, so she slept on the roll-out divan in the living room. Friday was the day of the funeral, and it seemed to Sandra that it would never pass. Finally, after a restless, almost sleepless night, Saturday dawned. All day long she felt uneasy, and there was a tension in the air that she found almost unbearable. When night came, Sandra asked that her mother share the couch with her. Neither woman had taken any tranquilizers or sleeping pills. Again they discussed the suicide from all angles, and again failed to arrive at any conclusions. Finally, they fell asleep.

Suddenly Sandra was awakened from deep sleep by a clicking sound. It sounded exactly as if someone had snapped his fingers above her head. As Sandra became fully awake, she heard her mother stir next to her.

"Did you hear that?" her mother asked. She had also heard the strange snapping sound. Both women were now fully awake.

They both felt a tingling sensation from head to toe, as if they were plugged into an electrical socket! Some sort of current was running through them, and they were quite unable to move even a limb.

The living room was situated in the front part of the house. All the window blinds were closed, and there was no light shining through them. The only light in the room came from a doorway behind them, a doorway that led into the hall. Suddenly they noticed a light to their left. It had the brightness of an electric bulb when they first saw it. It appeared about two feet from the couch on the mother's side and was getting brighter and brighter as it moved closer to them. "What is it?" they called to each other, and then Sandra noticed that the light had a form. There was a head and shoulders encased in the light!

They were terrified. Suddenly Sandra heard herself cry out: "It's Neal!" At the moment she called out her late brother's name, the light blew up to its brightest glare. With that, a feeling of great peace and relief came over the two women.

Mrs. R., still unable to move her body, asked, "What do you want? Why did you do it?"

Then she started to cry. At that moment, waves of light in the form of fingers appeared inside the bright light, as if someone was waving goodbye. Then the light gradually dimmed, until it vanished completely.

At that instant, a rush of cold air moved across the room. A moment later they clearly heard someone walking up the stairs. They were alone in the house, so they knew it could not be a flesh-and-blood person. When the footsteps reached the top stair, it squeaked as it always had when Sandra's brother walked up the stairs. Over the years, Sandra had heard this noise time and again. There wasn't a sound in the house, except those footsteps upstairs. The two women were lying quite still on the couch, unable to move even if they had wanted to. The steps continued through the hallway, and then went into Neal's room, which was directly over the living room. Next they heard the sound of someone sitting down on the bed, and they clearly made out the noise of bedsprings giving from the weight of a person! Since the bed was almost directly over their heads down in the living room, there was no mistaking these sounds. At this moment their bodies suddenly returned to normal. The tension was broken and Sandra jumped up, turned on the light, and looked at the clock next to the couch. The time was five o'clock Sunday morning—

the exact moment Neal had been scheduled to leave, had he not committed suicide!

With this, all was quiet again in the house. But Sandra and her mother no longer grieved for Neal. They accepted the inevitable, and began to realize that life did indeed continue in another dimension. The bond between Neal and themselves was reestablished and they felt a certain relief to know he was all right, wherever he was.

At different times since that initial goodbye visit, Mrs. R. and Sandra smelled in the house the strong aroma of Neal's favorite aftershave lotion. At the time of his death, he had a bottle of it in the glove compartment of his car. No one else in the house used aftershave lotion.

Neither Mrs. R. nor her daughter is given to hysterics. They accepted these events as perfectly natural, always carefully making sure that no ordinary explanation would fit. But when all was said and done, they knew that Neal had not let them down, after all. The bond was still unbroken.

It seems hard to understand why, with all the compelling evidence of cases such as Neal's, which can be found in many works on psychic subjects, the vast majority of the public still considers the question of spirit survival an iffy one. Yet almost every family in the United States has at least one event of this kind to report—whether it is a visitation of a dead relative, a prophetic dream, or a warning from someone "over there" concerned with helping a living member of the family.

Only in recent years has the scientific exploration of reincarnation been pursued. Until the latter part of the nineteenth century, psychical research was in the hands of amateurs or, at times, quacks; with the emergence of an orderly scientific approach to the many phenomena of human personality now classified as ESP, the subject of reincarnation was raised. Today, after a gap of perhaps fifty years, the subject of reincarnation is again being examined, because it seems to answer so many questions left unanswered both by science and by establishment religions. Particularly among the young, the cries for information on previous and future lives are very loud, for the process of reincarnation does furnish them with an explanation for the many injustices they see all around.

It stands to reason that a universally and scientifically accepted conviction that reincarnation is factual would have deep and long-lasting consequences in our way of life. The common attitude toward death, for instance, would undergo rapid and profound change, for if there is more than one life to live, surely one could not fear death as the inevitable end. Surely one might even welcome death at times, if the existence one suffers could be exchanged for a better one. The hopelessly ill particularly might well welcome a continuing life cycle.

Reincarnation has always had a place in the great world religion. The ancient Jews continually expected the reincarnation of their great prophets. To them, Moses was Abel, the descendant of Adam; and their Messiah was to be the reincarnation of Adam himself, who had already come a second time as David. It seems significant that the closing words of the Old Testament (Malachi 4:5) contain this prophecy: "Behold, I will send you Elijah the prophet before the great and terrible day of Jehovah comes."

Of course, Elijah had already lived among the Jews. But the first book of the New Testament refers to this prophecy on three occasions, thus linking the Old and New Testaments on the idea of rebirth (in the King James Version of the New Testament, the Greek form of "Elijah," namely "Elias," is used).

In the Hindu view, spirit no more depends on the body it inhabits than body depends on the clothes it wears or the house it lives in. When an outfit is too small or a house too cramped, we exchange these for roomier ones that offer our bodies freer play. Souls do the same. This process by which an individual jiva passes through a sequence of bodies is known as reincarnation or transmigration of the soul—in Sanskrit, *samsara.* On the subhuman level, the passage is through a series of increasingly complex bodies until at last a human one is attained. Up to this point the soul's growth is virtually automatic. It is as if the soul were growing steadily and normally, as a plant, and receiving at each successive stage a body that, being more complex, provides the needed room.

According to the Hindus, with the soul's graduation into a human body, this automatic ascent ends. Its assignment to this exalted habitation is evidence that the soul has reached self-consciousness, and with this estate come effort, responsibility, and freedom.

In the Koran, Islam's holy book, we read: "God generates beings, and sends them back over and over again, till they return to Him."

Reincarnation memories come to some people at various times in their lives, but most of us have never had them. It is my conviction that only where a previous life has been in some way cut short, has been tragic, is the individual given part of the memory, as a sort of bonus to influence him in his present conduct. People who had full lives prior to their present one never remember those prior lives, neither in dreams nor in so-called waking flashes, nor in a déjà vu, which is a phenomenon sometimes related to reincarnation memories. Most of the déjà vu phenomena are simply precognitive experiences that are not realized at the time they occur but are remembered when the knowledge gained through precognition becomes objective reality. Some déjà vus, especially those that are complex and contain precise and detailed information about places and situations the perceiver is not familiar with, are due to reincarnation memories. All déjà vu experiences occur in the waking state, but they are related to reincarnation dreams in that they also disclose to the individual some hidden material from his own past.

It is rare that a person can recollect large segments of an earlier existence in the physical world, and it is even rarer that they recollect their earlier lives from the beginning—that is to say, from birth onward. Occasionally there are cases of recollections in which the person does actually recall his or her own birth. In general, average people may remember as far back as their early school years.

Typical is the case of Mrs. N.A. She is twenty-six years old, a licensed practical nurse, and she is married to a professional musician. They have one son and live in a city in Alabama. Her interests are music and the arts. She and her husband enjoy reading books, but they have never had any particularly strong interest in the occult or in psychic research. Ever since she was a small child and able to speak, Mrs. A. had insisted to her mother that she did recall the moment of her birth into this world. She vividly described the day she was brought home from the hospital—a sixteen-day-old baby.

> My birth memories consist of an awareness of being blasted into a place where extremely bright lights and what seemed like the resounding echoes of human voices were imposed on my small person. I vaguely seemed to remember a detached observance of this affair, including blurred visions of figures clothed with masks and caps. The day I was brought home I remember riding snuggled in the arms of a woman with light brown hair and a prominent nose, arriving at a house where my aunt Jeff and sixteen-month-old brother were coming out the front door, onto the front porch, I suppose to greet my mother and me. I do remember it was the first time I had seen trees, and I was impressed by them. More clearly than anything is my memory of observing my mother, and in the thought language of the newborn, wondering, Who is she? What am I, and who are

those people standing on the porch? Since I was a young child I have always had the feeling of total detachment from myself and others, as if I were on the outside looking in.

As far as I have been able to discover, it is no more difficult to recall an episode that took place several millennia ago than to recall one from the current or the preceding century. Author Joan Grant writes of her "return" to Egypt in 1935, annoyed "that certain avenues of trees no longer led from Hat-shepsut's temple to Karnak, and feeling depressed that there were so many ruins instead of being pleased that there was so much left to see. I had no intimations that I had spent the best part of two thousand years in the Nile Valley. Eighteen months later, through the trivial catalyst of psychometrizing a scarab, I did the first of the 115 total recalls which became a posthumous autobiography of over 120,000 words."

All great philosophers accepted reincarnation as natural. Victor Hugo said, "The tomb is not a blind alley; it is a thoroughfare. It closes on the twilight, it opens on the dawn."

19

Psychic Dreams and Astral Projection

MAN HAS ALWAYS wanted to know how and why we dream, and what dreaming means in relation to the waking state. The shaman or priest of the early societies was asked these questions. However, as man became more sophisticated, he consulted his medical practitioner about his dreams, at the same time retaining the religious consultant in his life as a secondary source of information. When neither the medical nor the religious experts sufficed and his quest for a better understanding of his dreams continued, he turned to occult sources for definitions and explanations. We have long searched for the hidden meanings of dreams, meanings that can be explained and interpreted only by those familiar with the language of the occult.

A significant number of dreams contain material of a psychic nature, material that later becomes objective reality in the lives of those who dream it. This is common knowledge, not only among those who have studied these subjects but among laymen as well.

There are four kinds of dreams: those due to physical problems, which result in nightmares or distorted imagery; dreams due to suppressed material, which are useful in psychoanalytical processes; dreams of a psychic nature; and, finally, out-of-the-body experiences, also referred to as astral projections.

Dreams due to physical discomfort or environmental pressures and those stemming from emotional difficulties are not nearly as vivid as psychic dreams or out-of-the-body experiences.

One is rarely able to "shake" psychic dreams or out-of-the-body experiences, even if one does not write them down immediately. Some psychic dreams are so strong that they awaken the dreamer. In many cases the dream remains vivid in the memory for a long time afterward. These two types of dreams occur with great frequency.

Psychic dreams contain information in the form of messages, warnings, or other communications from individual entities outside the dreamer's consciousness, or they may contain material obtained through the psychic abilities of the dreamer himself, abilities that he does not normally use when awake. A psychic dream is one in which material from an *external* source, or from an *internal* source not ordinarily active in the conscious state, is received.

Prophetic dreams are those that involve some situation or event pertaining to someone's future, and they are remembered upon awakening. Sometimes, prophetic material can also be obtained in the waking state.

In 1969, Mrs. Elaine F. of Chambersburg, Pennsylvania, had a dream in which she saw a group of people having a party. She seemed to be off "in the trees," looking on. The group was celebrating something; they seemed like Girl Scouts to her. Suddenly, some people came "out of nowhere" and began to kill the "Girl Scouts." The killers were dressed in black, and had bushy hair. In the dream, she was particularly frightened by the eyes of the leader, whom she saw clearly. When she awoke the following morning she described the scene and how she had seen blood running from the wounds of the victims. Ten days later, the Sharon Tate murders shocked the nation. As soon as Mrs. F. saw a picture of Charles Manson in the newspapers, she recognized him as the man she had seen in her dream.

On the other hand, some psychic dreams take a long time to come true. Take for instance the case of C.G. He is fifty-two, worked in New York in advertising and publishing for ten years, and currently owns his own antique-restoration business on the West Coast. Because he has had a number of paranormal dreams over the years, he began to write them down, on the chance that some of them might later become reality. In one dream, he found himself riding on a train that, as it approached a city, went underground, and finally came to a stop beside a long platform. He got off the train and walked along the platform with a large crowd of people. In the distance ahead he could see a flight of stairs; there was a light at the end, outdoors. He went upstairs and saw before him a roofed platform stretching into the distance, with railroad tracks on both sides. In his dream, he could see a large city stretching to the right horizon; but on his left he saw complete destruction—nothing but piles of rubble. He awoke, and recorded his dream. One year later, in September 1942, he went into the armed services and served in New Guinea, the Philippines, and ultimately in Japan, where he arrived in September 1945, and was stationed in a small town about thirty miles south of Tokyo. On a weekend pass he decided to take a train into Tokyo. As he approached the city, the train went underground and came to a stop beside a long platform. He joined the throng of people going to a flight of stairs ahead in the distance, and he had a strong feeling of déjà vu at the moment when he began to climb the stairs. When he arrived at the roofed platform, he recalled his dream in vivid detail. On his right stood, indeed, the intact portion of Tokyo; on his left were the results of many months of bombing by the Americans, aimed at the industrial sections of Tokyo—devastated right up to the railroad tracks.

A special category of psychic dreams are the so-called warning dreams, which allow the dreamer to take steps to avoid danger of disability.

Mrs. M. of Kentucky dreamed in July 1952 that she saw a casket in the local funeral home, and she noticed that the furniture, which had never been changed, was somewhat different from what she knew it to be. In the dream, a couch that had always faced the casket was to the right side of it. She saw her Sunday-school teacher come in, and she saw herself seated in the middle of the couch. The teacher passed to an empty spot on the left in front of her and sat down to her right. She put her arm around her and said, "I feel so sorry for you; I don't know what to do." Mrs. M. saw flowers with a large white lily cross in the middle. When she dreamed the dream a second time, she told her husband about it, remarking that she feared something might have happened to her Sunday-school teacher's grandson, who had been seriously ill when they had left town for a short trip. She decided to write the Sunday-school teacher a letter, telling her how much she meant to her and the church and the town. When she arrived home, however, she found that her teacher's grandson was well, and so she dismissed the dream. Then, in September 1952, her dream became stark reality: she found herself at the funeral parlor in her home town, the furniture had been moved just as she had seen it in her dream, and the flowers were exactly like the large white lily cross she had seen in her dream; but her husband was in the casket, having died suddenly from a heart attack, and her old Sunday-school teacher was comforting her, saying the same words she had heard her speak in the dream two months prior to the event!

Telepathic, or ESP, dreams are those in which the dreamer receives information from another person, either living or dead, but pertaining to the present, even if from a distance. In telepathic dreams, the dreamer simply picks up thought energies. These transmissions need not be conscious or exact. Both actual events and contemplated events may be subjects of such dreams.

Mrs. J.W. of New Jersey had a telepathic dream. In 1941 a dear friend of hers was serving on an oil tanker based at Fort Pierce, Florida. A German submarine torpedoed this tanker at sea and all but one of the crew perished. At that time, Mrs. W. had a vivid dream in which she saw her friend trapped in his cabin; he pounded the door with his fists. She noticed the porcelain doorknob, which he kept bearing down on. Over and over, he cried out for her, calling her by his pet name for her. At this point the dream ended. Several hours later she was notified that he had died in the attack on the tanker.

Mrs. C.H. lives in Pennsylvania with her family. Her husband and three daughters are very telepathic. She has had frequent precognitive dreams for many years. "I have precognitive dreams which are sifted from the rest of my dreams by the color *green* somewhere in the dream," she explains. In February 1971 she dreamed that she saw green mountains, and several trucks sinking into the black slime that was covering the entire mountain. She saw the trucks, and suddenly found *herself* trapped deeply under the trucks and some wood. She heard herself scream until she almost lost her voice. At that moment someone called out to her, warning her that she would lose her voice. There the dream ended.

Two weeks later, the great tragedy at Aberfan, Great Britain, shook the world: A coal slag slide had buried a schoolhouse and killed many children. The newspaper account, which reached Mrs. H. two weeks *after* her dream, stated that among other harrowing experiences, a worker had heard a child screaming, because she was trapped under the rubble. The worker called out to the child to stop screaming and asked for her name, to which she replied, Katherine. "Most experiences become a reality about two weeks after I dream them and most of them pertain to world disasters," Mrs. H. explained. "I also feel the pain of a stricken person in a tragedy." She consulted a doctor, because she did not want this talent and hoped he would rid her of it. But her psychic ability has remained with her.

Astral projection—also referred to as "momentary displacement"—is separation of the *inner* body (or etheric self) from the physical body, usually during sleep, but not exclusively. Astral projections have occurred in the waking condition; however, projections of any length are nearly always part of the dream experience. In this phenomenon, the sleeper travels various distances and remains connected with his physical self by a silver cord which, however, is not always visible to him.

There are two ways to accomplish astral projection: one, willfully projecting the inner self to a predetermined location and reporting back for purposes of information or research; two, involuntary dissociation of the inner self during sleep and travel to external locations. Many or all of the events experienced in the actual state are remembered, upon awakening, with the same intensity and clarity that is typical of all truly psychic dreams.

Often, an astral projection will occur when a person has been anesthetized for surgery. These artificially-induced dissociations seem to encourage astral flight, and there are many records of people describing how they watched their own operations while hovering in a corner of the ceiling above the operating table.

Mrs. P.H. of the Midwest was delivering her third baby when she began hemorrhaging and felt her inner self leave her body through her head. According to her account, she witnessed everything that happened in the delivery room, as she floated over it. Then she left the room and visited with "other souls," where she was given the choice of staying, or returning to the earth plane. She decided to return to earth, and presently awoke on the operating table, but she remembered everything she had seen when apparently "unconscious."

Robert Monroe is a businessman and psychic noted for his OBE (out-of-the-body experience) work. He was first known for the OBE work done on him in the late 1960s by Dr. Charles Tart, at the University of California. Mr. Monroe has since opened the Monroe Institute, where he has been teaching psychiatrists and psychologists how to have OBEs.

Monroe spontaneously began to have OBEs in 1958 and since then he's been "out" thousands of times. He kept a detailed log of his OBEs and published them in 1971 in a book titled *Journeys Out of the Body*. In August 1966 Tart had eight sessions with Monroe, in which brainwaves, eye movements, and heart rate were electronically monitored while Monroe tried to travel out of his body and read a five-digit number that was on a shelf in an adjacent room. He could never read the number, but twice when he said he was "out" he gave Tart descriptions of activities that were taking place in other parts of the building. Tart checked these out and Monroe was proved correct. Tart found that Monroe's brainwave patterns were typical to those of dreaming.

In the summer of 1968 Tart worked with Monroe again. Once again Monroe could not read the target numbers, but he did provide correct information of events outside the lab. During Monroe's wanderings out of his body, Tart observed definite physiological correlates. Monroe's blood pressure dropped, his eye movements increased, and his brainwave pattern switched to prolonged theta rhythms typical of the "twilight" period between wakefulness and sleep.

Prospective students (fifty percent are Ph.D.s and M.D.s) for the Monroe Institute are put through a rigorous psychological screening process. Out of approximately six hundred who pass this level, about fifty emerge as really "proficient" OBE practitioners, six actually gifted. A typical trainee begins with a rigorous weekend session. The program includes yoga breathing exercises, visualization techniques, and the use of an "audio pulsing device."

This device has been patented by Monroe, and, he claims, is used in university sleep research throughout the country. The instrument produces sounds that have the exact same pulsating rhythms as the brain's own sleep waves. As a person falls to sleep, his brain waves pass from wakeful beta waves (thirty to thirteen cycles per second) to the slower alpha waves (twelve to eight cps) characteristic of mild meditative states, to theta waves (seven to three cps), to delta waves (three to one cps). Monroe's device produces sounds that run through these waves in just the order and amount that is experienced in falling asleep naturally. But Monroe is not, of course, interested in putting his subjects to sleep. Instead, using the audio pulsing device, he "suspends" his subjects between theta and delta levels. In other words, he locks subjects in at the very threshold of deep sleep, but not sleep. This level of consciousness, Monroe believes (as do other researchers), is conducive to OBEs. Monroe says his device is used regularly at the Veterans' Administration Hospital in his area for sleep research.

Subjects have OBEs, travel to near and distant locations, and report back on their sightings and on the nature of their experiences. Many psychologists and psychiatrists have taken Monroe's course for the experience of being out of one's body. In this state, a person can be free of the physical shell, open to a free flow of imagery, strange voices, transcending space and time, viewing events that happened in the past—all these things, claims Monroe, greatly help therapists treat psychotics and other mentally disturbed people. The OBE, says Monroe, gives the psychiatrist some "feeling" for another-world type of existence, and permits him to better appreciate the "imaginary" voices, images, and experiences that are common to people who are considered mentally disturbed. Monroe says that some of his subjects report that they have been able to "reach" their own patients and help them make contacts with reality since the therapists themselves have had a glimpse of an alternate reality.

So the next time you feel you are not quite yourself, and get that floating feeling, it may not be imaginary after all. Many experts in the field of psychic research claim that projections are among the most common forms of "dissociation of personality," that they loosen the bonds of consciousness, and are harmless.

20

Ghosts and How to Deal With Them

A GHOST, according to famed "ghosthunter" Professor Hans Holzer, is a surviving emotional memory of people who have died tragically and are unaware of their own passing. A ghost is a split-off personality that remains behind in the environment of the person's previous existence, whether a home or place of work, but closely tied to the spot where the person actually died. Ghosts do not travel, do not follow people around, and they rarely leave the immediate vicinity of their tragedy. Once in a while, a ghost will roam a house from top to bottom, or may be observed in a garden or adjacent field. But they do not ride in cars or get on buses, they do not appear at the other end of town: those are *free* spirits, who are able to reason for themselves and to attempt communication with the living.

In the mind of the casual observer, of course, ghosts and spirits are the same thing. To the trained parapsychologist, ghosts are similar to psychotic human beings: incapable of reasoning for themselves or taking much action. Spirits, on the other hand, are the surviving personalities of all of us who die in a reasonably normal fashion. A spirit is capable of continuing a full existence in the next dimension, to think, reason, and feel and act, while his unfortunate colleague, the ghost, can do none of those things. All a ghost can do is repeat the final moments of his passing, the unfinished business, as it were, over and over until it becomes an obsession.

The majority of ghostly manifestations draw upon energy from the living in order to penetrate our three-dimensional world. Other manifestations are subjective, especially when the receiver is psychic. In that case, the psychic person hears or sees the departed individual in his mind's eye only, while others cannot observe it.

There is no sure way of knowing why some individuals make postmortem appearances and others do not. It seems to depend upon the intensity of feeling, the residue of unresolved problems, which they have within their system at the time of death. Consequently, not everyone who dies a violent death becomes a ghost; far from it. If it were otherwise, our battlefields and other horror-laden places, such as concentration camps and prisons, would indeed be swarming with ghosts, but they are not. It depends on the attitude of the individual at the time of death, whether the passing is accepted and the person proceeds to the next stage of existence, or whether he is incapable of realizing that a change is taking place and consequently clings to the physical environment with which he is familiar, the earth sphere.

Some places seem better suited than others for ghosts. According to Peter Underwood, renowned head of the London Ghost Club:

> There are more ghosts seen, reported, and accepted in the British Isles than anywhere else on Earth. I am often asked why this is so and can only suggest that a unique ancestry with Mediterranean, Scandinavian, Celtic and other strains and intrinsic island detachment, and enquiring nature, and perhaps our readiness to accept a supernormal explanation for curious happenings may all have played their part in bringing about this state of affairs.

Of course, there are such famous places as Hampton Court, which is just filled with specters. The spirit of King Henry VIII seems to brood heavily over the mellow Tudor palace itself. He was at Hampton with five of his six wives, and it was there, on October 12, 1537, that his third queen, Jane Seymour, bore him a son and died a week later. Her ghost walks here, or rather glides, clad in white, perambulating the Clock Court. Carrying a lighted taper, she has been seen emerging from a doorway in the Queen's Old Apartments, wandering noiselessly about the stairway and through the Silver Stick Gallery. Quite recently some servants handed in their notice because they had seen "a tall lady, with a long train and a shining face" walk through closed doors, holding a taper, and glide down the stairs.

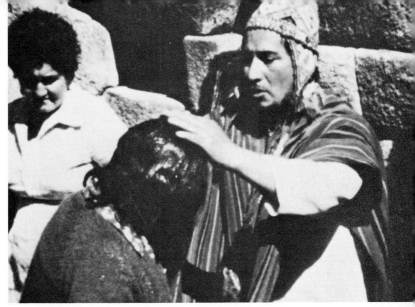

A Peruvian healer lays hands upon a patient.
Behind them are the expertly wrought, unmortared
stone walls built by the Incas.

A hat, or a pair of gloves, or a walking-stick may serve as
the focus for a Vodun (Voodoo) ritual. They are just signs
for an invisible presence that enters the worshippers.

The gods of Vodun "take possession" of those who believe
in them. The possessed may become violent and excited,
speak prophetically, or pronounce curses.

A 1508 woodcut of German witches preparing a charm. The same old women who preserved traditional folk medicine and herbal remedies were often attacked as witches when crops failed or livestock fell sick.

The Mother Goddess, central figure of the Old Religion. This statuette was made in the Turkish highlands more than 7,000 years ago—young compared to similar Stone Age fertility figures.

Turkish Embassy

A coelacanth caught in 1953, showing the limblike fins which reveal its relationship to the first land animals. Until then, paleontologists had thought this species extinct for two hundred million years.

A 19th-century illustration of a sea serpent which washed ashore at Hungary Bay, Bermuda.

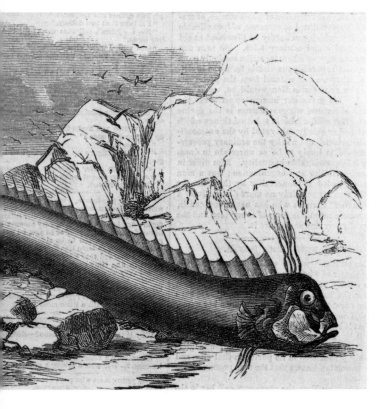

Sordus pilosus ("hairy devil"),
a flying reptile, was probably
warm-blooded. It had a coat
of fine, hairlike feathers.

Archaeopteryx, whose fossils were long thought to be those
of a primitive bird, is now classified as a dinosaur.
It was flightless, although its feathered front limbs
may have allowed it to glide for short distances.

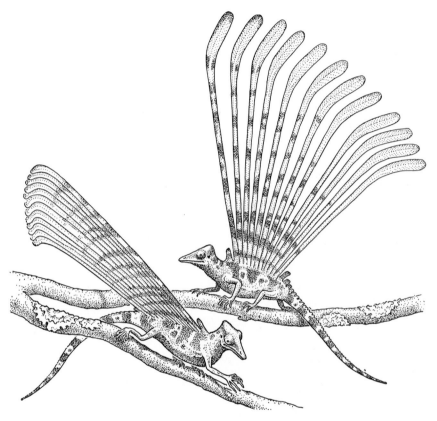

Longisquama, an animal that lived 220 million years
ago, was in the line of development that produced both
dinosaurs and birds. Its scales, with their central ribs,
were among the earliest forms of feathers.

The sea horse and sea cow are real enough, but some early naturalists believed that everything on land had a marine counterpart. This legendary sea monk of 16th-century Norway is from the book *Libri de Piscibus Marinis* (1554) by Rondeletius.

Aldus Archives

In the late 19th century, the vice-consul of Britain reported that fear of this sea monster—said to be the size of a small boat—was causing a sharp drop in the supply of sponges from Mount Lebanon, where the monster was said to reside. In this drawing, the monster is swallowing one of the sponge divers.

A SPONGE DIVER SWALLOWED BY A SEA MONSTER

Aldus Archives

The famous White Lady of Hampton Court is reputed to haunt the area of the landing stage, and a number of anglers reported seeing her one midsummer night a few years ago. There is also the ghost of Archbishop Laud (whose spirit is also said to appear in the library of St. John's College, Oxford, rolling his head across the floor!), which allegedly has been seen by residents at the palace, strolling slowly without a sound in the vicinity of the rooms he once knew so well.

Lady Catherine Howard is perhaps the most famous ghost of Hampton Court. In 1514 she came here, a lovely girl of eighteen, as the bride of the fat, lame, aging monarch. A year after her arrival, ugly rumors began to circulate that described her behavior before and after her marriage as a little better than a common harlot's. The night before she was arrested, her first step to the block, she broke free from her captors and ran along the gallery in a vain effort to plead for her life with her husband. But Henry was piously hearing vespers in the chapel and ignored her entreaties, and she was dragged away, still shrieking and sobbing for mercy. As you go down the Queen's Great Staircase you can see on the right-hand side the low-roofed corridor containing the room from which Queen Catherine escaped and to which she was dragged back, her screams mingling weirdly with the singing in the chapel. Her ghost reenacts this event on the night of the anniversary, running shrieking through what has come to be known as "haunted gallery." All the witnesses say that the figure has long, flowing hair, but usually the apparition disappears so quickly that no one has time to observe it closely.

The common term *poltergeist*, which is German for "noisy ghost," used to be applied mainly to physical phenomena occurring in haunted houses. These phenomena—such as objects moving mysteriously by themselves, flying through the air without apparent natural cause, and clearly defined noises such as heavy thumpings—are noticeable to all, not just to the psychic person.

It was believed that the presence of a child below the age of puberty was necessary to cause these phenomena, and that, indeed, the youngster unconsciously created them by the force of his untapped libido. It was felt that it was a young person's way of expressing himself and of getting attention from the family that might have been lacking. But in the majority of cases, this force appears to be used by an intelligent, if warped, nonphysical entity *outside* the child's mind. The youngster is the tool, not the creator of the disturbances.

M.D., a medical journal, had this to say about poltergeists:

The strangest aspect of poltergeist manifestation is the violation of ballistic principles: dozens of bemused observers have noted thrown objects traveling at unnaturally slow speeds and along impossibly curved paths, even circles; objects also hover motionless and make such soft landings that not even fragile china is broken. In a celebrated case in England in 1849, witnesses swore they saw salt and pepper emerge from their respective shakers, whirl and mix in the air like a swarm of bees and return, unmixed, to their proper receptacles.

Poltergeist-propelled objects are frequently found to be warm or hot on landing, even in Iceland and Siberia.

Psychical researchers use the term recurrent spontaneous psychokinesis (RSPK), and believe that the phenomena are usually associated with a child or young adult. In one study of poltergeist cases, more than three fifths of the manifestations were associated with a "central body," most of whom were females; in all but five instances the central party was under twenty; the average age was thirteen years for boys, fourteen for girls.

Although poltergeist phenomena occur quite frequently, today's ordinary observer is just as baffled by them as were his ancestors. A typical case was reported in the *Los Angeles Times* in 1962 by reporter Charles Davis, who witnessed the incident at Big Bear City, California:

Don Beasley, 20-year-old student, described Saturday how he watched in amazement as stones floated down out of the sky and landed on a cabin and the ground around it.

First public disclosure of the phenomenon was made Friday.

Beasley and John Holdorf, former Redlands student, moved into the cabin after it was vacated by Mr. and Mrs. W. M. Lowe and their five children. The cabin is at 301 Division Rd.

Beasley, who is employed with Holdorf at the nearby Rebel Ridge Ski area, said they had dinner with the Lowes in the cabin before they moved and were told jokingly that the house was haunted.

"Then the stones started falling," said Beasley, "and I couldn't believe it.

"I thought at first maybe kids were throwing these stones, but then I saw that wasn't possible. The stones were coming straight down from the sky. The stones actually seemed to float down.

One guy was standing outside and one of the stones hit him on the arm but it didn't hurt him. They didn't hit hard.

"One time my car was hit while I was standing right beside it. I had the sunroof open and I heard a plunk. I found the rock on the seat."

Not all ghostly manifestations have physical aspects. In fact, most ghosts restrict themselves to visual phenomena such as apparitions, or to auditory experiences such as footfalls, voices, and miscellaneous noises of human presence, which may be re-creations of noises heard when the ghost was actually in his physical body or at the time of his death. Chills, unexplained cold spots, and drafts are also part of the sensory experiences connected with hauntings. These are by no means created by Dracula-like ghosts to frighten people, but are natural phenomena due to the presence of psychic energy or electromagnetic fields. Whenever a ghost is present in a house, the area of main activity may feel clammy, and even people who have no psychic talents whatever will feel this.

Others complain of shivers and a sense of bodily chill. These experiences are not due to fear or imagination, as one might quickly assume; they are uncontrolled natural reactions to a change in the atmosphere of a room or an entire house. Most important, these changes can be measured by sensitive instruments designed to record temperature fluctuations and electromagnetic disturbances.

In at least one case, a ghostly presence was proved by a Geiger counter in the hands of a totally skeptical engineer. When he approached the area of the room in which the alleged ghost was standing, his intrument indicated radiation in the area. There was no other explanation for this result, and the engineer is a little less sure of his prejudices now.

Ghosts have rarely harmed anyone except through fear on the part of the observer, of his own doing and because of his own ignorance about ghosts. In the few cases in which ghosts have attacked people, it is simply a matter of mistaken identity, where extreme violence at the time of death has left a strong memory in the individual ghost. By and large, it is not dangerous to be a ghost hunter, or to witness phenomena of this kind.

21

Psychic Phenomena at Work

MANY PEOPLE believe that while ESP and other psychic phenomena may have much to tell us about human nature, they have little or no practical importance. To show how far this is from the truth, let us examine three areas where their application can be very important indeed. These are the clinic, where psychic surgery and healing are well documented; criminal investigation, in which clues provided by psychics have helped to "break" baffling cases; and the laboratory, where the study of Kirlian auras is pointing the way to new discoveries about the nature of life.

One of the most controversial subjects in the field of parapsychology is psychic surgery—opinions go all the way from cries of outright fraud to complete belief. So far, nobody has made a completely foolproof investigation to determine the full truth, but I am convinced, from my own research, that the truth lies somewhere in the middle. Certainly, the evidence of cases of genuine psychic surgery is strong.

The late Jose Arigo saw thousands of patients at his clinic in Congohas Do Compo, Brazil. Arigo's guide, Dr. Fritz, was a spirit doctor, who spoke with a marked German accent or in German, which Arigo did not understand. Through the entranced Dr. Fritz, Arigo would prescribe various medicines and treatments for his patients. In some ways the approach resembled that of the late Edgar Cayce. Dr. Andrija Puharich, who spent much time with the late Arigo, is fully convinced of the genuineness of the phenomenon; he himself had a growth removed from his arm by the spirit healer.

Arigo was killed in an auto accident at a time when he finally was getting recognition and protection from a jealous medical establishment that had attempted to jail him several times, and when a special hospital of 160 beds was being built in his honor and for his use. But he, the Brazilian psychic surgeons, the Philippines' Tony Agpaoa, and others less well known, who practice along similar lines, are by no means isolated cases.

In 1967 a British medium and healer, Isa Northage, performed psychic surgery on Scottish bus driver Tommy Hanlon, who suffered from a stomach ulcer. The surgery was witnessed by Hanlon's aunt, a registered nurse named Margaret Sim. Miss Sim closely observed the healer's work. To begin with, the healer massaged the patient's abdomen. Then, before the witness's astonished eyes, Hanlon's stomach wall was opened up—in her words, "opened like a rose"—and the ulcer was taken out in two pieces, with forceps. The healer then closed the wound. There was no trace of a scar. According to a reporter for the *Psychic News*, Hanlon was able to eat normally an hour after the operation.

Isa Northage, of Nottingham, works with a spirit doctor by the name of Dr. Reynolds. Photographs of malignancies were offered in evidence of another successful psychic surgery by Mrs. Northage. These malignancies came from the jaw of Mrs. Sylvia Hudstone, who signed a testimonial to the effect that she was cured completely by Mrs. Northage. During the operation, the patient felt no pain whatever, and the entire proceedings took place in front of a large audience in Mrs. Northage's Spiritualist church at Pinewoods, Nottingham.

Harold Sherman, the "grand old man of psychics," investigated the Filipino "wonder healers," as he calls them, in person. Sherman quoted Filipino investigator Ulpiano Guiang, a lawyer by profession, concerning the most prominent of the Filipino surgeons, Tony Agpaoa:

"As of now, I would evaluate Tony's healings as definitely divine in nature. His towering, bare-hand surgical performances are, in my opinion, above the knowledge and skill of professional medical practitioners. Tony moves freely, modestly, without any extraordinary physical culture; no special skill in any field of athletic or mechanical know-how. He knows little of medical terms, and has had no training, except the experience that has come to him through functioning of this divine power.

"Jealousy of Tony and his work is inevitable. He lives under the threat of being arrested for violation of medical practice at any time, despite the great following that he now has. Yet, I am continuing my investigations as best I can to find out more and more of the truth about Tony's healings."

Charges of fraud persisted, however, against Tony and the several lesser-known Filipino psychic surgeons. B. S. Sharma, a Spiritualist from Delhi, India, observed Filipino psychic surgeons at work in Manila. Sharma claimed that the material taken from the bodies of the patients was in fact "a waxy substance dexterously palmed and skillfully twisted to make it appear as if it is drawn out of the patient's body." However, a team of would-be investigators visited Tony Agpaoa to obtain this body tissue and had it examined in a laboratory. The tissue was then declared, on the opinion of one medical researcher, to be of animal origin, and, again on the testimony of one researcher, the entire field of psychic surgery was called fraudulent and the "wonder healers of the Philippines" were referred to as charlatans and frauds.

Unorthodox healing—that is, healing procedures that are contrary to current medical thinking—includes a number of approaches. First, there is *psychic healing*. This is a form of mediumship in which the healer draws psychic energy from himself, principally from the solar plexus area and the top of the head, and through his hands places this energy on the body of the patient, particularly on the areas in which he has seen or felt the presence of illness. Diagnosis always precedes healing. Psychic healers are able to look at a person and see discolorations in the person's aura or magnetic field. They will then tune in on that area. The psychic healer rarely touches the skin of his patient. His healing takes place at the periphery of the personality where the aura ends and where it is therefore more sensitive, just as nerve endings are more sensitive than the middle parts of nerve tissue.

Physical healers are those who touch the body of the patient and apply a combination of psychic energy and directional massage. The physical healer may or may not manipulate the body of his subject, and his healing is due primarily to the laying on of hands, through which the process of healing takes place. When a priest or, in rare cases, a layman places his hands on a patient in order to heal him, physical healing is involved even though the process may contain spiritual overtones.

For thirty years the work of the late John Myers has been respected in psychical-research circles and somewhat controversially in scientifically oriented and lay circles. The respect was due John Myers, who passed away in May 1972, because of his unusual contributions to the fields of psychic photography and psychic healing.

The cases Myers cured number several hundred and are on record. Interestingly, Myers was even able to heal himself, something very few psychic healers can do. In 1957 he suffered a serious hemorrhage and in the middle of the night was taken to Medical Arts Hospital in New York City. His personal physician, Dr. Karl Fischbach, examined him and discovered a growth over the right kidney. Several cancer experts examined Myers subsequently, and biopsies were taken in the operating room to determine whether the growth was malignant. The unanimous verdict was that an immediate operation was imperative, that any delay might prove fatal.

John Myers steadfastly refused. He informed his doctors that he had no intention of being operated upon but would do for himself what he had often done for others. Myers remained in the hospital for one week for observation. During that time he healed himself, calling upon the divine powers that had helped him so many times before. His cancer disappeared at the end of the week, never to return.

Probably the world's most famous psychic healer is England's Harry Edwards. Edwards heard the call at a spiritualist seance, when he was told by the medium that he should use his gifts for psychic healing. Soon afterward he developed trance mediumship and realized that he had been chosen as an instrument to manifest healing from the spirit world. He is convinced that his spirit guides are Drs. Louis Pasteur and Lord Lister, but he attributes the essence of his powers to God.

From time to time Edwards undertakes mass healing services at London's Albert Hall or Royal Festival Hall, which are large enough to hold several thousand people at one time. He welcomes the spotlight of press, radio, and television, and has an impressive record of actual healings performed in the glare of precisely such spotlights. Crippled individuals step up and explain their affliction. He then makes some passes over them or touches their bodies, at the same time praying for divine assistance. Not infrequently, the healing is instantaneous and the crippled person walks off the platform briskly—cured. At other times, several consultations or healing sessions are necessary.

Healing is the major component of the teaching of the late "sleeping prophet" Edgar Cayce. Many interesting books have been written about him, and his work is being carried on by his sons at the Association for Research and Enlightenment (ARE) in Virginia Beach, Virginia. Cayce, an untutored photographer, went into trance states during which he was able to diagnose the illnesses of people about whom he knew nothing. The language and contents of these diagnoses were such that only a trained medical doctor could have made them. Nevertheless, Edgar Cayce had no such training, nor was there any fraud or delusion involved. Many of the prescriptions given to the thousands of people who sought Cayce's help turned out to be unknown to the orthodox medical fraternity. Nevertheless, all these remedies worked, and much was learned by those willing to profit from the study of Cayce records.

ARE maintains a special clinic at Phoenix, Arizona, where medical doctors function in accordance with Edgar Cayce material. The clinic is housed in a pleasant suburb of Phoenix, with the mountains as a backdrop. It consists of a complex of one-story buildings and a small garden. By no means comparable to a hospital or a large research establishment, the clinic is nevertheless run along orthodox lines in the sense that patients are seen by appointment, medical records are kept, and the entire operation is undertaken with the full approval and blessing of the Arizona medical authorities.

Law enforcement agencies are using ESP more and more often. This does not mean that the courts will openly admit evidence obtained by psychic means. However, it does mean that a psychic may help the authorities solve a crime by leading them to a criminal or missing person—it is then up to the police or other agency to establish the facts by *conventional* means that will stand up in a court of law.

One of the most talented psychics who helped police and the FBI was the late Florence Sternfels, who was also a great psychometrist. She would pick up a trail from such meager clues as an object belonging to the criminal or missing person, or even merely by being asked what had happened to the person. Of course, she had no access to any information about the cases she helped with, nor was she ever told afterward how the cases ended. Police and other law enforcement agencies like to come to psychics for help, but once they've gotten what they came for, they are reluctant to keep the psychics informed of progress they have made as a result of the leads provided. They are even more reluctant to admit that a psychic has helped them.

The Dutch psychic Peter Hurkos, whose help was sought by the Boston police, was able to describe in great detail the killer in the case under investigation: that of the Boston Strangler. Hurkos, who had come to Boston to help the authorities, soon found himself in the middle of a power play between the Boston police and the Massachusetts attorney general. The police had close ties to Boston's Democratic machine, and the attorney general was a Republican.

Hurkos, certain that he had picked the right suspect, returned to New York, his job done. The following morning he was arrested on the charge of impersonating an FBI man several months before; he had allegedly said as much to a gas station attendant and shown him some credentials when the gas station man noticed some rifles in Hurkos's car. The "credentials" were honorary police cards that many grateful police chiefs had given the psychic for his aid. Hurkos, whose English was fragmentary, said something to the effect that he worked with the FBI, which was perfectly true.

Those in the know realized that Hurkos was being framed, and some papers said so immediately. Then the attorney general's office picked up another suspect, who practically matched the first one's appearance, weight, height, and even profession—that of a shoe salesman. Which salesman did the killing? But Hurkos had done his job well. He had pointed out the places where victims had been found and he had described the killer. And what did it bring him for his troubles, beyond a modest fee of one thousand dollars? Only trouble and embarrassment.

The well-known Dutch clairvoyant Gerard Croiset has worked with the police on a number of cases of murder and disappearance. In the United States, Croiset attempted to solve the almost legendary disappearance of Judge Crater, with the help of his biographer, Jack Harrison Pollack. Although Pollack succeeded in adding new material, he was not able to actually find the bones in the spot indicated by him clairvoyantly. However, Croiset was of considerable help in the case of three murdered civil-rights workers. He supplied, again through Jack Pollack, a number of clues and pieces of information as to where the bodies would be found, who the murderers were, and how the crime had been committed, at a time when even the question of whether they were dead had not yet been resolved!

Croiset "sees" in pictures rather than in words or sentences. He need not be present at the scene of a crime to get impressions, but it helps him to hold an object belonging to the person whose fate he is to fathom.

One of the schools that specialize in work with clairvoyants who cooperate with police is the University of Utrecht, Netherlands, where Dr. W. H. C. Tenhaeff is the head of the Parapsychology Institute. Between 1950 and 1960 alone, over forty psychics were studied by the institute, including twenty-six men and twenty-one women.

The University of Utrecht is, in this respect, far ahead of the other schools. In the United States, Dr. Joseph B. Rhine made a brilliant initial effort, but today Duke University's parapsychology laboratory is doing little to advance the research in ESP beyond repeat experiments and very cautious theorizing on the nature of man. There is practically no field work being done outside the laboratory, and no American university is in a position to investigate or work with such brilliant psychics as does Dr. Tenhaeff in Holland.

"Kirlian [pronounced keer-lee-an] photography is actually pretty old," said Dr. Thelma Moss of the Department of Clinical Medicine, UCLA at Los Angeles. "Electrical photography started about one hundred years ago and was considered an interesting curiosity. Nobody ever did very much about it until in the Soviet Union a man was able to learn something about living organisms—leaves, plants, people—by using an electrical current and pulsing it through an object.

"For example, a living leaf is quite green, but as it dies, all its luminescence goes. When photographing it repeatedly over two days, we see that it gradually fades away until we cannot photograph it anymore. It would be very easy for us to say, certainly when something is alive it has a lot more brilliance and luminescence than when it dies.

"The question, of course, is, What is it we are looking at in Kirlian photography? We have mummies that we suspect are four thousand years old. As a layman I would expect a less brilliant emanation than from the hand of a living person. But taking a mummy's hand that is four thousand years old and applying the Kirlian effect to it and seeing it luminesce so brilliantly is mind-blowing. All I can say is this is a fascinating field to explore and maybe in ten years' time we will know what we are doing. Up to this moment in time, nobody knows.

"Through Kirlian photography we've seen fascinating variations in people. You know, we tend to think of ourselves as living, emotional people that interact with other people in love and hate and so on. Though we think of this abstractly, there is such a thing as love and there is such a thing as hate. For example, when we get two loving people to put their hands quite close together, the emanations from the two are just intermingled with each other; whereas if they are registering something like antipathy or dislike for each other, the emanations literally repel each other, and sometimes brilliantly: you can see a barrier of light between them, as if there were something invisible cutting them off from one another.

"These things are awfully difficult to explain in terms of conventional physics."

Dr. Moss added that there are many different words used to describe this effect. Conventional physicists call it a corona discharge, which is an electrical emanation caused by the current and the voltage going through the object. People who are more inclined to the occult or to the mystical call it an aura. They compare it, for example, with famous paintings of saints or of Jesus—there are auras around the heads. These people believe that what we are photographing with this electrical photography is a representation of that, i.e., something invisible to the eye but existing in and around the body. People who are noncommittal call it an emanation or some outpouring of energy. The Russians use a technical term to describe it—bioplasma.

Dr. Moss explained that there may be practical applications for this kind of photography: "We are doing some preliminary work with cancerous and noncancerous rats. Cancerous rats show a visibly different pattern than do healthy rats without tumors. This has led to a more recent technique that detects heat changes in the body, which reveal areas of possible cancers. A series of experiments with the Orthopedic Hospital in Los Angeles has been planned. But only thousands of trials will decide the correlation between pictures."

The emanations do reveal certain kinds of information about communication between people. "We talk frequently about nonverbal communication," Dr. Moss explained. "I think if you look at emanations between people you will see that they are certainly communicating on a nonverbal level. Anger, antagonism, love, and other emotions are distinctly seen. Anxiety, or fear, vividly shows as a violent red blotch in the photograph."

The first hint that there was more to the human body than had previously been thought began back in 1939 in Krasnodar Krai, the capital city of the Kuban region in the south of Russia near the Black Sea. "Where can I get technical equipment repaired?" a research scientist asked a colleague. Soviets at research institutes, labs, and various businesses all agreed: "Go to Semyon Davidovich Kirlian, if you want a repair done properly. He's the best electrician in Krasnodar."

Kirlian was called. While picking up the equipment at the research institute, Kirlian chanced to see a demonstration of a high-frequency instrument for electrotherapy. As the patient received treatment through the electrodes of the machine, Kirlian suddenly noticed a tiny flash of light between the electrodes and the patient's skin. "I wonder if I could photograph that," he mused. "What if I put a photographic plate between the patient's skin and the electrodes?"

But the electrodes were made of glass and the photoplate would be spoiled by exposure to light before the machine could be switched on. He would have to use a metal electrode, which would be dangerous. He considered this a sacrifice for science, and attached the metal electrode to his own hand.

As he switched on the machine, Kirlian felt a stabbing pain in his hand under the metal electrode. It was a severe burn. Three seconds later, the machine was switched off and Kirlian rushed the photoplate into the emulsion. As the picture developed he could make out a strange imprint on it, a kind of luminescence in the shape of the contours of his fingers. "I studied the picture with pain, excitement and hope all combined," said Kirlian. "Did I have a discovery? An invention? It wasn't clear yet."

He discovered that scientists had observed this phenomenon before, but the information had been filed in their research reports and forgotten. He followed his hunch and soon his talent and ingenuity at electronics were at work on this new project. Other techniques of photographing without light—X-ray, infrared, radioactivity—were of no help. He therefore had to devise a whole new process to record on film the luminous energy coming from the human body. And so, with his wife, Valentina, a teacher and journalist, Kirlian invented an entirely new method of photography, which holds some fourteen patents.

But the photographs showed only static images. Soon the Kirlians developed a special optical instrument so that they could directly observe the phenomenon in motion. Kirlian held his hand under the lens and switched on the current. And then a fantastic world of the unseen opened before them.

The hand itself looked like the Milky Way in a starry sky. Against a background of blue and gold, something was taking place in his hand that looked like a fireworks display. Multicolored flares lit up, then sparks, twinkles, flashes. Some lights glowed steadily like Roman candles; others flashed out, then dimmed. Still others sparkled at intervals. In parts of his hand were little dim clouds. Certain glittering flares meandered along sparkling labyrinths like spaceships traveling to other galaxies.

The investigators examined under their high-frequency instrument every conceivable substance—leather, metal, wood, rubber, paper, coins, leaves. The pattern of luminescence was different for every item, but living things had totally different structural details from nonliving things. A metal coin, for instance, showed only a completely even glow all around the edges. But a living leaf was made up of millions of sparkling lights that glowed and glittered like jewels. The flares along its edges were individual and different from one another.

Soon many great Soviet scientists traveled to Krasnodar Krai. There were the famous and the curious. There were members of the Academy of Science as well as ministers of the government. Over some thirteen years, there were hundreds of visitors. Doctors, biophysicists, biochemists, electronics experts, criminology specialists—all appeared at the door of the little one-story, prerevolutionary wooden house on Kirov Street in Krasnodar.

The philosophical implications were even more extraordinary. It seemed that living things had two bodies: the physical body that everyone could see, and a secondary "energy body," which the Kirlians saw in their high-frequency photos. The energy body didn't seem to be only a radiation of the physical body. The physical body appeared to *mirror* what was happening in the energy body. If an imbalance in this energy body of the plant occurred, it indicated illness, and gradually the physical body would reflect this change. Would this be true of human beings too? they wondered. Fatigue, illness, states of mind, thoughts, emotion, all make their distinctive imprint on the pattern of energy that seems to circulate continuously through the human body.

Sheila Ostrander and Lynn Schroeder, in *Psychic Discoveries Behind the Iron Curtain,* summed up the Kirlians' contribution to sci-

ence: "S. D. Kirlian and V. C. Kirlian had created a way for us to
see the unseeable. . . . The Kirlians' 'window on the Unknown'
might revolutionize our entire concept of ourselves and our universe."

Over the years, psychic research has come from the metaphysical
world into the full glare of scientific inquiry. Today it may be establishing links with physical science through the findings of Kirlian
photography, with psychology in studies of out-of-the-body experiences. More people than ever are willing to keep an open mind—an
attitude that will be needed if we are to keep learning from strange
phenomena.

Part Five

MYTHS
and MONSTERS

22

Monsters: Missing and Presumed Nonexistent

WHAT IS a monster?

In modern English we use the word in two very different senses. Commonly it means either "something of remarkable size"—even a monster cabbage or a monster wedding cake—or "a creature of peculiar savagery," which we likewise use hyperbolically more often than literally; that is, children tend to be called little monsters unless they are little angels.

The practical Romans were skeptical, as most Americans are, of mythical monsters. The poet Horace, for example, poked fun at such "unnatural" forms as centaurs and satyrs, never realizing that eyewitness tales of them were more or less truthful. Witnesses had seen Pelasgian Greek tribes who disguised themselves as horses and goats in ritual dances.

Similarly, the Incas and Aztecs, who had never seen horses, much less men on horseback, were horrified by the invading Spaniards' cavalry; they thought that man and horse were one. When a rider fell, the warriors fled in panic, thinking that somehow a monster had split into two creatures. Similar optical illusions might lie at the root of Greek mythology's half-human half-horse Chiron, the centaur.

Such unlikely mythological monsters as the unicorn and the chimera were also proved long afterward to be less fanciful than the Romans had assumed. The unicorn (the one-horned horse) was supposed to have dwelt in faraway regions where, we now know, the one-horned rhinoceros flourished; travelers had seen it, and their descriptions got blurred with the passage of generations.

The word "chimera" is still used in English to mean an illusory fancy or a wild incongruous notion. Most scholars agree that the chimera is "the one creature that seems most likely to have started only in man's imagination," as Daniel Cohen wrote in his blithe book, *A Modern Look at Monsters.*

Yet Homer, who recorded that this monster lived in Asia Minor and breathed flames, suffered no chimerical delusions. Myths always described the chimera identically, and always localized it; it was always composed of a lion, a goat, and a snake, it vomited fire, and it always ravaged the wooded mountains of Lycia.

Classical prose writers portrayed the phenomenon of the chimera with curious accuracy, as it turned out later. Seneca wrote, "In Lycia is a remarkable region. The ground is perforated in many places; a fire plays harmlessly without any injury to growing things." Strabo explained, "The neighborhood is the scene of the fable of the chimera, and at no great distance is Chimaera, a sort of ravine." Servius knew the geographical underpinning of the myth. He specified, "The flames issue from the summit of Mount Chimaera. There are lions in the region under the peak. The middle parts of the hills abound with goats, and the lower with serpents."

There the matter rested until, at the end of the last century, a British admiral named Beaufort anchored off Lycia on hydrographic work. Every night he saw flames on a mountaintop. Natives told him it had always burned. He climbed the mountain and found flames of natural gas spouting from crevices. The ancient Phoenician word *Chamirah* means "burning mountain." I could see how, as Greek settlements spread over Lycia, the meaningless Phoenician names were retained like Indian names in America, and how the tale trickled back to the Greek homelands of a strange mountain called Chamira, from which flames escaped, and then of a monster Chimaera with its lions and goats and snakes, ravaging the mountains of Lycia. And so the story was finally fitted for the manipulation of Greek poets, who made stout Bellerophon kill the chimera, never dreaming they sent him on a quixotic tilt against a burning gas well.

Even in solid fact rather than hazy legend, various large creatures have shown remarkable ability in escaping documentation by scientists. The mountain gorilla, the pygmy hippopotamus, the white-haired snow monkey, and the giant panda were all well known to native villagers, yet they remained unknown to science for decades. The kouprey, a large wild bison, wasn't discovered by Western science until 1936, when the first specimen was identified at the Paris zoo.

This beast roams the open savanna and woodland areas of Cambodia, where the terrain leaves it highly visible. But zoologists, quick as they are to accept fossil evidence, usually deride eyewitness reports of large unclassified creatures that appear only briefly. So who knows what undiscovered giants may come slithering out of the dark someday, just as the terrible giant squid (described in myths as Scylla) arose from ocean depths to confound experts who had always insisted it was merely mythical?

In fact, science now admits that there are creatures all around us that should have been extinct aeons ago. The turtle, the alligator, the horseshoe crab, some snails, a few of the spiders and cockroaches, and all the snow fleas have remained unchanged by evolution over millions of years.

Conversely, we believe that certain large species died off, when there seemed no reason for their deaths, simply because later strata show no traces of them.

But of course all strata aren't available for inspection, and there's no law that says a living species has to leave any fossils at all. The possibility is strong that there are still large, unknown, and truly monstrous creatures alive in the world.

Why not, when a supposedly extinct lungfish from the dim past, a neoceratodus, turned up in an Australian river.

A takahe, a nonflying bird like the dodo, was discovered on the South Island of New Zealand.

The king crab or horseshoe crab, unchanged by evolution for at least two hundred and perhaps five hundred million years, has been found from Maine to the Gulf of Mexico, and in Asian waters.

"These stories all prove the same thing," writes Willy Ley at the end of his *Dawn of Zoology*. "Zoology is not yet a static science and the days of discovery are not yet over."

Indeed they aren't. The discoveries include several animals now alive and well (and in some cases here for fifty million years or more) whose fossils have never been seen at all. Until confronted with the actual creatures zoologists were skeptical and amused by natives' descriptions of them. The reports were filed under "mythical and imaginary creatures."

Which is understandable. Scientists must be skeptics. But sometimes they get dogmatic about their skepticism. Many zoologists still blindly follow the lead of Baron Georges Cuvier, Europe's most respected nineteenth-century pioneer of their profession, who chuckled at the idea of unknown survivors from past ages. He declared firmly,

"There is little hope of discovering new species of large quadrupeds." But his statement was proved wrong even in his own day.

The shy, solitary tapir had been known to Indians and Chinese for centuries, but Europeans refused to believe that any such creature could exist. When Europeans eventually "discovered" this large oddly colored animal with the droopy nose, Cuvier considered their testimony incredible. He finally got interested when a European shot a tapir and brought back its carcass.

The duck-billed platypus undoubtedly lives, and has been living for fifty million years, even though savants were suspicious when they read the first descriptions of it from a roving biologist, David Collins. He claimed to have seen the creature in New South Wales, and went on to report, "The most extraordinary circumstance observed in its structure was its having, instead of the mouth of an animal, the upper and lower mandibles of a duck."

He did not exhaust the remarkable list of peculiarities that distinguish this mixed-up amphibian. He could have added that it lays eggs and then suckles its young by exuding milk from its abdomen; it is equipped not only with webbed feet, enabling it to swim, but also with sharp claws for digging burrows on land, and with poison spurs on its hind ankles for kicking at enemies; it can't see straight ahead, only sideways and upward; it swims under water with its eyes shut, guided by its sensitive bill; in addition to the bill, it possesses horny teeth for crushing the worms it eats; it doesn't mind swallowing large mouthfuls of dirt if its favorite worms are inside.

No wonder zoologists feared a hoax when Collins told them about this nonesuch. Even after the British Museum received a pair of pickled specimens in a cask, some said the things couldn't be genuine. Several decades passed before the museum sent a distinguished scientist, Dr. W. H. Caldwell, to New South Wales to try to find a platypus egg, if any existed. He found two. Eventually the Bronx Zoo in New York obtained two live specimens and kept them in good health for ten years. Scientists don't know why platypus fossils, to say nothing of live specimens, were never found through a century of intensive exploration and research.

Since 1858 ichthyologists had been collecting samples of sea-bottom deposits from all the oceans. They had also been studying rock strata on land that had been sea bottom in bygone epochs. In 1938, after eighty years of painstaking work, they were certain that no large creatures unknown to them had swum the seas during the last three hundred million years—because a satisfactory cross-section of fossils from all those millennia had been cataloged and classified.

They knew all about coelacanths, they thought.

Coelacanths (pronounced see-la-kanths) were the commonest small fish in the Devonian era, when the only life on earth existed under water. Using their stumpy fins, these fish stirred up the mud of sea floors in search of prey.

But they became "extinct" about the time the dinosaurs did, roughly seventy million years ago. Not one fossil of a coelacanth appeared in any later rocks. And of course no live coelacanths had ever been reported. So there was no chance whatever that the species had hidden out somewhere and continued to exist. Thus spake the experts.

Then came the discovery of December 22, 1938. A fishing boat was trawling off the southern coast of Africa. When it hauled in its nets and dumped the catch on the deck, the three-ton pile of fish included something the crew had never seen before.

It was a fish more than five feet long, weighing as much as a small man, and still very much alive, flinging itself about furiously and snapping at anyone within reach. Its bulging blue eyes were so savagely alert that nobody dared to come too close. It seemed able to breathe air. Not until three hours later did it grow feeble, and finally gasp its last.

It was an unusually ugly fish—rough-hided and heavily scaled, with a powerful jaw and padded fins that stuck out like rudimentary legs. When the trawler returned to port, the manager of the fishing company telephoned the inquisitive curator of the local museum, Ms. Courtenay-Latimer, who often acquired specimens from the trawler captains. She hurried to the waterfront.

She had never seen such a fish before, nor could she find it pictured in any reference book. She made a sketch and sent it to Professor J. L. B. Smith, a well-known authority on fish from Rhodes University College in South Africa, who unfortunately was on vacation. The letter didn't reach him for ten days.

Professor Smith, who has discovered and named more than a hundred species of fish, looked at Ms. Courtenay-Latimer's sketch, and felt the tingling excitement of a man on the verge of a sensational discovery. Her sketch showed a coelacanth—a sheer impossibility, since this fish was known only from fossil impressions on rocks laid down millions of years ago. Moreover, the ancient coelacanths were five to eight inches long, not five feet.

The fish had been mounted because it had begun to decompose in the heat of the South African summer, but the skin, skull, and part of the spine had been saved. When Professor Smith got to the museum and confirmed his identification, he showed his appreciation of her work by naming the fish Latimeria.

Newspapers all over the world front-paged the discovery. Here was a specimen of an incredibly ancient group of fish. In fact, it belonged to the group that first crawled out of the sea onto the land. The first amphibians developed from coelacanths, so the coelacanth is a rather direct descendant of our own fishy ancestors. How had it perpetuated itself through the ages, without ever coming to the attention of scientists?

Of course Professor Smith wanted more specimens—fresh-caught ones with internal organs intact. He tried to organize a search expedition, but in September 1939 the outbreak of World War II torpedoed his plans. Nevertheless, he offered a reward of four hundred dollars for another coelacanth, and distributed a descriptive leaflet in English, French, and Portuguese. After the war he and his wife tramped the coast, sailing on fishing boats, distributing the leaflets, and personally impressing on local authorities the importance of the search.

The professor's patience was rewarded after almost fourteen years of waiting. On Christmas Eve 1952 the Smiths got a cable from an English sea captain, Eric Hunt, who ran a trading schooner in the Indian Ocean: HAVE COELACANTH IN COMORO ISLANDS. COME AND FETCH IT.

The Comoro Islands were two thousand miles away, north of Madagascar, and the professor did not have enough money to charter a plane. Knowing that the fish would decay quickly, he appealed to South Africa's prime minister, Dr. Daniel F. Malan, who put a military seaplane at his disposal.

Hoping that Captain Hunt had not made a mistake, Professor Smith flew to the schooner. "To my unspeakable relief," he said later, "the fish turned out to be a true coelacanth. When I knelt down to look at it lying on its bed of cotton wool, I'm not ashamed to say that I wept."

The fish had been caught off Anjouan Island by a native fisherman, Ahmed Hussein, who had been amazed to pull in a thrashing hundred-pound catch of a kind he had never seen before. Even after being landed, it fought so malevolently that he had to club it again and again. Hussein was unaware of the quest for the coelacanth, and didn't realize that he was damaging the brain of one of the most amazing specimens ever brought up from the sea.

In fact, it was only by luck that this second coelacanth became available for scientific study at all. Hussein hauled it off to market. There it was, about to be chopped up for food, when a native school-teacher recognized it as the kind of fish shown in Professor Smith's leaflet. To qualify for the reward, he sent the carcass by bearers twenty-five miles on mountain trails across the island to Captain Hunt, who had given him a leaflet. With great presence of mind, the captain salted the fish and wired for the professor, who arrived just in time to ensure its proper preservation with copious injections of Formalin.

The fish's brain was ruined by the clubbing, and Captain Hunt's crewmen had badly lacerated the body when they incised it for salting. Nevertheless, the body was otherwise well preserved. The skeleton was almost an exact replica—enlarged about ninefold—of primeval coelacanths. Professor Smith would spend the next two years in research on its various parts, including the rudimentary lung-bladder that had kept it alive so long after it was removed from the sea.

The following September a third coelacanth appeared and to date more than twenty-five of these supposedly extinct fish have been caught, ranging in weight from 43 to 209 pounds. Some came from depths of 2,000 feet, all from deeper than 650. Professor Jacques Millot of the Paris Museum of Natural History and other experts who have studied them say that the angle of their fins varied by as much as 180 degrees between one fish and another, and even sometimes between the two sides of the same fish.

This astounding feature may shed new light on how fins evolved into arms and legs as fish began spending part of their time ashore. But so far it sheds scant light on how this one species survived the extinction—or disappearance, at least—of so many other forms of life at the time the dinosaurs vanished.

Professor Millot credits the coelacanths' survival to "their great anatomical robustness and the great depth of their habitat." He adds that their reappearance "has been rightly described as 'the most amazing event of the century in the realm of natural history.'"

23

The Reign of Monsters

It is astonishing that fossils exist at all. Living tissue, even bone, decays quickly. It becomes powder and returns to the soil, unless it happens to be buried immediately in some soft material that later becomes rock-hard. Occasionally this does happen; and the earth's long life has allowed it to keep happening. Molds or imprints of billions of organisms great and small are preserved in the ancient rocks that encrust the earth.

Consequently, long ago men began finding strange shapes embedded in sedimentary rocks such as limestone and sandstone. These discoveries took many forms—impressions of weird plants and fishes, pressed into the solid rock as if into soft clay, and hard stony objects that look like little statues of living organisms.

The ancients invented fantastic explanations for these. But paleontologists read the riddle, and learned where to find many more remains of primeval life forms. From caves, bogs, swamps, stream beds, ice sheets, tar pits, and other places where decay had been prevented, they dug out fossils of creatures that lived millions upon millions of years ago. Footprints, crawl tracks, and sometimes the delicate tracery of feathers and fins were perfectly cast in solid, enduring stone. Occasionally minerals had seeped into the cells of organic matter, transmuting it to rock (petrifying it) without changing its shape.

And so from the abyss of time and from the depths of the earth, the dead came to life. Animals were resurrected from stone, and an astonishing parade of long-dead things marched before man's eyes. But the parade did not include monsters, because the first paleontologists found few monster-size fossils. The age-old talk of such creatures must have arisen from man's own imagination, they decided.

Pieces of fossilized dinosaur bone were dug from Connecticut sandstone in 1820. They caused some curiosity among American scientists, but no one believed that these fossils were valid evidence of monsters. The bone fragments found their way into drawers of museum storerooms and were quietly forgotten.

Soon afterward, a few oversized, unclassified teeth and bones came to light in England. Experts admitted, after long debate, that these might be evidence that some bulky creature unknown to science had existed at some time in the dim past. A country doctor named Gideon Mantell, whose hobby was paleontology, kept digging near the site of the discovery, and found more teeth of the same kind.

He took them to London's great museum of natural history, the Hunterian. He and the chief curator went around the collections for hours comparing the teeth with those of every animal, likely or unlikely, to which they might belong. At the end of a discouraging afternoon, Mantell was about to leave when the curator asked, as an afterthought, if he would like to see a model of a strange little lizard from South America, recently mounted for the museum. The two were glumly contemplating it when Mantell bent forward excitedly. In the lizard's mouth he saw miniature replicas of the big teeth he still carried in his hand.

The lizard was an iguana. Mantell named his hypothetical monster "iguanodont" (genus *Iguanodon*) to show its kinship. From other fossilized bones in the region, he and other scientists (including the great Thomas Huxley) gradually conjured up an image of a truly awesome reptile between thirty and sixty feet long. It was shaped like a lizard but walked upright, to judge from its thigh bones. It seemed to date back many millions of years, because its remains were found in very old rock strata.

The whole notion of a colossal lizard seemed fantastic—but was confirmed in 1878 when a group of iguanodonts emerged from a coal mine in Belgium. They were a thousand feet underground, not in coal but in a fissure filled with marl (muddy limestone). Evidently no less than thirty-one full-grown iguanodonts had tumbled into a deep ravine. It was literally filled for hundreds of feet with the stranded monsters. They had been unable to escape and were entombed in mud as the fissure filled with flood water. The Belgian authorities stopped the coal digging, hewed out thousands of blocks of marl-encapsulated bone, and entrusted a paleontologist named Louis

Dollo, still only in his mid-twenties, with reconstructing the skeletons. He devoted the rest of his life to the task. By the turn of the century the Brussels Royal Museum's group display of monsters was a worldwide sensation. The resurrected iguanodonts proved to paleontology that undiscovered apparitions might have been real.

Not only iguanodonts but other enormous unknowns evidently had roamed the land and sea during early tropical ages, long before the first glaciers. In 1868 an unidentified thigh bone as tall as a man was found in the rocks north of Oxford. Excited by the possibility of unearthing vast shapes totally new to science, diggers began to pry into all the earth's strata as vast burial grounds of the past.

Some strata did contain evidence of supposedly mythical monsters; museum reconstructions of dinosaurs reminded people of dragons. Beginning in the 1870s, two decades of intense activity exhumed the remains of an astounding assortment of colossal beasts. Sir Richard Owen coined the word *dinosaur*, from the Greek for "terrible reptile" or "terrible lizard."

The scientific community divided the vast span of geologic time in which the fossil record seems clear into eras called the Paleozoic (Greek for the time of "ancient animals"), the Mesozoic, or time of "intermediate animals," and Cenozoic, when the "recent animals," the birds and mammals, began contesting for dominant places on land. Manlike fossils appear only in rocks laid down during the last two million years.

If modern methods of geologic dating are correct, the Paleozoic era covered perhaps 350 million years. It was divided into ages, beginning with the Cambrian age (named for an area in Wales where these strata were first uncovered). In this time shelled sea creatures developed their casing and armor and became the most complex life form of their age.

The rise of the monsters began no less than three hundred million years ago—maybe four hundred million—sometime during the Paleozoic era's closing age, the Devonian (from "Devonshire").

They evolved from underwater predecessors—as did all living things. Even now there is no land animal, nor land plant, that does not owe its structure to slow deviations from a water-inhabiting ancestor. There are today certain kinds of lungfish in Africa and Australia that show the evolutionary process by which other creatures worked their way out of the water. During the rainy season these fish swim in rivers, breathing through gills like other fish. But their rivers dry up in summer. Then the lungfish burrow into the mud flats and stop using their gills. They keep alive by gulping air and swallowing it—pressing it down into a bladder that was previously a gas-filled organ enabling the fish to remain buoyant. Now the bladder doubles as a rudimentary lung.

A newt in a pond breathes similarly. These creatures are still in transit—moving ever so slowly across a threshold where countless long-ago forerunners of the higher vertebrated animals made their first gasping ventures into the dreaded atmosphere.

Some of the primitive amphibians had strange shapes, suggestive of certain hideous creatures imagined by myth-makers long afterward. There was one that looked like a monstrous salamander with a head bigger than a crocodile's. There was something that would be called a mesosaur—a spike-toothed, gap-jawed, tail-lashing sea lizard. There were popeyed, grinning things like serpents with horned heads. Some creatures had grotesque raised nostrils and raised eyes so that they could breathe and see while keeping their bodies under water. Some, if they lost a tail or a leg, could grow a new one.

It took a few million years for reptiles to develop from amphibians. One of the most innovative qualities of the reptiles was that their eggs had tough cases and could be deposited anywhere, and their young did not need to pass through a gill-breathing, water-dwelling stage before crawling onto land. So at last they were freed from bondage to the swamps—and they went on to conquer both lowland and upland. More active than any previous land animals—and more formidable—they filled every niche open to medium-size and large creatures.

Reptiles ushered in the teeming, tumultuous Mesozoic era, during which they were the supreme lords of the earth for roughly 120 million years. Throughout the Mesozoic era, reptiles flowered in a great variety of shapes.

Until lately, man thought of dinosaurs as cumbersome, dim-witted animals that blundered their way to extinction. "Dinosaur" became the term for anything clumsy, overgrown, ineffective, and obsolete—as though dinosaurs were a laughable example of evolutionary failure, a proof that a small brain in a big body made survival impossible. But science has learned much more about dinosaurs in the past decade.

The picture as it still looked in 1968 was reported by Robert T. Bakker of Yale University:

Generally, paleontologists have assumed that in the everyday details of life, dinosaurs were merely overgrown alligators or lizards. Crocodilians and lizards spend much time in inactivity, sunning themselves, and compared to modern mammals, most modern reptiles are slow and sluggish. Hence, the usual reconstruction of a dinosaur as a mountain of scaly flesh which moved around only slowly and infrequently.

But there was double-think in this view. Man, supposedly well adapted and brainy, has been here only two million years, most of that time in mean condition, and is already in danger of extinction if someone presses the wrong button. Dinosaurs were known to have ruled the earth, after snatching it from the mammals, for sixty times longer than man. Nobody tried to reconcile their "evolutionary failure" with their inconceivably long reign.

Another aspect of double-think was that dinosaurs admittedly had to be devourers and destroyers in order to find and seize the huge meals they needed—and were simultaneously assumed to be lazy, cold-blooded sunbathers like the lizards, crocodiles, and snakes we know. (A python, for example, needs only one good meal a year.) Bakker and others began to ask whether the species might have been misnamed. Maybe dinosaurs were not basically reptilian in some respects. "Analysis of energy flow indicates," Bakker wrote, "that dinosaur energy budgets were like those of large mammals, not elephant-size lizards."

We know that lizards eat little food and have little energy. They run for only short spurts before flopping on their bellies to rest in the sun, and cannot remain on their legs for more than a tenth of their "active" life. But mammals and birds need and have enormous energy. A rat burns ten times more fuel for its size than an alligator; hummingbird muscle uses five hundred times more oxygen than frog muscle of the same size. Because of their energy, mammals and birds stand and walk (or run) for almost all their waking life. Their limbs are under the body to assist them in ambulating. The body of a lizard or an alligator is slung between its legs.

Most dinosaurs did walk and run, not waddle or crawl. Their tracks and trails proved this (some fossilized tracks show just the claws of the front feet touching the ground, like a kangaroo). So did their bones. A solid leg bone means a sluggish creature or one of aquatic habits. Most dinosaurs had hollow bones, indicating that they were active land animals, and disproportionately long hind legs, implying that they walked erect with the short front legs dangling.

Such finds made ever clearer the fact that dinosaurs were not inherently doomed to extinction; they adjusted to their world in marvelous ways and developed all the qualities needed for long survival. Researchers began to suspect, therefore, that many kinds of dinosaurs were warm-blooded rather than cold-blooded like reptiles.

The test of a good theory is whether it fits together previously unrelated and inexplicable facts. Warmbloodedness not only explains the stance of the dinosaurs but also helps us understand why they grew so huge. The dinosaurs, unlike furry mammals whose insulation helps them stay warm, lost heat through their leathery skins. The dinosaur needed its large size, and could never have kept its temperature high enough had it been much smaller than it was. This is why no fossils of midget dinosaurs were ever found.

When certain saurians (suborders of reptiles) instinctively learned, somewhere in the long Mesozoic era, to generate heat from their own muscles and tissues instead of relying on the sun, as lizards and snakes do, it triggered the rather sudden emergence of dinosaurs from the swamps. Like the fish breathing air, and the amphibian laying shelled eggs out of water, the reptile raising and stabilizing its own internal temperature was a colossal step in the history of life—a major break with heredity.

No sizable mammals could survive around dinosaurs, because the monsters could run their choice of prey on the ground, or rear up to pluck it out of trees. For at least a million centuries—and perhaps a third longer than that—dinosaurs dominated the world as completely as men would later. The earth shook to their tread. The waters sprayed and spouted when they dived. All other beasts fled or hid when they approached.

But then something happened to them.

"The most hardheaded, blasé geologist is apt to get excited when he becomes involved in a discussion of the extinction of the dinosaurs," said one of the world's leading experts on dinosaurs, Dr. Edwin H. Colbert of the American Museum of Natural History. "The problem is one to which we return time and again, even though very little is known about it."

H. G. Wells in his *Outline of History* called it "beyond all question the most striking revolution in the whole history of the earth before the coming of mankind."

Cambridge's noted zoology lecturer Barry Cox wrote, "To a vertebrate paleontologist, this dramatic event is the most fascinating problem of all."

There is not even one single survivor of ancient dinosaurs that we can see, after a century of searching everywhere for their bones, eggs, and tracks.

The record of the rocks seems clear. We know that in rocks from all parts of the world there is a lower layer dating back seventy million years in which dinosaur fossils were found by the thousands. Right up to the top strata of the Mesozoic era, we find all these reptilian species still flourishing unchallenged. There is no sign that they were dwindling in numbers or in health. We can find no traces of enemies or competitors.

Then the record is broken. The next rock layer, many feet thick, contains few fossils of any kind. We don't know how long a time this represents. Many pages may be missing here—pages destroyed, perhaps in some worldwide cataclysm.

When next we find abundant traces of the earth's animals and plants, in the Cenozoic era, all the multitude and diversity of the dinosaurs have vanished. Monster reptiles of every kind are gone. For the most part they apparently left no descendants. Only the crocodiles and turtles and tortoises carry on in noteworthy number. Of the giant lizards a few small relatives remain; the largest are the twelve-foot, dragonlike monitor lizards that live only on the island of Komodo in the East Indies.

Instead of dinosaurs, a new kind of life inherited an earth that may have seemed empty. The new layers are crowded with bones of mammal predecessors of the elephant, the camel, the bison, and the horse. The Cenozoic era became the time of mammals.

The fossil record reveals many species that gradually died out when a competing group became more numerous or better adapted. But this wasn't the case with dinosaurs. They had no competitors, and their decline wasn't gradual; it was sudden and complete.

Just how long did their annihilation take? Some experts guess five million years, which in geologic time is rapid. Other authorities estimate less than one million years. However, M. N. Bramlette of the Scripps Institute of Oceanography estimates that most Mesozoic sea life disappeared in a few thousand years. Still others think that nearly all kinds of life went into steep decline within a few days.

To judge from what we can see today, world conditions changed sharply (a marked drop in temperatures, for instance), ending what we call the Mesozoic era. Monstrous reptiles died off quickly, together with much—if not most—sea life and plant life. Then later, after a time of trouble for all living things, the environment grew milder again, whereupon mammals developed and spread to fill the vacant world.

But things aren't always what they seem. Biologists, like other scientists, are beginning to understand the treacherous nature of circumstantial evidence.

Even Professor Adrian Desmond, the most eloquent expounder of the theory that climatic change killed the dinosaurs, has his doubts.

"If cold was responsible for the dinosaurs' annihilation, why did they not persist in the warm equatorial regions?" he asked. "Is it conceivable that the entire globe was subjected to intense cold? It seems unlikely. Even though America and Eurasia were in middle and high latitudes, South America and Africa were more favorably situated climatically."

There are other conjectures.

One is that the earth heated up, rather than cooled, and withered most plant life for a time—which could have starved the herbivorous dinosaurs, and indirectly doomed the carnivorous ones that hunted them. Moreover, sex glands of male reptiles are sensitive to heat; they become sterile when the temperature climbs too high.

Another guess is that the dinosaurs exterminated themselves. Roy Chapman Andrews, the famous naturalist, wrote:

When the Central Asiatic Expedition, under my leadership, discovered the first dinosaur eggs in the Gobi Desert, we found the skeleton of a small toothless dinosaur right on top of the nest of eggs. There is every reason to believe that it lived by sucking the eggs of other dinosaurs. Possibly it was in the very act of digging up these eggs when it was overwhelmed by a sandstorm. This group of toothless dinosaurs may have become so numerous that they actually exterminated their relatives by eating the eggs as fast as they were laid.

A related theory is that as small furry animals began to evolve in greater numbers, they too raided dinosaur nests for eggs, finally eating them out of existence. Andrews found skeletons of little mammals near where he discovered the eggs. But of course these theories don't account for the simultaneous disappearance of seagoing dinosaurs and other animals and plants.

Some scientists surmise that a global epidemic either wrecked the ecology (perhaps turning many plants poisonous, blighting others, and tainting all the seas, leading to widespread starvation) or directly attacked vast numbers of animals. Perhaps a virulent microbe or virus or insect parasite got a foothold and spread quickly.

A great sickness might not kill all monsters, but might rob them of their vital drive, and leave them indifferent to problems of survival. Or it might affect the eggs they laid. Today's birds react to stress by laying eggs with thinner shells; dinosaurs might have reacted the same way.

In recent years Bonn University's Institute of Paleontology has been studying late Mesozoic dinosaur eggshells in different strata, and computing trends. Working with thousands of fragments from successive rock layers in the Pyrenées, a grim sequence has been discovered. Eggs from the older layers are thick-shelled. But in higher (and thus younger) strata, the shells get ever thinner until the last ones are only two-fifths as thick as normal. They must have been pitifully fragile.

The institute found many whole eggs; these obviously had survived the ordeal of being laid but failed to hatch. Perhaps they didn't contain as much calcium as the embryos required. With their hormonal systems hopelessly out of kilter, the dinosaurs would have reacted by laying weak-shelled eggs, and so sealed the fate of their own young.

In 1973 the institute team confirmed its earlier findings when it located eight more eggs from the last layer of Mesozoic rocks. Through an electron microscope the eggshells could be seen to be so poor that the embryos couldn't possibly have absorbed enough calcium to build complete bodies. The majestic dinosaurs, overlords of the long Mesozoic era, went out not with a bang but a whimper—the whimper of the unborn as they perished entombed in tiny prisons.

At least this is how some dinosaurs went out.

Did all dinosaurs die out the same way, even those species that lived under water?

And are they really extinct, every one of the many varieties? Since we can only guess at the kind of fate that overtook them, can we be sure that none survived?

I do know this: deep down in the perpetual night of the ocean depths, right now and for a long time past, strange things have been happening. I know because I went and looked at evidence, talked with people who had made inexplicable discoveries.

24

Dark Worlds Below

THE THREE FISHERMEN felt their rowboat rise out of the water. The night was dark, and nothing was visible to them on the surface of Loch Ness.

For an instant their boat lifted; then it tilted, almost capsized, but righted itself as it slid back down onto the water. The men, scrambling to stay upright, thought they glimpsed something sleek and dark submerging ahead of them; it seemed about the size and shape of an overturned whaleboat. Presumably this was what had pushed their craft up out of the water.

To this day, the fishermen are sure that they encountered the Loch Ness Monster. They may have been closer to it than anyone else has ever been. But, being close-mouthed Scots and knowing the dour skepticism of their countrymen, they have never reported their experiences to the Loch Ness Phenomena Investigation Bureau, which sifted evidence from 1962 to 1972. What would be the use? They have no real evidence, and not even their own firsthand accounts are valid, for they can't give any precise description of what they saw and felt under them. Moreover, their story is unsubstantiated.

But since 1970 there have been more than a hundred other circumstantial reports—usually with some sort of corroboration—of sightings in the loch or on its shores. In this century the witnesses have included priests, lawyers, gamekeepers, naval officers, and policemen. One eyewitness was a member of Parliament. Another, who commanded a women's auxiliary army-corps unit in Britain during World War II, was the sister-in-law of former Prime Minister

Harold Macmillan. Another was a Nobel Prize-winning chemist, Dr. Richard Synge. Still another was a member of the Royal Observer Corps who studied, through binoculars, a large unidentified beast in the loch.

"There is no doubt in my mind, and never was, that there was something odd in Loch Ness," a local man wrote several years ago. "It was common knowledge; but people did not like being laughed at and you only heard little bits as you got to know the people. . . . After the first war, I had a talk with a priest with whom I had been friends for years, and he frankly said that the story had been going around to his knowledge since before the monastery was built."

It was in 1933 that the Loch Ness mystery first hit front pages all around the world. This might never have happened had not a road been built that year around the once-lonely loch, as part of a new Inverness–Glasgow highway.

Dynamite blasted the rocky slopes, pitching boulders and timbers into the dark waters, sending shock waves and echoes rumbling through the glen and the loch. The commotion may have stirred up whatever dwelt there. Or perhaps the highway itself brought more outsiders who talked. And certainly the clearing away of forest and scrubland gave an almost unobstructed view.

For whatever reason, in 1933 there were no less than fifty-two separate reports by individuals or groups who were willing to go on record as having seen something big and unidentifiable in the loch.

Many of these accounts merely spoke of a mysterious commotion in the water, or a great boiling without visible cause, a wake like that of a motorboat sweeping across the surface—a narrow, widening track of heaving waves and froth—when no boat was in sight.

As I delved back through news accounts of the carnival of monster seekers in 1933, I wondered whether E. G. Boulenger, director of the aquarium at the London Zoo, might have been partly right when he wrote that the Loch Ness Monster was "worthy of consideration if only because it presents a striking example of mass hallucination. . . . [We] should find no difficulty in understanding how the animal, once being said to have been seen by a few persons, should have shortly after revealed itself to many more."

Autosuggestion—a preconceived idea planted by the desire to see something—may indeed have been at work among hundreds of people who reported strange sights at the loch since 1933. But the photograph taken by Hugh Gray was not imagination.

On Sunday, November 12, 1933, Gray took his usual after-church walk near his house on the shore at Foyers. The path led along a cliff about thirty feet high. Suddenly he saw the calm water below him heave up, and a rounded back and tail burst into sight.

Nothing he could identify as a head appeared. He was carrying his camera, as was usual on his walks, and managed to snap five pictures during the few moments the animal thrashed on the surface. Because of the spray it was throwing up, Gray didn't think his snapshots would show much. He was a long-time employee of an aluminum works at Foyers, and he said later, "I was afraid of the chaff which the workmen and others would shower upon me." So he left the film in a drawer. He knew that hoaxes had been attempted in other years. Once a dark object on the loch turned out to be a string of barrels with a make-believe animal's head attached. Another time, tracks ascribed to a monster were found to have been made by pranksters with a stuffed hippopotamus foot.

Weeks later, Gray's brother took the film to Inverness to be developed. Only one of the five shots came out. It showed a long writhing body, shrouded in spray, as Gray had described to his brother. Kodak technicians examined the negative and certified that it hadn't been doctored. Newspapers published the photo; zoologists at first could think of nothing to say.

Pressed for comments, Professor Graham Kerr of Glasgow University called the picture "unconvincing." J. R. Norman of the British Museum of Natural History said, "It does not appear to me to be the picture of any living thing. My personal opinion is that it shows a rotting tree-trunk which rises to the loch surface when gas has generated in its cells."

After a hiatus in widespread monster watching for almost a quarter century, interest began to pick up again in the late 1950s. Mrs. Constance Whyte, having spent eight years collecting accounts from people living near the loch, published her book *More Than a Legend* in 1957.

An educated woman with an interest in Scottish history, she was the wife of the manager of the Caledonian Canal, so she knew a lot about Loch Ness. She herself never saw any monsters, despite living nearby for twenty-three years—but, she wrote, "a book had to be written. Friends of mine had been subjected to ridicule and contempt, and I felt it was time to counteract the flippant and frivolous attitude of the media."

Her book contained several photographs taken in the 1950s. One seemed to show three humps in a line; their contours made it unlikely that all were part of the same animal. Another picture showed what might be a hump, and, slightly ahead of it, a smaller protuberance that might be a half-submerged head. If the two were connected, measurements indicated that this monster could be fifty feet long.

By piling up masses of consistent evidence, Mrs. Whyte moved a few technical researchers to investigate. Dr. Denys W. Tucker, a zoology lecturer at Oxford University and a scientific officer at the British Museum, told his students that the Loch Ness phenomena were worth probing. Thirty students from Oxford and Cambridge planned a month-long expedition during summer vacation—whereupon the British Museum dismissed Dr. Tucker from the post he had held for eleven years. The students took to the field with cameras and an echo sounder, but they got little except one brief sighting of a ten-foot hump and some unusual echo traces.

Meanwhile, a monster buff named Timothy K. Dinsdale, an aeronautical engineer, took a statistical approach. He broke down the details of hundreds of sightings, and put together a picture of the monster or monsters as reported by the preponderance of evidence: small head, long neck, large body with varying humps, four flippers, and short rounded tail. Wording that recurred in many reports made astonishing reading:

"Humps churning through the water leaving a foaming trail. . . . Head about the same width as neck, mouth twelve to eighteen inches wide. . . . Looked like an elephant's back, twelve feet long. . . . Wake like a torpedo. . . . Speed at least ten miles an hour."

Pondering the composite description, Dinsdale and Tucker and Mrs. Whyte all thought they saw the dim outline of a fantastic possibility—the ghost of a great dinosaur.

To judge from skeletal remains of those giant aquatic reptiles called plesiosaurs, found in both salt- and fresh-water deposits around Great Britain, they were very much like the description of today's denizens of Loch Ness.

Adapted for life in the open sea, plesiosaurs grew to thirty feet long. They had a barrel-shaped body with a hefty tail, four paddle-like limbs, a long slender neck, and a tiny head with a large mouth and pointed teeth. They ate fish, of course—which meant that they probably had to be fast swimmers to catch their prey. And they sometimes lurched onto land.

The Loch Ness Monster remains a mystery. No one yet has obtained *the* definitive picture; success depends largely on luck. Until a living specimen is captured for scientific study, we can only guess what kind of monstrous things have been living for so long in Loch Ness.

Loch Ness tales are not unique. They are merely better known than similar tales about a number of other deep mountain waters.

"There is a tradition in the Great Glen of Scotland and indeed in Inverness generally that a strange beast inhabits the depth of Loch Oich," travel writer Alister MacGregor noted in 1937. "Although many of the natives and not a few travellers profess to have seen it, the beast has been overshadowed by its more famous neighbor in Loch Ness."

At Loch Lochy I saw a photograph in a family album, supposedly of a monster surfacing. It wasn't clear enough to prove anything—just a dark, irregular mass surrounded by foam. But I also heard that in 1930, before the Loch Ness Monster became famous, a man living in Lochyside warned his wife not to wash their linen in Loch Lochy anymore. When she pressed for a reason, he said that he had seen something ghastly and to his mind unnatural in the loch. He never said what it was.

South of Clifden in the province of Connacht in Ireland, there is a wide bogland in which a stream connects a chain of three small lakes with the sea. In 1954 Mrs. Georgina Carberry, with three companions, was fishing in Lough Fadda, the largest of these lakes. They saw "a black object which moved slowly, showing two humps. The head was about three feet out of water, in a long curve." It swung around and dived.

Another time, Pat Walsh was in his boat on that same lake when a head and neck emerged from the water near him. He rowed ashore at top speed.

And there was the time when a family of seven watched "a black animal about twelve feet long," with the usual hump and neck, swimming around the lake. On a fourth occasion a local shepherd saw a monster on land near the lake.

The Scandinavians have taken lake monsters for granted since time immemorial. In 1765 a British correspondent noted in *The Gentleman's Magazine*, "The people of Stockholm report that a great dragon named Necker infests the neighboring lake." Because of this, he wrote, they tried to dissuade the visiting bishop of Avranches from swimming in Lake Mälaren one hot summer day. The doughty

French cleric would not be deterred. The Swedes "were greatly surprised when they saw him return."

Although Bishop Huet didn't believe in Necker, I think descendants of that monster may still dwell in some of Sweden's ninety-six thousand icy lakes. There are well-authenticated reports from a lake called Storsjön in the heart of the country. The lake covers 176 square miles—a small lake for Sweden—and is frozen in winter. But it is nearly nine hundred feet deep, and its middle levels are probably no colder than Loch Ness.

On the island of Forso in this lake, there is an ancient stone carved with a runic inscription and a sketch of a beast with a long neck and flippers. At the lake's east shore is the town of Östersund, where the local museum contains harpoons and some enormous spring traps. These were used in 1894, records show, in a sustained effort to catch the monster. The curator, in a letter to Tim Dinsdale, said that the creature seemed most active from 1820 to 1898, when "mostly trustworthy persons" saw it twenty-two times.

Many Indian tribes of North America believed in monsters or powerful spirits that lived in deep lakes. The belief is still strong among some surviving tribes in Canada, where the country is sprinkled with hundreds of thousands of lakes like puddles drying in the sun between the Great Lakes and the Arctic Circle.

Among the largest of these is Lake Okanagan in British Columbia, an area that was cut off from the sea only recently, geologically speaking. It covers about 127 square miles. The Shuswap Indians who live in the Okanagan Valley are in awe of it. Until a century ago they made ritual offers of chickens and puppies to Naitaka, the monster spirit who, they believed, dwelt in its dark forbidding depths. They gave the name of Monster's Island to a small rocky isle in the center of Okanagan.

The prehistoric Shuswaps in that area left crude drawings of Naitaka cut in stone, showing the familiar long neck and flippers. Their dread didn't fade away with the advent of white settlers, because sometimes these newcomers too saw apparitions in the lake. In 1854 two horses, swimming across the lake beside their owner in a canoe, suddenly sank. The half-breed canoeist claimed that they had been pulled down by some strong force.

Decades later, a settler named John McDougal saw the same thing happen to a pair of his horses, towing him across in a boat. If he had not cut them loose, he said, his boat would have been pulled down.

Ever since man first went into the sea by ship, sailors have returned with tales of strange behemoths plying the waves. Ships change through the ages, but the sea doesn't. During man's comparatively brief dominance of the land, how many strange beasts have been dragged from the sea or found on beaches, and either dumped back because they had no commercial value or boiled down because they had?

In that unchanging environment, amphibious mammals or reptiles might easily maintain themselves undetected at great depths for millions of years. We already know that creatures from that age are still with us—crocodiles and turtles, for example.

Despite all these possibilities, the hypothetical sea monsters have probably ignited more controversy—some of it wonderfully acrimonious—than any other creature ever reported on land or sea.

No matter how much it is scoffed at, dismissed as an invention of promoters, or explained away as seaweed and driftwood and processions of dolphins, the great unknown of the seas has been reported by so many reliable witnesses that it must be accepted as reality. Anyone scanning the data with at least a half-open mind will conclude that we cannot write off sea monsters for lack of credible evidence, even though the evidence consists mainly of eyewitness testimony.

It can be shown that a well-defined if nightmarish sea creature has been reported from somewhere almost every year since 1800. There is a remarkable similarity among many reports made by isolated people who never heard of one another or their reports.

It is a striking fact that most people who admit to having seen sea monsters are Englishmen, Scots, or Scandinavians, or particularly New Englanders and Newfoundlanders—seafaring people even if well educated. These regional folk are known as conservative, skeptical, and grimly honest. Why are these virtually the only groups that lay claim to sightings of sea monsters? Possibly because they are the kind of people who can stand up to the ridicule that comes from affirming an unpopular belief.

Let's consider the earliest sighting that is well authenticated by a formidable body of witnesses: the famous events of August 1817, when Massachusetts saw a "sea serpent."

One day during that month the skipper of a coastal vessel, forced into Gloucester by bad weather, made a strange statement in the town auction room. At the harbor entrance, he said gravely, he and his crew had seen an awful beast that looked like a serpent—sixty feet long. He was laughed out of the room.

But in two weeks Gloucester was agog. Everyone seemed to have caught sight of the creature at one moment or another. Crowds swarmed to the waterfront to see it. The Linnaean Society of New England, meeting in Boston on August 18, quickly organized a committee to gather evidence. Few committees can have been charged with a more fascinating task, and the Bostonians set to work with zest and diligence.

They wrote immediately to the Gloucester justice of the peace, asking him to take sworn depositions from those who saw the "strange sea animal." Their letter stressed that he should question the witnesses as soon as possible after sightings, when their memories were fresh, and should concentrate on people who hadn't yet widely discussed what they had seen. Twenty-five detailed questions, designed to elicit optimum information with minimum verbiage, were set forth.

Eight depositions were taken—two from ship captains, three from merchants, and one each from a carpenter, a sailor, and the seventeen-year-old son of a prominent citizen. The committee also interviewed three witnesses in Boston, and in Plymouth a Captain Elkanah Finney, who had forthrightly announced a similar sighting two years before.

These cautiously chosen witnesses' stories added up to an account of fitful appearances by the monster during thirteen consecutive days, occasionally for an hour at a time. Sometimes it lazed extended on the surface; sometimes it cavorted like a porpoise; but mostly it pursued and feasted upon schools of herring, which fishermen had been catching in record numbers that year. When it swam with its head high, the head and long neck turned watchfully from side to side, while the body proper rose in a series of humps or bunches, similar to the vertical movement of a caterpillar. It basked for one whole afternoon off Windmill Point, under the scrutiny of two hundred fascinated spectators.

If the "Great American Sea Serpent," as European zoologists jocularly called it, was a mass hallucination, it certainly didn't hypnotize everyone into immobility. On August 20, we are told, an unwarned ship from the fishing banks sailed into the bay, saw the monster, and fled in horror. Traps and nets were set out to capture the creature, but it eluded them gracefully. A local marksman named Matthew Gaffney fired a bullet at it from a distance of thirty feet, he claimed; someone in another boat said the distance was more like thirty yards. At any rate, the creature submerged and reappeared out of range.

There were a few later reports of sightings in Long Island Sound off Connecticut, and then silence. Two summers later, the leviathan, or one like it, turned up in the waters of Nahant, then a seashore retreat for Boston's elite. Hundreds watched it disport in July and early August. Certain Cabots wrote first-person narratives for Boston newspapers. On August 26 the creature was back at Gloucester again. There it confronted a U.S. Navy surveying ship, which took optical measurements and calculated its length at a whopping one hundred feet.

Subsequent appearances thereabouts, if any, were not recorded. Backed now by science, naval authority, and the Cabots, the Boston newspapers considered the monster no longer newsworthy. After all, as one editor wrote, "The existence of this fabulous animal is now proven beyond all chance of doubt."

His verdict was too optimistic. Disbelief persisted everywhere but in New England. A story, perhaps apocryphal, relates that a ship's crew sighted a sea serpent and sent word to the captain in his cabin. He refused to go on deck to look at it, explaining later, "Had I said I had seen the sea serpent, I should have been considered a warranted liar my life after."

Between 1940 and 1966 at least seventy-five sea monsters were reported. Many naturalists have begun to regard these great unknowns with respect. But the press—and consequently the public—seems to have lost interest. Shore dwellers and ships' passengers no longer mention seeing large strange organisms at sea. Nowadays, if someone observes what he once might have called a sea serpent or monster, he assumes that somehow he is mistaken, or he simply keeps quiet to avoid ridicule.

My opinion is that the ancient fables have become a fascinating fact. Out there in the wastes of sea, giants sometimes slither up out of the darkness onto the surface. Nonviewers may insist on their nonexistence, but I hold with the Encyclopaedia Britannica, which now says of sea monsters:

"When all these and similar possibilities have been explored, there still remain a number of independent and apparently credible stories which are not satisfactorily explained."

25

Monsters Who Walk Like Men

ON DECEMBER 14, 1972, two Americans and two Sherpa tribesmen left a base camp in northeastern Nepal for a journey into high fastnesses near the vaguely defined borders of Nepal and Sikkim.

They had been in the Himalayas for almost two years, with the Arun Valley Wildlife Expedition. The Arun, one of the world's deepest river valleys, slashes between the huge masses of Everest and Kanchenjunga, respectively the highest and third highest mountains on earth. Few people have been there, so it remains a primordial paradise for wildlife.

The Americans were Edward W. Cronin, Jr., an eminent zoologist and chief scientist of the Arun expedition, and Dr. Howard Emery, the expedition physician. The purpose of their trip was to reconnoiter the unknown shoulders of a mountain called Kongmaa La, and to "investigate the winter conditions of the ecosystem."

Cronin and Emery enjoyed the first few days of their journey, hiking slowly up through the winter-bare forests, breathing deep lungfuls of the diamond air, watching the glories that unfolded at each turn along the slopes. A spicy breeze refreshed them occasionally as they clambered over gigantic hogbacks in hot sunshine.

But later, at a height of nine or ten thousand feet, they went over a cruel pass in a storm when driven snow dust filled their eyes and ears and nostrils; they crossed a snowy tableland in cold moonlight, and watched the dawn flare windy-red above stark blue as

Mount Makalu took the first sunlight. Their porters had turned back the day before because of the cold, but the four men pressed on, searching for a place to make camp on the great slanting fold of rock connecting to Kongmaa La.

They found a half-acre basin in the ridge at about twelve thousand feet. The flat snowfield was unmarked by prints, so the men thought they were completely alone when they pitched their two light tents there on the afternoon of December 17.

The wind had died and the sun was warm, permitting them to loll in comfort on the ridge and gaze into the enormous pit below. Far down, they could see the Barun River on the north and the Kasuwa River on the south like molten silver under the sun. They ate dinner around an open fire, then crawled into their sleeping bags soon after dark. No wind stirred. No noises broke the silence.

During the night they had a visitor, though they did not know it then.

Something walked up the steep north slope on two oddly shaped flat feet (nine inches long, almost five inches wide). It turned and approached their camp slowly, stalked directly between the tents, and finally strode away down the south slope.

Shortly before sunup Dr. Emery emerged from his tent, and let out a shout when he saw the footprints of the nocturnal wanderer. Seizing cameras, he and Cronin made a full photographic record before the sun touched any of the tracks. Later they made plaster casts.

Most of the footprints were perfectly clear, because the snow was firm and crystalline, smoothed by the winds of previous days. A few of the stranger's tracks merged with their own earlier ones, but elsewhere in the flat area he left some fifteen distinct prints, both left and right feet, showing every detail of spatulate toes, wide round heels, and flat soles.

Emery and Cronin began to follow these prints down the south slope, but there the sun had melted most of the snow, and they lost the track on the bare rock and scrub. They did not dare descend far in their search, because the slope fell away at a perilously steep angle.

As a professional biologist with ample experience in the Himalayas, Cronin was sure that the prints were not made by "any known, normal mammal," as he cautiously expressed it. He was not ready to say what had made the footprints.

The two Sherpas had no doubts. At the first glance, they identified the tracks as "yeti footprints." *Yeti* is a Tibetan word that means "dweller among the high rocks." But the word is now current in

A wall painting of St. Claire, combining imagery from Catholicism with African elements in a mixture unique to Haiti.

Night-long drumming and dancing are part of the excitement of Vodun.

A necklace or torque wrought in gold by Celtic tribesmen of Northern Europe. These were given by chieftains to their servants and kinsmen, and symbolized a magical link as well as faith and loyalty.

Seashells used to hold pigments for an early artist-magician. The techniques for extracting and preparing paints were as jealously guarded as any secret potion.

Eyes have always appeared in decorative designs. Are they intended to be more than ornamental—perhaps to ward off evil influences as well?

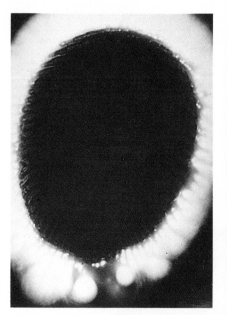
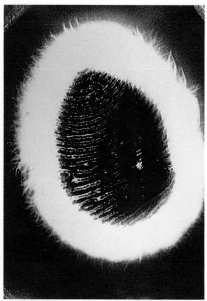

This is the aura of a subject immediately after hypnotic trance.

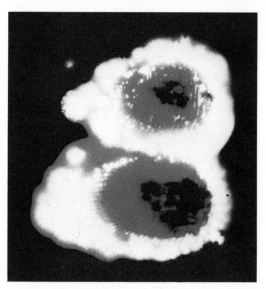

The aura of a subject under the influence of marijuana.

A portrait of Vlad IV Tepes, the Rumanian ruler whose cruelty made him one source for the story of Dracula.

Transylvania, the "land beyond the forests," remote and mysterious even today.

In 1976, an expedition jointly sponsored by MIT, the
National Geographic Society, and *The New York Times* spent months
in an inconclusive search for the Loch Ness monster.

Above and on facing page—Artists' renderings based on
descriptions of the Loch Ness monster and on what
is known of prehistoric sea monsters.

An aerial view of the wild country where most of
the sightings of Bigfoot (the "Sasquatch" of
Indian folktales) have taken place.

A frame from the most convincing film footage of Bigfoot.
Some scientists believe that the creature's way of moving
in this film, as well as measurements of its footprints,
rule out the possibility of a hoax. *Patterson/Gimlin. 67*

English, and our recent dictionaries define it simply as "the Abominable Snowman."

The Snowman, of course, is that mysterious mountain monster for whom so many intrepid Himalayan climbers have searched since 1889, when a British explorer, Major L. A. Waddell, found some sets of unidentifiable, oversized, five-toed footprints in the snows at seventeen thousand feet in Sikkim. Another report came out of Sikkim in 1914, from a British Forestry officer who saw similar footprints.

In 1942 a Polish soldier crossing the Himalayan foothills after escaping from a Russian prison camp was confronted by two manlike, hairy giants a hundred yards away, shambling toward him as if they were curious. He outran them. Afterward he estimated that they were about eight feet tall.

In 1948 two Norwegians announced that they had followed a set of yeti tracks, and had overtaken an awesome primate that they boldly tried to lasso. Their attempt failed. The Norwegians came down the mountain with a description of something that walked upright on thick legs, had no tail, and looked more like a human than an ape or bear.

But the scientific world, as we have already seen, is cool to reports of uncataloged creatures. "The yeti does not exist," proclaimed one notable scientist who visited the Himalayas. He based this dictum solely on his discovery that the sun could melt known animal tracks into a semblance of the many photos and plaster casts of alleged yeti tracks.

To him (and to eminent colleagues), this was enough to discredit all the references to yetis in Chinese manuscripts dating back to 200 B.C., as well as a total of forty reports by Westerners since 1832, when the British resident at the Court of Nepal—B. H. Hodgson, an esteemed naturalist of his day—published an account of a yeti seen on a collecting expedition. These witnesses included famous mountaineers like Eric Shipton, Colonel John Hunt, and Sir Edmund Hillary. However detailed and circumstantial their reports, however painstaking their reproductions of the tracks, scientific authorities at home always impugned their reliability: "They may be excellent mountain climbers but how qualified are they to examine spoor or interpret visual sightings? Were they tired or in some way affected by the high altitude? . . . Large unidentifiable footprints could belong to almost any of the wild animals that live in the Himalaya range. At certain gaits, bears place the hind foot partly over the imprint of the forefoot. This makes a very large imprint that looks as if it might be the print of a monster. . . . The Himalayan langur, a monkey with a long tail, often leaves prints that might be mistaken for those of a large unknown animal. . . . Markings thought to be left by the Abominable Snowman could very well have been caused by stones or lumps of snow falling from higher regions and bouncing across the slopes."

But Cronin, by matching his own footprints made on the night of December 17 with those he made the next morning, proved to his own satisfaction that all prints near the camp had remained unaltered by any night wind or early-morning sunshine.

He knew all about bear tracks, langur tracks, and other prints nominated as "explanations" for yeti tracks. He wrote in his report:

> During the expedition we devoted special efforts to examining all large mammal prints made in snow.
>
> We noted possible variations produced by different snow conditions, terrain, and activities of the animal (i.e., running, walking, etc.); a photographic record was made. We feel we can eliminate any possibility that the prints are referable to a local animal. . . .
>
> Based on this experience, I believe there is a creature alive today in the Himalayas which is creating a valid zoological mystery. . . . The evidence points to a new form of bipedal primate.

Or perhaps a very old form, he thought.

Paleontologists deduce from fossils that nine million years ago a breed of mighty apes, which they have christened *Gigantopithecus*, roamed widely in southern Asia. These hulking creatures flourished for at least eight and a half million years—so eventually they were contemporaries of man's ancestor, *Homo erectus*.

Suppose the huge apes came in contact with evolving man in India or thereabouts. The two species probably would have competed. A basic principle of population biology, the competitive-exclusion principle, lays down the rule that whenever two similar forms of life arise in the same area, one will flee or become extinct as it loses the competition for food and other necessities.

A half-million years ago, man had already learned about fire. He had learned to make tools of stone, bone, and wood. Thus his rivals, the giant apes, would have been at a fatal disadvantage. Perhaps they died out. Paleontologists think so, because their fossils have not been found in later strata. But what if *Gigantopithecus* simply moved out of man's way? What if he wandered up into the Himalayas? Might he not survive there, right up to the present?

White settlers in the Pacific Northwest of the United States built up their own legend of Bigfoot, a seldom-seen biped that sometimes left tracks of five-toed feet in lonely forest glades. The tracks were like a human's but much bigger—occasionally as long as seventeen inches, as wide as five. Bigfoot seemed to take commensurately long strides, up to fifty-six inches.

In The Dalles, in the heart of "Bigfoot country" on the Columbia River, is the Bigfoot Information Center, presided over by Peter Byrne.

Byrne was a wartime Royal Air Force pilot who later made a name in Nepal as an explorer, big-game hunter, and tracker. He often guided sportsmen on tiger hunts. But when he realized that the tiger was on the verge of extinction he changed to hunting with cameras instead of guns; he established Asia's first tiger sanctuary, and helped found the International Wildlife Conservation Society.

Byrne prowled the Himalayas on four expeditions in search of the Snowman, and photographed its footprints. When he studied yeti lore he saw the possibility that *Gigantopithecus* had not only fled into the Himalayas but had also wandered across the Bering Strait when it was dry land, and then had spread through American mountains—perhaps evolving into something bigger than their Asian cousins.

If any of these wild ape-men still survived, he yearned to find them. Tom Slick, a Texas oil millionaire and monster buff who had subsidized Byrne's last two yeti hunts, offered to back him in seeking Bigfoot. So Byrne went to Oregon in 1960. He and Slick found twelve sets of Bigfoot prints that year. Not a glimpse did they get, however, of Bigfoot.

Then Slick died in an air crash. Byrne went back to Nepal, but the Bigfoot bug was in his blood. In 1970 he returned to resume the search, this time pumping $100,000 of his own money into it. In 1972 he devised a way to make the quest almost self-supporting.

He put a fifty-five-foot mobile home on a permanent site at West Sixth Street in The Dalles, and mounted a collection of exhibits—photos and casts of the huge tracks, maps that pinpointed tracks and ninety-four "credible sightings," brochures that told details about them, and newspaper and magazine features. By charging admission to this exhibition hall, Byrne kept enough cash flowing in to pay most of his search and investigation expenses.

His Bigfoot Information Center began to receive letters, phone calls, and personal visits from people who said they had seen a giant or its tracks. Byrne gave everyone careful hearings, kept names confidential whenever asked to do so, and pursued every lead that sounded promising.

At fifty, he was the picturesque prototype of a rugged adventurer: tall and lean, handsome in an urbane patrician style, frosting at the temples.

When I asked him what made him keep searching for Bigfoot, he replied, "I've been asked that many times. I'm the only man who has made a profession of this extraordinary search. For most of my life I've been a hunter, professionally and emotionally—and for a hunter this is perhaps the ultimate hunt. The quarry is the rarest of all big game—a possibly highly intelligent, highly mobile, partially nocturnal creature with a habitat of a hundred thousand square miles in some of the most difficult country in the world."

"How far are we from finding this thing?"

"It has eluded me now for six years," he said. "We make progress, but it's very slow. If we had proper funding I think we could find one within two years. But we're not doing the kind of research we should, through lack of support. It may take many years.

"But I'm not discouraged. Every time my phone rings there's the thrill of knowing this call could lead to the quarry. Every time we race to the scene of a new sighting, we know we may find one of the giant primates around the bend."

He recalled that the chase had covered more than 150,000 miles. He had roped his way up cliffs, followed bloodhounds through snowstorms, and gotten himself shipwrecked and stranded for eight days in the British Columbian straits. Night after night he still crouched in high-altitude lookout posts, often in subzero cold, peering through a snooperscope on loan from the army.

It was obvious that he was driven by almost obsessive determination to confront this hairy enigma, even if it took a lifetime—almost like Ahab and the white whale. I said, "Hunters are itching to bring back a dead Bigfoot. Why has nobody gotten a shot at one?"

"Shooting one of these creatures would be criminal," he replied angrily. "There aren't many alive—maybe as few as two hundred. They're nearly human, or anyhow less vicious than our kind. In all our investigations there's no report of aggression. Think of all the fishermen, hikers, snowmobilers, and young children who go into these dense forests. If Bigfoot were dangerous I think there would be attacks, abductions, disappearances—and there is no such record during the past two centuries. So we look on them as benign, inoffensive creatures. We hope to get an executive order to protect them from hunters."

Byrne's files listed five sightings worth checking in 1971, three in 1972, and four each in 1973, 1974, and 1975. Altogether he has compiled details of ninety-four reported sightings that seem believable. As for tracks, the files bulge with listings, including one trail of three thousand prints that Byrne photographed in the dust of a lonely logging road in the Cascade Range.

And so out of the ancient darkness of superstition and myth the hairy man-monsters have come to our times. Recent reports of them haven't been confined to the United States and Canada. In the forests of Indonesia there is rumored to be a manlike monster called an *orang pendek*. Jesuit missionaries to South America have brought back stories of shadowy giants seen striding through certain jungle areas.

The southern Florida swamplands are said to harbor big-footed things known locally as "skunk-apes," but their tracks indicate two species: the larger one has three toes and a violent nature, while the smaller five-toed kind is shy and harmless. Plaster casts of both types of tracks have been taken, and more than a hundred sightings of skunk-apes have been reported in the Everglades during the past five years. Any swamp could have been a good refuge for a "Bigfoot" or "Snowman" who strayed south from the mountains a million years ago. The vastness of forest areas, too, would have offered countless hiding places. Until modern times our continent had a thin *Homo sapiens* population. After the end of the Ice Age there were few large predators on the continent to disturb this shy giant.

Therefore, it may be that *Gigantopithecus*, or something like him, still lives—free as the beasts, and an affront to science—in various secluded pockets of wilderness across the world.

As long as the giant is at large and uncataloged, revealing himself but briefly, he remains a powerful and shimmering symbol of gaps in our knowledge—a mystifying reminder that the human family tree may still have branches we haven't seen.

26

Dracula, Vampires,
and Werewolves

CENTRAL EUROPEAN CITIES tend to be drab, heavy, and gloomy. The massive masonry of the medieval piles weighs one down; windows are slits in ancient walls three feet thick, and iron-barred. These are cities of ogres' towers, of dungeons and dormers, casements and embrasures, posterns and wickets and drawbridges.

Romania had a history of stern repression by its own Iron Guard before it became the most regimented and conventional of all communist nations. But its capital, Bucharest, struck me when I visited it as happier and more relaxed, at least on the surface, than Prague or Budapest. It had fewer great gray fortress buildings. It had music and wine and good food.

Strolling through the city, I felt faint tingles of the romantic and the occult. The broad main thoroughfare, Victory Street, was almost deserted. I wandered down ancient, tired alleys with tiny tired houses built into the masonry of quays and bridges—houses that leaned to one another for support.

I had come to Romania to track down possible origins of those ghoulish monsters called vampires and werewolves—but already I had learned more than I really wanted to know.

I had seen a disagreeably lifelike oil portrait of Prince Vlad IV, nicknamed Tepes, which means "the impaler." He had a narrow, sallow face. I had read the facts about his terrible reign from 1455 to 1462, during which he maintained order in his realm by putting thousands of people to death in picturesque ways.

Vlad enjoyed the process of eliminating potential enemies, critics, insufficiently flattering courtiers, and others who caught his attention unfavorably. Sometimes he scheduled impalements or other tortures as dinnertable entertainment. A German writer described him walking under conscious victims who "twisted around and twitched like frogs. After that he spoke: 'Oh, what great gracefulness they show!' "

Vlad was known by another name too: Dracula.

Yes, there was an authentic historical Dracula who made the fictional one in Bram Stoker's novel *Dracula* seem tame. He was Vlad IV of Walachia.

The old Roman word *draco* meant "dragon," and *dracula* meant "dragon's son." Latin words were familiar to Romanians in medieval times and still are, even though the Romanians speak Slavonic languages; Romanians claim to be descendants of the conquering Romans who ruled there for two centuries, calling the province Dacia; hence, they insist on calling their nation Romania rather than Roumania or Rumania, as it used to be spelled in atlases and encyclopedias.

Why was Tepes, or Vlad IV, known as the Dragon's Son? Because his father, Vlad III, joined the Order of the Dragon, a central European league of kings and princes who hated the Turks' oppressive Ottoman Empire. Vlad III put the dragon emblem on his coins and battle flags, and was pleased to call himself Dracul, i.e. the Dragon. His son was equally proud of the Dracula sobriquet.

Wholesale, hideous executions earned the Walachian prince his tag "Tepes." According to the Bishop of Erlau, probably the most scholarly and reliable chronicler of that century, Vlad IV authorized the cold-blooded slaughter of approximately one hundred thousand people, including twenty thousand in Brasov on one day. Many were Turks or other outlanders, but he apparently killed at least a tenth of Walachia's population. Impalement was his hobby. He used it in various forms, depending on age, rank, sex, or special circumstances. He usually arrayed the screaming victims neatly in various geometric patterns—often concentric circles around a town, so that townspeople would be aware of them on all sides.

Even so, Dracula occasionally grew bored with skewering people, and tried other divertissements. Once he was annoyed by beggars, so he rounded up all the mendicants in Walachia, set out a feast for them, then burned them alive at their banquet table. Once a delegation of Turkish diplomats wore fezzes in accordance with their native custom while salaaming to Dracula; as a way of showing that he preferred visitors to be bareheaded, the prince ordered the fezzes nailed to their heads.

Vlad was surely gruesome, but none of the chronicles hinted that he might have been a vampire. I wanted to follow Vlad's track, see the places where he had thrived, and try to ascertain the connection, if any, between him and the Transylvanian vampire legends.

Not only the novel *Dracula* but the stage play and the movies about Count Dracula were laid in Transylvania. The name means "land beyond the forest," and the land really does exist. It was part of Hungary for almost a thousand years, until Romania seized it after the First World War. And it was still rich in folklore of were-wolves and vampires.

In the dawn as I set out from Bucharest, all the mountain line to the north was black and hard like the end of the known world. All through that long day, as I drove up through one village after another, I found that belief in ghouls grew stronger the deeper I went into the mountains. That a person may die and yet live on as a corpse, may sustain himself by sucking blood from the living, seemed to be a fact of life to the rural folk—a fact attested to by parents and grandparents, by wise men and priests.

Long ago, superstitions about vampires were nearly universal. I knew that folklorists had found legends of blood-sucking human monsters in chronicles of ancient Babylon, in India and China, in large stretches of the primitive world. Vampires were cited among the dead in Egyptian scrolls. Montague Summers, an eccentric but eminent English scholar, unearthed so many vampire stories that he devoted two large volumes to them. He said that the ancient Greeks believed in vampires, and that the barbarians picked up this part of Greek culture and spread it over Europe.

Vampires, in ancient belief, were malign spirits who left their graves at night in a kind of somnambulistic trance, prowling in search of stray people whose throats they might pierce with their teeth in order to drink their blood. The corpse of a vampire was always fresh, and could only be put to rest by impalement or burning.

Medieval European chronicles were full of accounts of villagers exhuming corpses and staking them down to keep them in their graves. Not until 1823 did England outlaw the practice of pounding stakes through the hearts of suicide victims. (Suicide victims were considered especially prone to vampirism, as were criminals, bastards, and excommunicated people.)

According to Eastern Orthodox doctrine, the body of anyone

bound by a curse will not be received by the earth, will not decay, cannot fully die and find peace. This teaching of the Church naturally fostered the vampire legend in Orthodox countries such as Romania.

In fact, the legend fits in smoothly with other beliefs that date back to pagan times. Romanian villagers like to think their dead are still among them in the parks and streets; life after death is much like life in this sphere, they say. Most of their village cemeteries look like chaotic harbors with gravestones tipped up every which way like sinking ships. This is because the markers settle into the soft soil. But to villagers it is proof that bodies climb from graves.

However, no one thinks that the walking dead are necessarily vampires thirsting for blood. I heard the word *moroi* ("undead") much more often than the harsher epithets *strigoi, vukodlak,* and *brukolak,* which all mean undead blood-drinkers and troublemakers, i.e. vampires. In such an atmosphere the legends grew, and ultimately endowed Dracula with a strange immortality through Stoker's 1897 novel.

I drove a lonely road up through the Borgo Pass. Across the pass, according to legend, stood Castle Bistrita, where Vlad the Impaler lived for five years. But after his death the Germanic peasants nearby sacked the castle, perhaps in retaliation for Vlad's atrocities against their kinsmen farther south in Brasov and Sibiu. Not a trace remained of the castle. Nor did I sense any hint of the miasma that I sometimes noticed in old places where evil had been strong.

A hundred miles to the southwest I found the forbidding Hunedoara Castle, dating back to 1260. This was the stronghold of the Hunyadi family, where Dracula was received as an honored guest in 1452. It looked much like the description of Castle Dracula in Stoker's novel, with massive walls, battlements, towers, and drawbridge. In its impressive Hall of Knights a portrait of Dracula once hung among its gleaming marble columns. But again I felt no aura, no vibrations.

Wherever I went in the mountains, I asked if the Dragon's Son was considered a vampire. He had been bloodthirsty enough. Was the famous fictional Dracula modeled after this prince?

Answers always were negative. No evidence indicated that peasants of the fifteenth century, or the twentieth, had any notion that their Dracula was a vampire—or that he became one after he was captured and beheaded by Turkish troops.

Bram Stoker wrote *Dracula* without ever visiting Romania, although he did study its folklore and that of other countries where vampires were feared. His book was an artful grab bag of Middle European tales from the Dark Ages. In the aristocratic figure of Count Dracula, that deadly ghoul and accursed victim who could not die, Stoker created the first and only vampire to grip the Western imagination, the greatest fictional monster of the day. Did anything more than imagination and myth go into the creation?

It's hard to see how there could be any factual basis for the vampire legends. The superstition is so absurd physically that it seems to be an example of what Karl Marx called "the idiocy of rural life." How could vampires get in and out of their graves? How could they stay alive by imbibing blood?

I came across Charles Fort's book *Wild Talents*, in which he cited four disconcertingly relevant news stories.

In 1867 the captain of a fishing smack outside Boston noticed that two crewmen were missing, and went below to seek them. In the dark hold he lifted his lantern and saw one of the men in the arms of a Portuguese sailor who called himself James Brown. Brown's mouth was on the man's throat, sucking blood. The body of the other missing sailor lay nearby; it apparently was bloodless. "Brown" was tried, convicted, and sentenced to be hanged, but an incredulous President Andrew Johnson commuted his sentence to life imprisonment. Twenty-five years later this putative vampire was transferred from the Ohio Penitentiary to the National Asylum in Washington, D.C., and his story was retold in the Brooklyn *Eagle* for November 4, 1892.

On September 17, 1910, a child was found dead in a field near the town of Galazanna, Portugal. The body seemed drained of blood, though very little blood was visible around it. The child had last been seen with a man named Salvarrey. He was arrested, and confessed that he was a vampire.

On December 29, 1913, a woman known as "Scotch Dolly" was found battered and dead in her room at 18 Etham Street, S.E., London. An inquest rendered a verdict of death from heart failure and shock. However, on one of her legs were thirty-eight little double wounds. The coroner asked, "Have you ever had a similar case?" The doctor who performed the autopsy answered, "No, not exactly like this."

In 1929 the people of Düsseldorf, Germany, were terrified by the similar murders of eight women and a man. Peter Kurten was caught and tried for the killings. He made no defense, but described himself as a vampire. The New York *Sun* for April 14, 1931, tells the story in detail.

These cases sound to us like grotesqueries. They might have sounded otherwise to various ethnic groups that often ate human flesh and drank human fluids, ostensibly in order to enhance their own strength, courage, or vitality. Chinese peasants sucked the bile of bandits they executed, according to Sir James Frazer, one of the greatest authorities on the folklore of magic, in *The Golden Bough*. Celebes headhunters quaffed the blood and spooned up the brains of their victims; the Nauras Indians of New Granada munched the hearts of captured Spaniards; the Italones of the Philippines ate enemies' entrails raw; the notorious Zulu chief Matuana drank the gall of thirty captured rival chieftains; mountain tribes in southeast Africa held initiation rites in which they fed young men a paste made of human testicles, human livers, ground-up human ears, and skin. When Sir Charles McCarthy was killed by the Ashantis in 1824, it was said that their chiefs shared morsels of his heart and flesh at a victory banquet.

Such dietary quirks might be highly nutritious, for all we know. Human blood contains carbohydrates, vitamins, minerals, and amino acids. Other organs contain other health-giving substances. We customarily cut these organs out of various animals and devour them.

So perhaps a human "vampire" needn't be thought so unnatural after all. Local customs and individual preferences could make quite a difference.

What of that other supposedly occult aberration, lycanthropy?

Belief in it used to be widespread, and I was told that countless families in the Balkans still believe in it.

Among modern psychiatrists, "lycanthropy" is a standard term for a peculiarly hideous state of mind. Dictionaries and encyclopedias define it in such terms as these: "A kind of insanity in which the patient imagines himself to be a wolf or other wild beast, and exhibits the tastes, voice, etc. of that animal. . . . A morbid desire for eating human flesh appears in certain extreme cases."

This syndrome could explain the cults of leopard-men and hyenamen with their bestial dances and rituals in African jungles—and not always just in the jungles. According to William Seabrook, a quiet little native clerk in one African town donned a panther skin with sharp claws and killed a girl. The clerk was totally convinced that he became a panther periodically, and told Seabrook that he much preferred panther ways to human ways.

Seabrook also reported a case of a Russian immigrant woman in New York, meditating on the mystical *I Ching*'s hexagram 49, which is associated with animal fur. She imagined that she was a wolf in the snow, and began to bay, then slaver. Someone tried to bring her out of the dream or trance, whereupon she sprang at his throat.

Folklore of many lands agreed that men might become animals. Pausanius recorded that Arcadian Greece was troubled by citizens who actually ran with the wolves. Ovid told of Lycaon, king of Arcadia, who served "hash of human flesh" at his banquet tables, and eventually turned into a wolf. Legend said that Vereticus, king of Wales, was transformed into a wolf by the punitory Saint Patrick. (For a long time afterward, Wales paid a yearly tribute of three hundred wolves to British kings.) The Neuri people assumed the shape of wolves at will, according to Herodotus.

Sir James Frazer tells in *The Golden Bough* of presumed tiger-men, cat-men, and even crocodile-men in China, adding that each part of the world had its own variations on this theme. To most believers the transformation into a beast wasn't just a figure of speech or a delusion; it was an actual metamorphosis.

During Dracula's lifetime an international council of theologians, convoked by King Sigismund of Hungary and Bohemia, studied certain data and decided that the werewolf was a real and present danger. It had the appetite of a wolf, they agreed, and prowled at night, devouring children, ravishing flocks and herds, sometimes digging up corpses. But they couldn't agree on whether it took the visible shape of the beast it emulated.

There was and is less uncertainty about werewolves among the unschooled. Their tales seem to prove the physical reality of such incarnations. One element is common to most of these tales: someone attacked by a werewolf manages to wound it; later a man or woman is found with a very similar wound, and confesses to being the werewolf. What could be more damning? they ask.

Frazer tells of a huntsman in Auvergne who hacked off the paw of a wolf that charged him, and kept the paw as a trophy. Later he found it to be a woman's hand, with a ring on the finger, which was recognized as belonging to a well-known lady of the town. The lady, nursing a wrist from which the hand had been severed, confessed to lycanthropy, and was burned.

Such stories were hardly credible. Assuming them to be false, could we then say that a metamorphosed human beast is only a figment of superstition? According to psychologists, it comes out of our subconscious, which seems to be populated with monsters that appear normal enough and yet terrify us. They are the predators we occasionally meet in a nightmare, huge animals with slavering jaws and glowing eyes who nonetheless act peacefully for the time being. The theory is that such dream creatures are projections of whatever traits are most threatening in ourselves—dangerous desires disguised as beasts.

Transformation of man into beast would seem physically impossible. One might also think it physically impossible for a fish to turn into a frog.

But that is what the tadpole does. Its gills disappear; its tail goes back into its body somehow; legs sprout; the tiny mouth widens fantastically; the eyes bulge larger and larger. Finally we see a rebuilt creature, sitting on dry land instead of swimming under water.

Even in maturity, a few animals make seemingly magical changes that humans apparently cannot. A starfish produces new parts if some are damaged. Newts and salamanders promptly replace lost limbs by growing new ones. Lizards regrow lost tails.

You can't always predict what a creature will turn into, even if you know the life history of others that look virtually identical. An underwater larva indistinguishable from many others will grow legs, then eat and digest its own skin, and emerge as a red salamander. Tiny plankton organisms in the ocean turn into jellyfish, snails, clams, octopuses, oysters, or sea urchins, as dictated by the blueprints of their genes.

Can genes go awry in higher species? Well, we know what cancer can do. We know of two-headed calves, of human freaks in sideshows, of baby monstrosities born to mothers who took thalidomide.

But can genes go so far awry as to turn a man into a wolf or hyena or a blood-sucking parasite? Surely not.

Well, almost surely not.

BIBLIOGRAPHY

Ahmed, Rollo. *The Black Art*. Arrow Press, 1966.

Archaeological Institute of America. *Archaeological Discoveries in the Holy Land*. New York: Thomas Y. Crowell, 1967.

Augusta, J. and Burian, Z. *Prehistoric Sea Monsters*. London: Paul Hamlyn, 1964.

Barclay, William. *The Bible and History*. New York: Abingdon Press, 1968.

Bibby, Geoffrey. "Before the Argo." *Horizon*, July 1960.

Botsford, George W. and Robinson, Charles A., Jr. *Hellenic History*. New York: Macmillan, 1969.

Bourne, Geoffrey. *The Gentle Giants*. New York: G. P. Putnam's Sons, 1975.

Bowra, C. M. *Classical Greece*. New York: Time-Life, 1965.

———. "Homer's Age of Heroes." *Horizon*, January 1961.

Bracewell, Ronald. *The Galactic Club*. San Francisco: W. H. Freeman, 1974.

Brewer, Ebenezer Cobham. *Brewer's Dictionary of Phrase & Fable* (revised). New York: Harper & Brothers, 1947.

Brian, Denis and Dixon, Jeane. *The Witnesses*. Garden City, N.Y.: Doubleday, 1976.

Byrne, Peter. *The Search for Bigfoot*. Washington: Acropolis, 1975.

Cambridge Ancient History. New York: Cambridge University Press, 1924.

Cameron, A. G. W. *Interstellar Communication*. New York: W. A. Benjamin, 1963.

Churchill, Winston. *The Birth of Britain*. New York: Dodd, Mead, 1956.

Clarke, Arthur C. *Profiles of the Future*. New York: Bantam, 1958.

Cohen, Daniel. *Curses, Hexes and Spells*. Philadelphia: J. B. Lippincott, 1974.

————. *A Modern Look at Monsters.* New York: Dodd, Mead, 1970.

Collingwood, R. C. *Roman Britain.* Oxford: Oxford University Press, 1937.

Conway, David. *Magic.* New York: E. P. Dutton, 1972.

Cooper, Henry S. F., Jr. "Profile—Carl Sagan." *The New Yorker,* June 21 and 28, 1976.

Cornin, Edward W., Jr. "The Yeti." *Atlantic Monthly,* November 1975.

Costello, Peter. *In Search of Lake Monsters.* New York: Coward, McCann & Geoghegan, 1974.

Cottrell, Leonard. *The Bull of Minos.* New York: Holt, Rinehart & Winston, 1961.

Crampton, Patrick. *Stonehenge of the Kings.* New York: John Day, 1968.

Cranston, S. L. and Head, Joseph. *Reincarnation.* New York: Julian Press, 1968.

DeCamp, L. Sprague. *Great Cities of the Ancient World.* Garden City, N.Y.: Doubleday. 1972.

Dent, J. M. *Everyman Dictionary of Non-Classical Mythology.* New York: E. P. Dutton, 1952.

Desmond, Adrian. *The Hot-Blooded Dinosaurs.* New York: Dial Press, 1976.

Dinsdale, Timothy. *Monster Hunt.* Washington: Acropolis, 1972.

Dole, Stephen H. and Asimov, Isaac. *Planets for Man.* New York: Random House, 1964.

Durant, Will. *Caesar and Christ.* New York: Simon & Schuster, 1944.

————. *The Life of Greece.* New York: Simon & Schuster, 1939.

————. *Our Oriental Heritage.* New York: Simon & Schuster, 1935.

Edwards, Frank. *Flying Saucers—Serious Business.* New York: Lyle Stuart, 1966.

Eiseley, Loren. "The Time of Man" in *Light of the Past.* New York: American Heritage, 1965.

Eliot, Alexander. *Greece.* New York: American Heritage, 1972.

Ellis, H. R. Davidson. *Gods and Myths of Northern Europe.* Harmondsworth: Penguin, 1964.

Evans, Sir Arthur. *The Palace of Minos.* London: Macmillan, 1921.

Farrar, Stewart. *What Witches Do.* New York: Coward, McCann & Geoghegan, 1971.

Festinger, Leon. *When Prophecy Fails.* Minneapolis: University of Minnesota Press, 1956.

Finley, M. I. *The World of Odysseus.* London: Macmillan, 1956.

Frazer, Sir James George. *The Golden Bough.* New York: Macmillan, 1951.

Fuller, John G. *Aliens in the Skies.* New York: G. P. Putnam's Sons, 1959.

Gardner, Gerald. *The Meaning of Witchcraft.* New York: Samuel Weiser, 1971.

Gatti, Arthur. *The Kennedy Curse.* Chicago: Henry Regnery, 1976.

de Givry, Émile Grillot. *A Pictorial Anthology of Witchcraft, Magic and Alchemy.* New York: University Books, 1958.

Gold, T. "Cosmic Garbage." *Space Digest,* Vol. 3, No. 5, May 1960.

Gonzalez, Arturo F., Jr. "Lost Island of Atlantis?" *Science Digest,* May 1972.

Gould, Rupert T. *Enigmas.* New Hyde Park, N.Y.: University Books, 1965.

——. *The Loch Ness Monster and Others.* London: Geoffrey Bles, 1934.

Grant, Joan and Kelsey, Denys. *Many Lifetimes.* Garden City, N.Y.: Doubleday, 1967.

Grumley, Michael. *There Are Giants in the Earth.* Garden City, N.Y.: Doubleday, 1974.

Gwyne, Peter. "Visit to a Small Planet." *Newsweek,* August 2, 1976.

Hale, William Harlan. *Ancient Greece.* New York: American Heritage, 1965.

Hamilton, Edith. *The Greek Way.* New York: W. W. Norton, 1930.

Hawkins, Gerald. *Stonehenge Decoded.* Garden City, N.Y.: Doubleday, 1965.

Herskovits, Melville J. "What is Voodoo?" *Tomorrow,* 1954.

Hogg, Garry. *Odd Aspects of England.* New York: Arco, 1969.

Holzer, Hans. *Beyond Medicine.* New York: Ballantine, 1974.

——. *Born Again.* Garden City, N.Y.: Doubleday, 1970.

——. *ESP and You.* New York: Ace, 1972.

——. *The Handbook of Parapsychology.* New York: Manor, 1975.

——. *Haunted Houses.* New York: Crown, 1972.

——. *The Human Dynamo.* Millbrae, Calif.: Celestial Arts, 1975.

——. *Life After Death: The Challenge and the Evidence.* Indianapolis, Ind.: Bobbs-Merrill, 1969.

——. *The New Pagans.* Garden City, N.Y.: Doubleday, 1972.

——. *Patterns of Destiny.* Plainview, N.Y.: Nash.

————. *Possessed—An Exorcist's Casebook.* New York: Fawcett, 1973.

————. *The Prophets Speak.* New York: Manor, 1975.

————. *The Psychic Side of Dreams.* Garden City, N.Y.: Doubleday, 1976.

————. *The Truth About Witchcraft.* Garden City, N.Y.: Doubleday, 1969.

————. *The Witchcraft Report.* New York: Ace, 1973.

Hunter, Don and Dahinden, Rene. *Sasquatch.* Toronto: McClelland & Stewart, 1973.

Huson, Paul. *Mastering Herbalism.* Briarcliff Manor, N.Y.: 1974.

————. *Mastering Witchcraft.* New York: G. P. Putnam's Sons, 1970.

Hynek, J. Allen. *The UFO Experience, a Scientific Inquiry.* Chicago: Henry Regnery, 1972.

Ivimy, John. *The Sphinx and the Megaliths.* New York: Harper & Row, 1975.

Jung, C. G. *Flying Saucers, A Modern Myth of Things Seen in the Skies.* New York: Harcourt, Brace, 1959.

Keller, Werner. *The Bible as History,* translated by William Neil. New York: William Morrow, 1956.

Keyhoe, Major Donald E. *Aliens from Space.* Garden City, N.Y.: Doubleday, 1973.

Kramer, Samuel Noah. *Cradle of Civilization.* New York: Time-Life, 1967.

The Last Two Million Years. London: Reader's Digest Assn., 1973.

Ley, Willy. *Dawn of Zoology.* Englewood Cliffs, N.J.: Prentice-Hall, 1969.

Linnaean Society of New England. *Report Relative to a Large Marine Animal.* Boston: Linnaean Society, 1817.

Lore, Gordon I. R., Jr. and Deneault, Harold H., Jr. *Mysteries of the Skies.* Englewood Cliffs, N.J.: Prentice-Hall, 1968.

Lorenzen, Jim and Coral. *UFOs Over the Americas.* New York: Signet, 1968.

Lum, Peter. *Fabulous Beasts.* London: Thames & Hudson, 1952.

Lunan, Duncan. *Interstellar Contact.* Chicago: Henry Regnery, 1975.

MacCulloch, John A. and Gray, Louis H. *The Mythology of All Races.* New York: Cooper, 1922.

Mackal, Roy P. *The Monsters of Loch Ness.* Chicago: Swallow Press, 1976.

Marinatos, Spyridon. "Thera, Key to the Riddle of Minos." *National Geographic*, May 1972.

Marple, Eric. *Witchcraft*. Octopus, 1973.

Maximilien, Louis. "Voodoo, Gnosis, Catholicism." *Tomorrow*, 1954.

McKendrick, Melveena. *Spain*. New York: American Heritage, 1972.

McNally, Raymond T. and Florescu, Radu. *In Search of Dracula*. New York: Warner, 1973.

Michell, John F. *The Flying Saucer Vision*. London: Sidgwick & Jackson, 1967.

Moulton, Richard G. *The Modern Reader's Bible: Book of Ezekiel*. New York: Macmillan, 1897.

Mumford, Lewis. *Technics and Civilization*. New York: Harcourt, Brace, 1934.

——. "The First Megamachine." *Daedalus*, Spring 1965.

Napier, John. *Bigfoot, the Yeti and Sasquatch in Myth and Reality*. New York: E. P. Dutton, 1973.

New Larousse Encyclopedia of Mythology. London: Hamlyn, 1976.

Ostrander, Sheila and Schroeder, Lynn. *Psychic Discoveries Behind the Iron Curtain*. Englewood Cliffs, N.J.: Prentice-Hall, 1971.

O. T. A. "The Seventh Day" (pamphlet), 1975.

Oudemans, A. C. *The Great Sea Serpent*. London: Lonzac, 1892.

Pendlebury, J. D. S. *The Archaeology of Crete*. London: Methuen, 1939.

Ross, Nancy Wilson. "Sir Tashi and the Yeti." *Horizon*, Spring 1965.

Sagan, Carl. *The Cosmic Connection*. Garden City, N.Y.: Doubleday, 1973.

Sagan, Carl (ed.) and Page, Thornton. *UFOs, A Scientific Debate*. Ithaca, N.Y.: Cornell University Press, 1972.

Schliemann, Heinrich. *Ilios*. London: John Murray, 1880.

Scott, David. "Closing In on the Loch Ness Monster." *Reader's Digest*, February 1967.

Sherman, Harold. *"Wonder" Healers of the Philippines*. Psychic Press, 1974.

Shklovskii, I. S. and Sagan, Carl. *Intelligent Life in the Universe*. San Francisco: Holden-Day, 1966.

Slate, B. Ann and Berry, Alan. *Bigfoot*. New York: Bantam, 1976.

Smith, J. L. B. "The Second Coelacanth." *Nature*, Vol. 171, London, 1953.

Smith, Ronald. "The Abdication of Human Intelligence." *The Humanist.*

Smith, Warren. *Strange Monsters and Madmen.* New York: Popular Library, 1969.

Smyth, F. *Modern Witchcraft.* London: Macdonald, 1970.

Stanford, W. B. *The Quest for Ulysses.* New York: Praeger, 1974.

Sterrett, J. R. S. "Vampires." *The Nation,* August 31, 1899.

Sullivan, Walter. *We Are Not Alone.* New York: McGraw-Hill, 1964.

Summers, Montague. *The Vampire: His Kith and Kin.* New York: E. P. Dutton, 1929.

Tester, M. H. *The Healing Touch.* New York: Taplinger, 1970.

Thom, Alexander. *Megalithic Sites in Britain.* London: Faber & Faber, 1959.

Underwood, Peter. *A Gazetteer of British Ghosts.* New York: Walker, 1975.

Vallee, Jacques. *Challenge to Science.* Chicago: Henry Regnery, 1966.

Voss, Gilbert. "Squid." *National Geographic,* March 1967.

Walker, E. D. *Reincarnation.* New York: University Books, 1965.

Wells, H. G. *Outline of History.* Garden City, N.Y.: Doubleday, 1971.

White, R. J. *England.* New York: McGraw-Hill, 1971.

Whyte, C. *More Than a Legend.* London: Hamish Hamilton, 1957.

Wilson, Edmund. "Voodoo in Literature." *Tomorrow,* 1954.

Witchell, Nicholas. *The Loch Ness Story.* Baltimore: Penguin, 1975.

Woolley, Sir Leonard. *Excavations at Ur.* London: Ernest Benn, 1954.

Wyckoff, Charles W. "Filming the Loch Ness Monster." *Filmmakers' Newsletter,* June 1976.

INDEX